T0234028

The Definitive Guide to AWS Infrastructure Automation

Craft Infrastructure-as-Code Solutions

Bradley Campbell

Apress®

The Definitive Guide to AWS Infrastructure Automation

Bradley Campbell
Virginia, VA, USA

ISBN-13 (pbk): 978-1-4842-5397-7   ISBN-13 (electronic): 978-1-4842-5398-4
https://doi.org/10.1007/978-1-4842-5398-4

Managing Director, Apress Media LLC: Welmoed Spahr
Acquisitions Editor: Celestin Suresh John
Development Editor: Matthew Moodie
Coordinating Editor: Aditee Mirashi

Cover designed by eStudioCalamar

Cover image designed by Freepik (www.freepik.com)

Distributed to the book trade worldwide by Springer Science+Business Media New York, 233 Spring Street, 6th Floor, New York, NY 10013. Phone 1-800-SPRINGER, fax (201) 348-4505, e-mail orders-ny@springer-sbm.com, or visit www.springeronline.com. Apress Media, LLC is a California LLC and the sole member (owner) is Springer Science + Business Media Finance Inc (SSBM Finance Inc). SSBM Finance Inc is a **Delaware** corporation.

For information on translations, please e-mail rights@apress.com, or visit http://www.apress.com/rights-permissions.

Apress titles may be purchased in bulk for academic, corporate, or promotional use. eBook versions and licenses are also available for most titles. For more information, reference our Print and eBook Bulk Sales web page at http://www.apress.com/bulk-sales.

Any source code or other supplementary material referenced by the author in this book is available to readers on GitHub via the book's product page, located at www.apress.com/978-1-4842-5397-7. For more detailed information, please visit http://www.apress.com/source-code.

Printed on acid-free paper

It's a dangerous business, Frodo, going out your door.
You step onto the road, and if you don't keep your feet,
there's no knowing where you might be swept off to.

—J.R.R. Tolkien, *The Lord of the Rings*

Dedicated to my amazing wife,
Patricia, who's been pushing me out my
figurative door since the day we met. Her belief in me and
the sacrifices she made to give me the opportunity to write
this book are what have made it possible.

Table of Contents

About the Author

Bradley Campbell is a self-taught technologist. He got his start in technology in college, picking up a copy of the *HTML 4.01 Bible* before an academic break and learning to hand-code his first web sites. From these beginnings, he forged a career for himself as a full-stack developer after several years of freelance application development work. He has worked with Ruby, ColdFusion, Perl, Python, Golang, C++, Java, Bash, C#, Swift, and JavaScript (and probably some others he's forgotten about) across all kinds of server and database backends.

With many years of application development, systems administration, database design and administration, release automation, and systems architecture under his belt, his current role is as a hands-on principal cloud architect at Cloudreach. He currently holds all 11 AWS (Amazon Web Services) certifications and holds several other industry certifications. Specialties include full-stack software engineering, SQL and NoSQL databases, application architecture, "DevOps," application migration and modernization, automation, cloud-native app design and delivery, AWS, Python, Golang, Terraform, CloudFormation, and Ansible.

About the Technical Reviewer

Navin Sabharwal has 20+ years of industry experience and is an innovator, thought leader, patent holder, and author in the areas of cloud computing, artificial intelligence and machine learning, public cloud, DevOps, AIOps, infrastructure services, monitoring and management platforms, big data analytics, and software product development. Navin is responsible for DevOps, artificial intelligence, cloud lifecycle management, service management, monitoring and management, IT Ops analytics, AIOps and machine learning, automation, operational efficiency of scaled delivery through Lean Ops, and strategy and delivery for HCL Technologies. He is reachable at navinsabharwal@gmail.com and www.linkedin.com/in/navinsabharwal.

Introduction

This book is for aspiring and intermediately experienced cloud practitioners. This book is designed to be extremely hands-on, focusing primarily on outcomes and code necessary to arrive at those outcomes without a great deal of additional discussion.

The book begins with a day in the life of a fictional cloud engineer who lives in a world devoid of infrastructure-as-code frameworks and tooling to make his life easier. In the absence of these tools, the engineer undertakes the daunting task of building a bespoke set of tools to tackle the requirements of his daily tasks. Through his experiences, we begin to realize that simply maintaining and extending such tooling just to meet a very basic set of needs is a full-time job in and of itself.

With the reader primed to understand the critical enabling role that this class of tools plays in modern environments, we take a look at the general landscape of infrastructure-as-code tools, discussing general-purpose tools and also examining some of the more niche tools that exist and what problems they aim to solve. With this general survey completed, we begin to take a more in-depth look at several representative tools.

CloudFormation is the first stop. CloudFormation represents the vendor solution; we analyze the benefits bestowed to users by virtue of this fact. From there, we look at the semantics used by CloudFormation code and how to deploy and manage resources using it.

Next, we take a look at the third-party heavyweight, Terraform. Terraform is differentiated from CloudFormation in many key areas, areas we discover in this chapter. We also explore resources defined as-code with Terraform. We also discuss how to leverage Terraform's multifaceted command set to create and manage infrastructure.

INTRODUCTION

Following Terraform, we reprise CloudFormation, looking at the tools that have emerged to form an ecosystem around CloudFormation since its 2011 launch. Tools have emerged to address several pain points with the offering. We examine those pain points and how the tools address these pain points. While many tools exist in many domains, we focus on DSL providers and orchestrators. By focusing on a leading tool in each domain, we keep the scope of the chapter small enough to focus on these two key domains. While we only address two tools throughout the chapter, the Appendix contains a mind-bogglingly long list of tools from each class if you find that you might need tooling that aligns to a different set of needs than those addressed in the chapter.

"Next-gen" infra-as-code frameworks follow. Emerging tools such as the AWS CDK and Pulumi are shaking up how we are creating infrastructure these days, all the while continuing to lean on the lessons and power of our two mainstays: CloudFormation and Terraform. This chapter provides insight on how these newer tools are set up for success by leaning on the strengths of their predecessors. We also look at how to work with these tools and create and manage infrastructure with each of them.

With a firm understanding of several well-known and emerging technologies in this space, we put each through its paces by using it to build a mainstay of AWS architecture: a high-availability (HA) (or non-high-availability, as desired) VPC that supports HA features via toggles built directly into the code base itself. In the course of doing so, we are able to clearly establish tradeoffs made between building the same bundle of resources across multiple tools.

We end not with a protracted rehashing of previously discussed topics but with some additional "lessons learned" over the last few years of functioning within multiple roles primarily focused on cloud architecture, engineering, and automation of software delivery into such environments.

CHAPTER 1

Infra the Beginning

Infrastructure: the word has this weight about it. Bridges, roads, racks, servers.... The word carries this connotation of tangibility – that if something is infrastructure, that there is something substantial, bulky, heavy, and real – not some ephemeral or abstract notion that can be destroyed or recreated at a moment's notice. IT practitioners these days are thinking of infrastructure in much different terms than they were five years ago. In the mind of the cloud-enlightened IT pro, servers are now abstract units of raw computing power dynamically allocated when needed by a system and disposed of when their task is completed. Users get the resources they want when they need them, forsaking bygone capacity planning exercises that have traditionally led to data centers and server racks overprovisioned for peak loads, only to sit underutilized most of the time. These days, IT infrastructure scaleout is defined by API calls and the speed of the Internet/cloud provider, no longer by purchase orders and six- to eight-week lead times. While we all realize that this paradigm is the new normal, it's worth taking a moment to reflect on how we got here, evaluating the current landscape, and looking forward to things to come. In many ways, this indeed is a golden era of computing; in this book, we're going to embrace that notion fully by both taking in a broad view of the AWS infrastructure automation landscape and casting a deep lens (pun intended) toward the many different tools and services that comprise this landscape.

© Bradley Campbell 2020
B. Campbell, *The Definitive Guide to AWS Infrastructure Automation*,
https://doi.org/10.1007/978-1-4842-5398-4_1

We begin this chapter by exploring the foundations of virtualization, the beginnings of software and API-defined infrastructure, the advent of the cloud, and the progression and maturity of the current set of API-driven infrastructure tools and practices. These tools, concepts, and practices have enabled not just rapid innovation, better time to market, and more significant value realizations for "the business" but increasing returns for IT-centric objectives such as security, compliance, stability, and so on. As we progress to the current day, we examine the evolution of these tools from basic control mechanisms to the powerful declarative DSL-based frameworks and languages that dominate the current landscape to the tools that are currently defining the cutting edge of this space. Such tools include the language-based tooling that looks to finally help (truly) begin to bridge the gap between dev and ops.

A New and Novel Approach to Infrastructure

Public cloud platforms have indeed brought API-driven infrastructure to the masses. In my research, Amazon was one of the first (if not *the* first) platforms to offer such functionality. As early as 2004,[1] Amazon was offering API-based functionality to create and manage Simple Queue Service (SQS) queues. In the years that followed, Amazon would release the S3 and EC2 services, formally relaunching as Amazon Web Services (AWS) in 2006.[2] This suite of products formed the cornerstone of Amazon's offerings and – willingly or unwillingly – set a benchmark for the rest of the industry.

---

[1]Amazon Simple Queue Service REST Operations. https://web.archive.org/web/20041207090145/http://www.awszone.com/scratchpads/rest/sqs/index.aws
[2]Wikipedia – Amazon Web Services. https://en.wikipedia.org/wiki/Amazon_Web_Services

Those who weren't ultra-early adopters of Amazon's nascent platform wouldn't have similar functionality available for several years, with the 1.0 version of VMWare's vCloud Director dating back to August of 2010.[3] The earliest incarnations of vCloud Director offered a CLI-style interface, with references to the vCloud API going back as far as April of 2010.[4] As such, it would seem that Amazon led the way in providing API-based infrastructure resources, with others following. In the intervening eight-and-a-half years, the public cloud has become *the* ubiquitous computing platform, supplanting private clouds (signaled by organizations such as the "Department of Defense" even adopting public clouds for critical and sensitive workloads).

The pace of innovation has been staggering for Amazon since its 2006 release of its three-service platform. As of January 2019, the AWS platform boasts more than 130+ services. Each of these services now supports multiple methods of orchestration, from simple CLI-style interfaces, to SDKs supported in multiple modern languages, to complex infrastructure-as-code tools, to modern language-based tools that now sit as abstractions over infrastructure-as-code tools and concepts. Of course, each of these families of tools is simply a consumer of REST-based APIs, meaning that if you were so inclined, you could come up with an SDK for your own language or create your own custom tooling to interact with Amazon's APIs. Of course, Google's Cloud Platform and Microsoft's Azure cloud platform have followed the leader, by offering API-based mechanisms to interact with their respective platforms. Regardless of the platform, these APIs typically support the entire lifecycle of a given cloud resource, allowing a user to create, update, read, and delete new instances of objects provided by each service in the platform. Coupled with the multitude of

---

[3]Cloud Director Release History. `https://anthonyspiteri.net/vcloud-director-release-history/4` Cloud API Programming Guide

[4]`https://pubs.vmware.com/vca/index.jsp?topic=%2Fcom.vmware.vcloud.api.doc_56%2FGUID-86CA32C2-3753-49B2-A471-1CE460109ADB.html`

other benefits that cloud platforms provide – such as elasticity, access to deep resource pools, and pay-as-you-go pricing – the flexibility and power of being able to create a 2,000 server grid computing cluster by writing a simple Bash or Python script is almost mind-bending.

As interesting as the notion of using scripted tooling to control infrastructure is, the logistics of managing large, critical estates through such means is fragile and perilous. CRUD-style APIs typically present different interfaces for create, update, and delete functions. Out of the gate, we're dealing with the additional complexity of maintaining three separate sets of scripts for create, update, and delete operations.

Alternatively, though no more pleasant, we could create a single set of scripts that conditionally handle each scenario. In either case, it's clear to see that even for small deployments, the complexity of the solution increases quickly. Ultimately, CRUD-style APIs implemented at the resource level lack the expressiveness needed to manage deployments in situations where:

- Resource sets are complex (heterogeneous – e.g., compute in addition to base networking)

- Resource sets are updated frequently or have short lifecycles

- Resource sets represent large-scale deployments

In addition to the challenges mentioned previously, these types of scenarios present additional considerations, such as

- Dependency resolution and management

- Ensuring that shared resources aren't deleted (or that end users are at the least informed of the fact that a common resource is about to be deleted and are able to make a decision appropriately)

- Intelligently sequencing the operations to maximize success rates

- State tracking

As you think through these issues at a high level, we're going to walk through this in a (pseudo) real-world scenario.

Into an Unknown World

Congratulations! It's your first day as a cloud engineer at InfraCo, a startup whose product line is a digital service. The products are standard full-stack applications, with backend servers running serving APIs consumed by web frontends (with a mobile app soon to follow). You're relatively new to the world of cloud and AWS. After getting settled in your first day, one of the developers comes by to say hi and to hit you with your first task. He'd like two new EC2 instances for some backend development. ***It's also worth mentioning that in this (highly contrived) example, we live in a world where tools like CloudFormation, Terraform, and friends don't yet exist – in short, you're constrained to scripts using the AWS CLI or to leverage the AWS SDKs to develop your solutions.*** With that very unexpected caveat out of the way, you begin work on your first solution: a script to create two EC2 instances (Listing 1-1).

Listing 1-1. create_ec2.sh (Creates EC2 Instances)

```
#!/bin/bash region="${1}"
aws --region "${region}" ec2 run-instances \
    --image-id ami-0de53d8956e8dcf80 --count 2 \
    --instance-type t2.nano --key-name book \
    --security-group-ids sg-6e7fdd29 \
    --subnet-id subnet-661ca758
```

Your script handles our basic need to create new EC2 instances –
not well parametrized, not very robust, but it does meet our most basic
requirement to create a few instances. Your job done, you check your script
into the git repo you store your infrastructure management scripts in and
jump to the next task. A few days later, the developer comes back to tell
you those *t2.nano*s just aren't cutting it; you decide to upgrade to *t2.xlarge*s
to take care of the immediate need of the app developers. You find the
command you need from the AWS CLI reference docs and cook up a script
to manage the upgrades. Listing 1-2 shows what you come up with:

Listing 1-2. update_ec2_attrs.sh (Update EC2 Instance Attributes)

```bash
#!/bin/bash

region="${1}"
attribute="${2}"
value="${3}"
instance_id="${4}"

aws --region "${region}" ec2 stop-instances \
    --instance-ids "${instance_id}" sleep 30
aws --region "${region}" ec2 modify-instance-attribute \

    --attribute "${attribute}" \
    --value "${value}" \
    --instance-id "${instance_id}" sleep 30
aws --region "${region}" ec2 start-instances \
    --instance-ids "${instance_id}"
```

The good news here: you're learning! You've parametrized the bits of
the script that will likely change between invocations of the script. Don't
start prematurely patting yourself on the back, though. Your efforts to
parametrize the script to provide an extensible, forward-thinking solution
to a problem that's sure to manifest itself again later have actually revealed

a larger problem with your overall strategy (yes, even with your extremely modest footprint of two EC2 instances). First problem: you need to retrieve the instance IDs of the instances you created previously when you ran your **create_ec2.sh** script (Listing 1-1); you have a few options:

- Login to the AWS console, find the instances, record the instance IDs somewhere, and feed them into the script.

- Use an *ec2 describe-instances* command from the CLI to grab the instance IDs.

- Rework **create_ec2.sh** so that it does something meaningful with the output of the command, storing the instance IDs it created somewhere so that they can be ingested by any downstream "update_ec2_*.sh" script.

Second problem: you have to run the script individually for each instance you want to update. You run out for lunch with a colleague. Over lunch conversation, you present your quandary for coming up with a better long-term scripting solution to maintain your infrastructure to your colleague. Her thoughts are that the third option, while presenting the most upfront work, will likely yield the greatest dividends in the long run. Back from lunch, you set about refactoring your **create_ec2.sh** script. Listing 1-3 shows your efforts.

Listing 1-3. create_ec2.sh (Modified Based on Your Colleague's Feedback)

```
#!/bin/bash
region="${1}"
ami="${2}"
how_many="${3}"
itype="${4}"
key="${5}"
```

```
sg_ids="${6}"
subnet="${7}"

aws --region "${region}" ec2 run-instances \
    --image-id "${ami}" --count "${how_many}" \
    --instance-type "${itype}" --key-name "${key}" \
    --security-group-ids "${sg_ids}" \
    --subnet-id "${subnet}" \
    --query 'Instances[*].[InstanceId]' \
    --output text >> .ec2_instance_ids.out

# Remove any empty lines from inventory file sed -ie '/^$/d'
.ec2_instance_ids.out
```

There's no doubt that this is a considerable improvement over your first script, right? Everything's parametrized. You even learned about that awesome *--query* flag AWS has in their toolkit. Here, you've used it to grab your newly created EC2 instance IDs and store them in a text file alongside your scripts. Your brilliant colleague showed you a few other tricks at lunch that she mentioned may be helpful for your project.

After some trial and error and a StackOverflow visit or two, you incorporated her feedback to make some changes to your **update_ec2_attrs.sh** script, which follows in Listing 1-4:

Listing 1-4. update_ec2_attrs.sh (Modified Based on Your Colleague's Feedback)

```
#!/bin/bash

region="${1}"
attribute="${2}"
value="${3}"
```

```
while read instance do
    echo "==== Stopping ${instance} ===="
    aws --region "${region}" ec2 stop-instances \
        --instance-ids "${instance}" >/dev/null sleep 90
    echo "==== Changing ${attribute} on ${instance} ===="
    aws --region "${region}" ec2 modify-instance-attribute \
                            --attribute "${attribute}" \
                            --value "${value}" \
                            --instance-id "${instance}" >/
                            dev/null    if [[ "$?" == "0" ]]
    then
    echo "==== ${instance} updated successfully ===="
    fi
    echo "==== Starting ${instance} ===="
    aws --region "${region}" ec2 start-instances \
        --instance-ids "${instance}" >/dev/null done
        < .ec2_instance_ids.out
```

This script really gives you the feeling that you're really starting to build out something useful. Your colleague pointed out how you might enhance your scripts by including some useful output with echo statements, how to check whether or not commands might have failed, and how to loop through an input file. Putting all this together in combination with your work from the script in Listing 1-3, you now have a solid solution for creating EC2 instances, tracking their IDs locally once created, and using that same tracking mechanism to feed later updates. You decide to go ahead and run your script just to see how it all works. You first decide to see what your inventory file looks like (Listing 1-5):

Listing 1-5. Contents of .ec2_instance_ids.out

```
$ cat .ec2_instance_ids.out i-03402f2a7edce74dc
i-078cdc1a2996ec9ab
```

Satisfied that this should work with your freshly updated script, you run the script. Its output is captured in Listing 1-6.

Listing 1-6. Output of update_ec2_attrs.sh

```
$ ./update_ec2_attrs.sh us-east-1 instanceType t2.large
==== Stopping i-03402f2a7edce74dc ====
==== Changing instanceType on i-03402f2a7edce74dc ====
==== i-03402f2a7edce74dc updated successfully ====
==== Starting i-03402f2a7edce74dc ====
==== Stopping i-078cdc1a2996ec9ab ====
==== Changing instanceType on i-078cdc1a2996ec9ab ====
==== i-078cdc1a2996ec9ab updated successfully ====
==== Starting i-078cdc1a2996ec9ab ====
```

Excited, you fire off a quick email to your colleague to thank her for her insightful wisdom, letting her know how wonderfully your refactored scripts worked when running your latest round of experimental updates. You feel like there's probably a better way to handle the wait than the sleep statement, but that can be a problem for another day. You commit your new inventory file and your updated scripts in your git repo and head home for the evening.

The next day, you arrive fresh, ready to tackle the day's challenges. You're greeted by a member of one of the application development teams, who informs you that he needs you to use a different AMI than the one you used to create the instances when you created them yesterday. You visit the documentation page for the *modify-instance-attributes* call, only to discover that AMI isn't one of the attributes that can be changed – in fact, you discover that if you want to change the AMI of the instance, it is necessary to create new instances.

You immediately think of running your **create_ec2.sh** script to spin up a few new instances with the new AMI. You are immediately confronted with the need to create yet another script to delete the existing instances.

In your mind's eye, you start thinking about how to write your deletion script in a forward-thinking manner. What if you need to run this script again at some point in the future when you've amassed a much larger inventory of instances? Is simply tracking instances by instance ID truly an effective way to track your inventory? As you think through the problem, you remain convinced that you need to track the instance ID somewhere, as the few CLI calls for which you're familiar with all utilize the instance ID as a parameter to the underlying AWS CLI calls. But, what about human operators? If some person, at some later time, wanted to selectively filter out some subset of instances for targeted operations, how would that work? How could we guarantee that our scripts would allow such flexibility?

If we handle that now, what impact and additional work will it require for us with the scripts we've already created?

You decide to revisit these issues later and address the immediate need: your deletion script. You set off to work; Listing 1-7 shows the fruits of your labors.

Listing 1-7. delete_ec2.sh

```
#!/bin/bash
region="${1}"
# Create a temp file to use for program logic,
# while program manipulates actual inventory file cp .ec2_
instance_ids.out .ec2_instance_ids.out.tmp

# Read in inventory from temp file, while updating #
inventory per operations in actual inventory file.
# We use the "3" filehandle to allow the "read" command # to
continue to work as-normal from stdin.
while read instance <&3; do
    read -p "Terminate ${instance} [y|n]? " termvar if [[
    ${termvar} == [yY] ]]; then
```

```
        echo "==== Terminating ${instance} ===="
        aws --region "${region}" ec2 terminate-instances \
            --instance-ids "${instance}" >/dev/null if
            [[ "$?" == "0" ]]; then
            echo "==== ${instance} terminated successfully ===="
            sed -ie "/^${instance}/d" .ec2_instance_ids.out
        fi else
        echo "==== Keeping ${instance} ===="

    fi
done 3< .ec2_instance_ids.out.tmp

# Cleanup inventory file
sed -ie '/^$/d' .ec2_instance_ids.out

# Remove temp file
rm .ec2_instance_ids.out.tmp
```

Looking back through the collection of scripts you've created and maintained, you see that your scripts are getting much better. You're now working with shadow copies of your inventory file, dealing with user input, and considering long-term solutions and maintenance in your code (that Apress *Expert Shell Scripting* book by Ron Peters that you've been reading in the evenings has really helped you hone your skills). You do notice and are concerned, however, by the increasing amount of complexity that your scripts need to keep up with the day-to-day requirements coming from the development teams. "Is this really a sustainable solution?," you ask yourself. In the meantime, you run your **delete_ec2.sh** script, its output captured in Listing 1-8.

Listing 1-8. Output of delete_ec2.sh

```
$ ./delete_ec2.sh us-east-1
Terminate i-03402f2a7edce74dc [y|n]? y
==== Terminating i-03402f2a7edce74dc ====
==== i-03402f2a7edce74dc terminated successfully ==== Terminate
i-078cdc1a2996ec9ab [y|n]? y
==== Terminating i-078cdc1a2996ec9ab ====
==== i-078cdc1a2996ec9ab terminated successfully ====
```

With that task successfully completed, you begin to think again about the myriad issues with your budding EC2 resource management system. Just as you're getting in the zone, the developer who started this cascading series of events returns to your desk for a quick chat. He and a few developers were talking; as it turns out, they can utilize some additional AWS technologies to deliver their work this sprint. In addition to the updated EC2 instances, they ask you to deliver backend APIs; they've been reading some Jeff Barr blogs and discovered they can use CloudFront distributions backed by S3 buckets to deliver static web resources from nearby edge locations for basically any user in the world. The developers are voraciously eager to start playing with these new technologies; knowing you have been working feverishly on a scripted solution to manage infrastructure resources, they ask you if you can deploy three buckets with three accompanying CloudFront distributions. Before you can even mutter a hesitant "yes...," the developer is on his way back to his work area to continue work on the web site, clamoring on about something called "Route 53" and how we can add that to the mix later.

Your mind turns back to the issues you wanted to tackle with the EC2 scripts. As you mull through those issues, you begin to think about how you'll begin to integrate the management of new classes of resources into your current solution. Once again, the more you think about it, the more you are overwhelmed with questions and the work involved in building out a solution, like

- Should resource IDs of different types be managed in a single file with some sort of additional field to specify resource type?

- If you decide to keep resource inventories instead in different files, does it make sense to adopt some sort of naming convention based on resource type so that scripts can be somewhat generic in how they look for files?

- Does it make sense to begin to factor out what is sure to be common functionality across scripts that handle different resources into library code?

- Going back to our EC2 management issues, is a simple list file up to the tasks that we currently have on our plate, as well as being flexible enough to handle any foreseeable future needs?

- If a simple list file isn't going to cut it, what kind of file format should we use? CSV? JSON? YAML? While these formats might be a better fit in terms of data expression, what is the impact of using them going to be on our current solution? Would it make more sense to drop the shell scripts now and migrate them all to something like Python? Isn't all that work possibly a bit premature? Or is it exactly what's called for?

- Files are, well, files. While you think you've got a somewhat effective solution for managing inventory by keeping files synced up to a git repository, is that a real-time and scalable enough solution for the practical needs of a growing team? Your manager mentioned your group was looking for another cloud engineer to work with additional delivery teams that

were being hired in the development group, so it's not
unreasonable to think someone else might be using
this solution in short order. Would it make more sense
to keep all of that information in some sort of database?
If you need to support interoperability with a database,
there's no doubt you'll need to refactor your scripts –
extensively.

You're getting a headache thinking through all these challenges.
Once again, you have an immediate demand placed on you by the
developer who visits your desk just a bit too frequently: creating new
EC2 instances and S3 bucket/CloudFront distributions. You dig into
the AWS documentation and come up with a script to manage S3
bucket/CloudFront distribution pairings. Listing 1-9 captures your work.

Listing 1-9. create_web_bucket_with_cdn.sh

```
#!/bin/bash
region="${1}"
name="${2}"
corp="${3}"

BUCKET="${name}.${corp}"

aws --region "${region}" s3api create-bucket \
    --bucket "${BUCKET}" >/dev/null

if [[ "$?" == "0" ]]; then
    echo "==== Bucket ${BUCKET} created successfully ====" echo
    "${BUCKET}" >> .s3_buckets.out

    aws s3 website "s3://${BUCKET}/" \
        --index-document index.html \
        --error-document error.html
```

```
    if [[ "$?" == "0" ]]; then
        echo "==== Website hosting successfully set up on
        bucket ${BUCKET}
===="
    else
        echo "==== Website hosting failed to set up on bucket
        ${BUCKET} ====" exit 1
    fi

    CFDIST=$(aws cloudfront create-distribution \
        --origin-domain-name "${BUCKET}.s3.amazonaws.com" \
        --default-root-object index.html \
        --query "Distribution.[join(',', [Id,DomainName])]" \
        --output text)

    if [[ "$?" == "0" ]]; then
        echo "==== CloudFront distribution created successfully
        ====" echo
        "${BUCKET},${CFDIST}" >> .cloudfront_distributions.out
    else
        echo "==== CloudFront distribution failed to create ===="
else fi
fi

echo "==== Bucket \"${BUCKET}\" failed to create ===="
```

You stand back for a moment and marvel at your work for a moment before using this script to create the three bucket/CloudFront distribution combos the developer asked you for. After you've finished basking in the glory of a well-written shell script, you sit back down and let it do the hard work creating these resources for you, as we see in Listing 1-10.

Listing 1-10. Output of Several create_web_bucket_with_cdn.sh runs

```
$ ./create_web_bucket_with_cdn.sh us-east-1 web1
definitiveawsinfraguide.com
==== Bucket web1.definitiveawsinfraguide.com created
successfully ====
==== Website hosting successfully set up on bucket web1.
definitiveawsinfraguide.com ====
==== CloudFront distribution created successfully ====

$ ./create_web_bucket_with_cdn.sh us-east-1 web2
definitiveawsinfraguide.com
==== Bucket web2.definitiveawsinfraguide.com created
successfully ====
==== Website hosting successfully set up on bucket web2.
definitiveawsinfraguide.com ====
==== CloudFront distribution created successfully ====

$ ./create_web_bucket_with_cdn.sh us-east-1 web3
definitiveawsinfraguide.com
==== Bucket web3.definitiveawsinfraguide.com created
successfully ====
==== Website hosting successfully set up on bucket web3.
definitiveawsinfraguide.com ====
==== CloudFront distribution created successfully ====
```

You also inspect the inventory files for each type of resource, just to make sure things look as you would expect they would, as seen in Listing 1-11.

Listing 1-11. .s3_buckets.out and .cloudfront_distributions.out

```
$ cat .s3_buckets.out
web1.definitiveawsinfraguide.com
web2.definitiveawsinfraguide.com
web3.definitiveawsinfraguide.com
$ cat .cloudfront_distributions.out
web1.definitiveawsinfraguide.com,E2EZUHPOLOOU8I,d2lrcbdlg2446m.
cloudfront.net
web2.definitiveawsinfraguide.com,E129E6KQVF4FJ7,d7il3up2alO33.
cloudfront.net
web3.definitiveawsinfraguide.com,EVNKZ610XI94T,d4vdfuuz2gfn8.
cloudfront.net
```

You made some very wise decisions in capturing the CloudFront distribution inventory. You decided to begin by capturing this output in a CSV format. You even decided to associate the source S3 bucket with the distribution as the first field. At this point, you're not quite sure how you'll leverage that information in the future, but you have an innate feeling that it was probably a good idea to go ahead and capture this information here to facilitate future scripting and management needs.

Out of the Dream

Stepping out of our incredibly contrived scenario for a moment, our new cloud engineer is two days in and, in no uncertain terms, certainly faces an uphill climb in the days, months, and years to come. As demonstrated, there is a tremendous amount of power in API-driven infrastructure: our engineer was able to quickly provision virtual machines and petabyte-scale storage over a period of days (and in fact, the actual provisioning was mostly instantaneous once the automation scripting was put into place), not months or years as in times past. Each shell script presented the power of dealing with some API, whether to provision, update, or delete some aspect of the deployed infrastructure. As our engineer attempted to scale out his solution to actually manage the lifecycle of resources in a carefully planned and directed notion, the frailty of the solution as a general-purpose tool became more and more apparent as new and changing requirements emerged.

Hopefully, the example of a few days in the life of our cloud engineer, while highly contrived, brings home the point of the perils, fragility, and difficulty of developing, maintaining, and extending a bespoke solution to the problem of automated infrastructure lifecycle management. Our cloud engineer was already in over his head, and we are yet to tackle really hairy subjects like resource dependencies or the impact of dealing with large-scale deployments (hint: our simple loop-based mechanisms and sleep-based hacks would be largely inadequate in this dimension). Terraform's web site actually addresses this very issue on its site.[5]

Most organizations start by manually managing infrastructure through simple scripts or web-based interfaces. As the infrastructure grows, any manual approach to management becomes both error-prone and tedious, and many organizations begin to home-roll tooling to help automate the mechanical processes involved.

These tools require time and resources to build and maintain. As tools of necessity, they represent the minimum viable features needed by an organization, being built to handle only the immediate needs. As a result, they are often hard to extend and difficult to maintain. Because the tooling must be updated in lockstep with any new features or infrastructure, it becomes the limiting factor for how quickly the infrastructure can evolve.

---

[5]Terraform vs. Other Software. `www.terraform.io/intro/vs/custom.html`

Once again, it is my hope that our exercise in walking through a few days in the life of a fledgling cloud engineer gives some form to the claims made on the Terraform site. In very short order, our engineer was not only overwhelmed with the immediate needs of his organization but also, at every point and turn, was forced to continually assess the future needs his tooling might be required to meet and balancing that against the need to continually refactor tooling he had already created. As also pointed out so succinctly in this quote, our cloud engineer's scripts were very much "tools of necessity, ... represent[ing] the minimum viable features ... needed by [the] organization, being built to handle only the immediate needs." In fact, any software developer who's worked in an agile shop will recognize the paradigm of delivering solutions that looks only to solve immediate challenges.

New Tools for New Problems

Our shell scripts were pretty amazing. Honestly, it's hard to imagine a solution better than whatever great framework was bound to eventually emerge from their continued iteration and improvement, right? In 2011, AWS gave us CloudFormation, a service that allows you to "describe the AWS resources you need to run your application in a simple text file called a template and AWS CloudFormation takes care of provisioning those resources in the right sequence and taking into account any dependencies between resources."[6] Back in 2011, you'd create resource definitions using JSON files that you could either upload straight to the CloudFormation service or stage from an S3 bucket. When you want to change something, you change your template, rerun CloudFormation with the updated template, and that's it. The CloudFormation services do the heavy lifting

---

[6]Introducing AWS CloudFormation. https://aws.amazon.com/about-aws/whats-new/2011/02/25/introducing-aws-cloudformation/

for you – no separate script to perform one type of update and another script to delete and recreate a resource if the change necessitates it (e.g., changing AMIs on an EC2 instance).

Conceptually, Terraform follows a similar paradigm. A declarative language is used to define resources, with an underlying service doing the heavy lifting of dependency calculation and managing resources. When you want to make changes, you update the template and rerun the executable to effect changes to your deployment. While other operations are supported, the core operation centers around a cycle of updating templates and rerunning the engine to assess what is defined in your templates, what currently exists in the target resource set, and what series of operations the engine needs to do through API calls to close the delta. While we don't know exactly what CloudFormation does under the covers, it's probably fair to assume it works in a somewhat similar fashion.

These types of tools are declarative systems (Kubernetes being another familiar modern example):

> … [I]n a declarative system, the user knows the desired state, supplies a representation of the desired state to the system, then the system reads the current state and determines the sequence of commands to transition the system to the desired state. The component that determines the necessary sequence of commands is called a controller.[7]

These tools let us keep up with the demands of infrastructure consumers. Specifically, we are going to look at CloudFormation, Terraform, Pulumi, the new AWS Cloud Development Kit (CDK), Troposphere, Sceptre, as well as tools that perform similar functions in specialized domains through the course of the book. These tools have shaped a generation of cloud deployments, but what benefits do they really provide?

---

[7]Imperative vs Declarative. https://medium.com/@dominik.tornow/
imperative-vs-declarative-8abc7dcae82e

For the Business

The value propositions of cloud – reduced time to market, increased agility, and the ability to iterate more quickly – are unconditionally enhanced by the existence of tools like CloudFormation and friends. There's no disputing that cloud has laid a foundation for the DevOps movement that has overtaken the industry in the last several years. Being able to move quickly and reliably has tangible benefits, as follows:

> *US companies experienced a $3 return for every $1 they invested in improving the customer experience. While improving the customer experience is often seen as the job of the marketing department, 52% of those surveyed said that technology plays a key role in their customer experience. In the CA Technologies study, 74% of those surveyed said that adopting DevOps had improved their customer experience.*[8]

As businesses continue to look to cloud to provide differentiators in time-to-market vs. competitors leveraging traditional IT operational models, so must businesses already in the cloud seek to continue to differentiate themselves among other competitors reaping the benefits of cloud-based technologies.

Making smart decisions in how to leverage and consume these technologies is certainly an important factor in the overall equation.

Working with infrastructure-as-code solutions provides a fast, scalable path to working in the cloud. It enables businesses to quickly and safely pivot, experimenting with new designs and products to test market performance. While these types of experiments are possible without the help of cloud-based technologies, they are certainly easier to facilitate with the help of on-demand, infinitely scalable resources – and these resources are managed much more effectively and easily through the use of the types of solutions we cover in this book.

---

[8]Business Benefits of Adopting DevOps. www.informationweek.com/devops/
8-business-benefits-of-adopting-devops/d/d-id/1328460?page_number=3

For IT

The benefits of infrastructure-as-code solutions are numerous in achieving IT objectives. Beginning with centralized git repositories like GitHub, GitLab, and so on, clear audit trails show who initiated a change and who allowed a pull request to be merged into a deploy branch; CI/CD systems in conjunction with tools like AWS CloudTrail show us who ran certain actions and when and how they performed them. In short, there is a verifiable audit trail from commit to release into production system. This approach has numerous additional advantages that have typically applied previously to purely software-based projects. For example, the code itself can be analyzed as part of a CI pipeline, incorporating innovative practices such as

1. Looking for potential policy violations, for example, wide open IAM permission sets, insecure security group settings, public S3 buckets, out-of-compliance EC2 instance class types (do you *really* need that x1.32xlarge instance type), and so on

2. Assessing basic code quality, for example, linting, template validation, and so on

3. Baking in quality testing, for example, spec-based infrastructure/service testing/validation, and so on

4. Introducing peer-based code review practices

5. Introducing compliance protocols such as separation of duties for infrastructure deployments

As tooling has matured, new avenues have opened up to continue to bridge the gap between dev and ops. As the current generation of declarative tooling has grown more mature, new imperative toolsets using developer-friendly languages have evolved as abstractions over top of the declarative frameworks (e.g., the AWS CDK and Pulumi). The emergence of these types of tools further empowers developers to take control of their own destinies when it comes to designing their own infrastructure to deploy their applications on.

CHAPTER 2

The Current Landscape

The current landscape is an interesting mix of proprietary, vendor-locked tooling and cross-cloud compatible open source tooling. Some of these tools are primarily focused on managing the lifecycle of IaaS and PaaS services from providers, while some of them are traditional configuration management tools – capable of automating host/virtual machine configurations – that have been "bolted onto" to work with IaaS and PaaS services (though mostly as an afterthought). As we consider these tools, we'll consider the following:

- *How Do We Interact with the Tool?* Is it declarative? Procedural?

- *What Is the Tool's Primary Function?* Is it an actual orchestration tool? Or does it add to or work alongside an existing orchestration tool?

- *What View of Resources Does the Tool Take?* Does it use some state-tracking mechanism to keep track of your estate? Does it care?

© Bradley Campbell 2020
B. Campbell, *The Definitive Guide to AWS Infrastructure Automation*,
https://doi.org/10.1007/978-1-4842-5398-4_2

Declarative Tools

CloudFormation

When it comes to AWS, every conversation around declarative tooling starts with CloudFormation. Why? Most importantly, CloudFormation is the default tool that AWS provides its users to give them access to declarative, infrastructure-as-code-based functionality. In fact, many of the third-party declarative tools that exist for AWS leverage CloudFormation under the covers, essentially offering extensions or augmenting functionality provided by CloudFormation to create an experience more closely aligned to that of a programming language – tools like Sceptre offer extensions, while tools such as Troposphere and even AWS' own CDK work in conjunction with CloudFormation to provide a programming language-based experience. Per AWS' documentation[1]

> *AWS CloudFormation provides a common language for you to describe and provision all the infrastructure resources in your cloud environment. CloudFormation allows you to use a simple text file to model and provision, in an automated and secure manner, all the resources needed for your applications across all regions and accounts. This file serves as the single source of truth for your cloud environment.*

---

[1]AWS CloudFormation. https://aws.amazon.com/cloudformation/

Benefits

In its most basic form, CloudFormation is relatively easy to use. Templates can be either JSON- or YAML-based documents and so are relatively straightforward to author. The AWS CLI has a built-in template validation function which can evaluate a template before it is used by identifying syntax issues and other possible deployment-time issues. Templates can be deployed locally using the AWS CLI or can be staged to an S3 bucket, giving the user the ability to deploy from either the CLI or the AWS console (usage of some of CloudFormation's more powerful features requires deployment from an S3 bucket). While new services aren't always supported at time of release by CloudFormation, support for most newly released services usually follows within a few weeks of product release. CloudFormation has support for macros (called "intrinsic functions" in CloudFormation parlance), which provide additional functionality.

For the beginning infrastructure-as-code practitioner, CloudFormation is a great starting point. It provides good support for core AWS services. As CloudFormation itself is an AWS service, you are entitled to support with problems related to CloudFormation itself (levels of support will depend on support tier for the given account). While end users are unable to peep into how CloudFormation works under the covers, as CloudFormation is itself an AWS service, it is a relatively safe assumption that the functionality provided by CloudFormation is safe to use in the deployment and management of critical assets and services. In fact, a very well-known third-party tool – the Serverless Framework – cites "the safety and reliability of CloudFormation" as its reason for relying on CloudFormation to actually handle resource management.[2]

---

[2]https://serverless.com/framework/docs/providers/aws/guide/
deploying#how-it-works

Perhaps one of the most compelling reasons companies use CloudFormation is that, as an AWS service, it is covered under AWS Support offerings. While third-party tooling is covered under the Business and Enterprise support offerings, Amazon would not be in a position to offer bugfixes or feature prioritization with a tool like Terraform, for example.

Drawbacks

While the services that are supported are generally supported in a robust manner (i.e., all facets/parameters of a service are supported), there are several aspects that are less positive and worth considering:

- *Service Support Availability*. There is often a lag from time of release of a new service until its support is available in CloudFormation. This continues to be a point of contention in the AWS user community.[3] This has anecdotally led to an argument that CloudFormation should not be considered a first-class service of the AWS, and early adopters are better served by looking at third-party tools which generally provide support for new services more quickly.

- *Limitations to Extensibility.* While there are native functions and limited support for macros, these are not extensible; custom logic is relegated to the context of Lambda functions only. Hence, if local logic is needed, it has to be supported through the use of a wrapper script or program. For example, Sceptre's hooks mechanism allows for local operations to be carried out

---

[3]"A Quick CloudFormation Update" – Reddit. `www.reddit.com/r/aws/comments/avx449/a_quick_cloudformation_update/`

before or after a stack is created, updated, or deleted.[4] While Terraform doesn't have a direct corollary to something like Sceptre's hooks (which are still being provided by an additional tool), Terraform provides interfaces where you would likely want to perform the same sorts of operations you would likely carry out in a hook, for instance, using an external data source[5] to execute an operation on some outside system to leverage from within your Terraform deployment.

- *Lack of Expressiveness in DSL.* Template logic isn't extensible, and many general-purpose logic mechanisms aren't supported. For example, there is no concept of a loop within CloudFormation. While this is available in third-party DSL wrappers that employ a programming language, like Troposphere, this functionality isn't available within CloudFormation itself. Once again, looking at Terraform, you get access to looplike constructs via its *count* metaparameter (which we will look at in Chapter 4). Additionally, traditional for loops are available in some contexts as of the release of Terraform v0.12.[6]

- *Inconsistent Experiences.* Though the CLI supports the deployment of local templates, templates must be staged from an S3 bucket to take advantage of features like Transform functions. Additionally, users who deploy templates locally are much more restricted in

---

[4]https://sceptre.cloudreach.com/latest/docs/hooks.html
[5]www.terraform.io/docs/providers/external/data_source.html
[6]https://github.com/rberlind/terraform-0.12-examples/blob/master/for-expressions/lists-and-maps-with-for.tf#L13

the overall size of their templates compared to users who opt to stage their templates in S3 buckets and deploy from there instead (approx. 50KB vs. 460KB).[7]

- *Feature Tradeoffs.* Features such as StackSets tout the promise of "extend[ing] the functionality of stacks by enabling you to create, update, or delete stacks across multiple accounts and regions with a single operation."[8] While on the surface this looks like a very powerful and promising feature of CloudFormation stacks, you actually end up sacrificing quite a few of CloudFormation's more useful features to use StackSets. While StackSets address pain points that at-scale CloudFormation users would otherwise address through third-party of bespoke tooling, users of StackSets are forced to give up access to powerful features such as Transform functions, which have a variety of uses within CloudFormation templates.[9]

Overall

Any tool discussed in this book is going to come with its fair share of issues, things users wish were different about it, and things it does well. I have spent the last year managing complex cloud-native estates in a serverless application environment with the use of CloudFormation (and in some

---

[7]https://docs.aws.amazon.com/AWSCloudFormation/latest/UserGuide/ cloudformation-limits.html

[8]https://docs.aws.amazon.com/AWSCloudFormation/latest/UserGuide/what- is-cfnstacksets.html

[9]https://docs.aws.amazon.com/AWSCloudFormation/latest/UserGuide/ transform-section-structure.html

cases, custom resources and local helper scripts to make things more automated); prior to that, I worked almost exclusively with Terraform for three years. CloudFormation is well suited for the task of managing complex applications. I have used it and seen it used at scale inside a Fortune 100 company.

Now that we've covered CloudFormation, the stage is set to discuss tools that augment CloudFormation's native functionalities. These tools generally exist in two classes: the first are tools that present domain-specific languages (DSLs) in general-purpose programming languages that then generate CloudFormation template code for you; the second are a class of tools that make the actual deployment of CloudFormation stacks less cumbersome for the user.

CloudFormation DSLs and Template Generators

In our exploration of tools that enhance the overall CloudFormation experience, we'll talk about DSLs and template generators. In my personal experience, one of the better-known tools representative of this class of tools is Troposphere. Troposphere allows developers with Python programming experience to author Python classes to model their deployments. In turn, Troposphere will generate CloudFormation templates that can be deployed using standard CloudFormation deployment mechanisms.

Troposphere

Troposphere[10] is a wrapper for CloudFormation based on the Python programming language. Its power lies in giving engineers the ability to model deployments using traditional object-oriented principles as well

---

[10]Troposphere. `https://github.com/cloudtools/troposphere`

as the additional logical constructs inspired by most general-purpose programming languages. For instance, an EC2 instance modeled in CloudFormation might look like what we see in Listing 2-1:[11]

Listing 2-1. ec2_instance_snippet.yml

```
EC2Instance:
  Type: AWS::EC2::Instance
  Properties:
    InstanceType:
      Ref: InstanceType
    SecurityGroups:
      - Ref: InstanceSecurityGroup
    KeyName:
      Ref: KeyName
    ImageId:
      Fn::FindInMap:
        - AWSRegionArch2AMI
        - Ref: AWS::Region
        - Fn::FindInMap:
          - AWSInstanceType2Arch
          - Ref: InstanceType
          - Arch
```

In comparison, that same EC2 instance modeled in Troposphere might look like Listing 2-2.[12]

---

[11]Borrowed from CloudFormation Template at https://github.com/tongueroo/cloudformation-examples/blob/master/templates/single-instance.yml

[12]Adapted from a Troposphere GitHub Repo Example. https://github.com/cloudtools/troposphere#duplicating-a-single-instance-sample-would-look-like-this

Listing 2-2. ec2_instance_troposphere.py

```python
#!/usr/bin/env python

from troposphere import Base64, FindInMap, GetAtt
from troposphere import Parameter, Output, Ref, Template
import troposphere.ec2 as ec2

template = Template()

...

ec2_instance = template.add_resource(ec2.Instance(
    "Ec2Instance",
    ImageId=FindInMap("AWSRegionArch2AMI", Ref("AWS::Region"),
    FindInMap(
        "AWSRegionArch2AMI",
        Ref("InstanceType"),
        "Arch"
    )),
    InstanceType=Ref(InstanceType),
    KeyName=Ref(KeyName),
    SecurityGroups=[Ref(InstanceSecurityGroup)]
))

print(template.to_yaml())
```

While this looks pretty similar on its face to the pure CloudFormation example provided earlier, consider the situation where you want to add two more EC2 instances to the deployment modeled in our infrastructure-as-code solution. Based on our previous CloudFormation example, our new template would look like Listing 2-3.

Listing 2-3. ec2_multi_instance_snippet.yml

```yaml
EC2Instance1:
  Type: AWS::EC2::Instance
  Properties:
    InstanceType:
      Ref: InstanceType
    SecurityGroups:
      - Ref: InstanceSecurityGroup
    KeyName:
      Ref: KeyName
    ImageId:
      Fn::FindInMap:
        - AWSRegionArch2AMI
        - Ref: AWS::Region
        - Fn::FindInMap:
          - AWSInstanceType2Arch
          - Ref: InstanceType
          - Arch

EC2Instance2:
  Type: AWS::EC2::Instance
  Properties:
    InstanceType:
      Ref: InstanceType
    SecurityGroups:
      - Ref: InstanceSecurityGroup
    KeyName:
      Ref: KeyName
    ImageId:
      Fn::FindInMap:
        - AWSRegionArch2AMI
        - Ref: AWS::Region
```

```
      - Fn::FindInMap:
        - AWSInstanceType2Arch
        - Ref: InstanceType
        - Arch
EC2Instance3:
  Type: AWS::EC2::Instance
  Properties:
    InstanceType:
      Ref: InstanceType
    SecurityGroups:
      - Ref: InstanceSecurityGroup
    KeyName:
      Ref: KeyName
    ImageId:
      Fn::FindInMap:
        - AWSRegionArch2AMI
        - Ref: AWS::Region
        - Fn::FindInMap:
          - AWSInstanceType2Arch
          - Ref: InstanceType
          - Arch
```

Now, let's consider what this might look like in the context of our earlier Troposphere example in Listing 2-4.

Listing 2-4. ec2_multi_instance_troposphere.py

```
#!/usr/bin/env python

from troposphere import Base64, FindInMap, GetAtt
from troposphere import Parameter, Output, Ref, Template
import troposphere.ec2 as ec2

template = Template()
```

35

```
...

for i in range(3):
    ec2_instance = template.add_resource(ec2.Instance(
        "Ec2Instance{}".format(i+1),
        ImageId=FindInMap("AWSRegionArch2AMI",
        Ref("AWS::Region"), FindInMap(
            "AWSRegionArch2AMI",
            Ref("InstanceType"),
            "Arch"
        )),
        InstanceType=Ref(InstanceType),
        KeyName=Ref(KeyName),
        SecurityGroups=[Ref(InstanceSecurityGroup)]
    ))

print(template.to_yaml())
```

Relative to the CloudFormation examples (e.g., Listing 2-1 and Listing 2-3), the amount of change necessary to add any arbitrary number of additional resources is quite minimal. With Troposphere, the inclusion of the **for** loop is all that is required to add new resources with a resource definition matching the original. Contrast this with the case of CloudFormation, where we essentially have to copy and paste our original definition (taking care to modify the resource identifiers as we do so), as no such looping construct exists in CloudFormation (for more advanced practitioners who note that a nested stack would reduce the boilerplate here, that observation is correct, but we would still have to add two more references to the stack template that creates our EC2 instance from our parent template).

Even from our small contrived example here, the power of a tool like Troposphere should be self-evident. Access to control structures, outside libraries, and the ability to model our deployments with modularity and reusability using object-oriented classes are extremely powerful features that we will explore more in-depth in future chapters. For now, though, consider the use of Troposphere if you have a bit of Python experience and find yourself building out an infrastructure deployment using CloudFormation. There are actually many tools similar to Troposphere that are available for other programming languages; a listing of these tools and their corresponding languages can be found in the Appendix.

AWS Cloud Development Kit (CDK)

The AWS CDK,[13] while possessing many of the attributes of a tool like Troposphere, is a bit different in the sense that outputting raw CloudFormation templates is not its focus (though, it does support this functionality). The CDK also contains a command-line tool that manages the actual deployment of the stacks – essentially making the actual underlying use of CloudFormation transparent to the end user. The CDK truly begins to bridge a long-standing gap between dev and ops tooling (even in the "DevOps" era), as developers with skill across a variety of languages (Python, C#/.NET, JavaScript, and TypeScript at the time of this writing) will find themselves able to author reusable, component-based infrastructure without the need to learn a new tool. Instead, developers just need to learn to work with new libraries and classes – a task commonplace to most development projects anyways. A wide variety of AWS services are supported by the CDK (in contrast to tools like AWS Serverless Application Model (SAM) or Serverless.js, which are targeted at a very narrow subset of AWS services).

---

[13]What is the AWS CDK? https://docs.aws.amazon.com/cdk/latest/guide/what-is.html

If you're not yet convinced of the power of this class of tools, consider this example from AWS' documentation page. The example (Listing 2-5) is TypeScript code that creates an AWS Fargate service.[14]

Listing 2-5. AWS CDK Example (cdk_example.ts)

```
export class MyEcsConstructStack extends cdk.Stack {
  constructor(scope: cdk.App, id: string, props?: cdk.
  StackProps) {
    super(scope, id, props);

    const vpc = new ec2.VpcNetwork(this, 'MyVpc', {
      maxAZs: 3 // Default is all AZs in region
    });

    const cluster = new ecs.Cluster(this, 'MyCluster', {
      vpc: vpc
    });

    // Create a load-balanced Fargate service and make it public
    new ecs.LoadBalancedFargateService(this, 'MyFargateService', {
      cluster: cluster,  // Required
      cpu: '512', // Default is 256
      desiredCount: 6,  // Default is 1
      image: ecs.ContainerImage.fromRegistry("amazon/amazon-
      ecs-sample"), // Required
      memoryMiB: '2048',  // Default is 512
      publicLoadBalancer: true  // Default is false
    });
  }
}
```

---

[14]What is the AWS CDK? https://docs.aws.amazon.com/cdk/latest/guide/what-is.html

Per the AWS documentation, these 20 or so lines of code in Listing 2-5 generate **over 600 lines** of raw CloudFormation template code with the help of the CDK. If you've ever spent a day (or several) cranking out CloudFormation code to build a deployment, you probably already have an appreciation for the power of the CDK.

Serverless.js

The Serverless Framework[15] differs a bit from the rest of the pack in that its target audience isn't your typical cloud/devops engineer whose primary focus is to define a cloud infrastructure on AWS. Instead, the primary audience of the Serverless Framework are application developers. Hence, the Serverless Framework is a much more application-centric framework than even the CDK (which isn't necessarily concerned with deploying applications per se, though it provides an application-*like* method by which to deploy applications' underlying infrastructure). Another key differentiator is Severless' support for several major cloud providers, including Google Cloud, Azure, AWS, and others. These two points illustrate key points of differentiation between the Serverless Framework and most of the other tools and frameworks this book covers.

With the points of differentiation with Serverless well understood, how does it interact with AWS specifically? Does it employ some sort of API implementation of its own abstracted over provider API layers? The Serverless Framework plainly describes its relationship to provisioning AWS resources in its documentation:[16]

---

[15]Serverless Framework. `https://serverless.com/`

[16]Serverless Framework – Deploying. `https://serverless.com/framework/docs/ providers/aws/guide/deploying#how-it-works`

> *The Serverless Framework translates all syntax in*
> *serverless.yml to a single AWS CloudFormation*
> *template. By depending on CloudFormation for*
> *deployments, users of the Serverless Framework get*
> *the safety and reliability of CloudFormation.*

From a user experience perspective, the Serverless Framework offers what could be best described as an augmented CloudFormation-like experience. For example, take the base unit of work for Serverless, the **serverless.yml** file. An example file might look what we see in Listing 2-6:[17]

Listing 2-6. Example serverless.yml Template

```
service: fetch-file-and-store-in-s3

frameworkVersion: ">=1.1.0"

custom:
  bucket: <your-bucket-name>

provider:
  name: aws
  runtime: nodejs8.10
  stage: dev
  region: us-west-1
  iamRoleStatements:
    - Effect: Allow
      Action:
        - s3:PutObject
        - s3:PutObjectAcl
      Resource: "arn:aws:s3:::${self:custom.bucket}/*"
```

---

[17]From Serverless repo, examples folder. https://github.com/serverless/
examples/blob/master/aws-node-fetch-file-and-store-in-s3/serverless.yml

```
functions:
  save:
    handler: handler.save
    environment:
      BUCKET: ${self:custom.bucket}
```

Much like CloudFormation, a template describes your resources. Serverless provides a CLI tool which then allows the user the provision of their resources into AWS. Under the covers, Serverless creates CloudFormation templates, stages artifacts in S3, and then provisions the templates using CloudFormation APIs.

AWS SAM

AWS' Serverless Application Model is another niche tool, very similar to the Serverless Framework. AWS describes SAM as follows:[18]

> *The AWS Serverless Application Model (AWS SAM)*
> *is an open-source framework that enables you to*
> *build serverless applications on AWS. It provides you*
> *with a template specification to define your serverless*
> *application, and a command line interface (CLI)*
> *tool.*

As with Serverless, the focus of SAM is on deploying resources that comprise a serverless backend. This type of deployment typically comprises Lambda functions, API gateway endpoints, other "glue" such as IAM permissions and roles, and other event dispatchers (e.g., CloudWatch Events Rules). At the highest level, both of these tools provide a layer of abstraction over CloudFormation. The biggest points of comparison between these tools worth considering are

---

[18]AWS SAM Documentation. https://docs.aws.amazon.com/serverless-application-model/index.html

- ***Multi-cloud Support for Serverless Framework.*** While
  the focus of this book is on AWS, this point should not
  be ignored in any context. AWS SAM only supports
  AWS, whereas Serverless (at the time of writing)
  supports AWS (via its Lambda offering), Google Cloud
  Platform's (GCP) Cloud Functions, Azure Functions,
  CloudFlare (via its Workers offering[19]), OpenWhisk[20]
  (upon which IBM's Cloud Functions service offering
  is based[21]), and Kubeless[22] (which supports GCP's
  Kubernetes Engine [GKE] offering).

- ***Extensibility.*** As Serverless and SAM both are intended
  to cover a small subset of the larger collection of AWS
  services, they bring additional considerations that
  other tools and frameworks may not necessarily need
  to consider, as each maintains a primary focus on
  developing applications. Mocks for online services, unit
  testing, integration testing, code linting, code coverage,
  and a multitude of other considerations typically come
  along with application code development. Serverless
  provides facilities to account for these facets of
  application development within the framework itself

---

[19]CloudFlare Workers Documentation. https://developers.cloudflare.com/workers/about/

[20]Apache OpenWhisk. https://openwhisk.apache.org/

[21]IBM Cloud Functions. www.ibm.com/cloud/functions

[22]https://kubeless.io/

through an extensible plugin architecture.[23] There are currently quite a few plugins developed for Serverless.[24] There is no corollary feature within AWS SAM.

CloudFormation Orchestrators

With a thorough treatment of DSLs and template generators behind us, we take a look at orchestration tools. Whereas DSLs and template generators are intended to address some of the perceived shortcomings and pain points of simply authoring CloudFormation templates, orchestrators address a different set of concerns: easily, reliably, and effectively provisioning and managing deployments centered around CloudFormation.

By way of example, let's take the simple case of deploying a Lambda function. We can work around complexities in deployment by simply inlining our function code in our CloudFormation templates; this comes with serious limitations and really not a viable option except in cases of the simplest, standalone functions. If we no longer consider inlining our code to be a viable strategy, we now have a few tasks that we must take care of before we even get to run an **AWS CloudFormation – CLI** command. First, if our code consists of more than one file, we have to zip all of the necessary files up in a single archive. Once the code is in a state where it's represented by a single file (whether a single code file or a zip archive), it needs to be deployed to S3. CloudFormation's CLI options provide no facility to perform these operations. To accomplish these tasks, it is up to you to craft some sort of script (bash, Python, etc.) to perform all of these bootstrapping functions. If your scripting skills are really up-to-snuff, you may opt to simply abstract all of these tasks into some sort of subcommand for your script, additionally adding in functionality to kick off (or update)

---

[23]Serverless Blog – How to Write Your First Serverless Plugin - Part 1.
   https://serverless.com/blog/writing-serverless-plugins/
[24]Serverless Plugins. https://serverless.com/plugins/

the actual stack build using the CloudFormation calls from whatever library or context your script is built with. While this simple example highlights the type of boilerplate task that's addressed by a preexisting framework like the Serverless Framework, there are myriad other tasks that could potentially need to be done as a precursor to a deployment: fetching configuration values from a third-party API; archiving and staging Ansible, Chef, or Puppet artifacts (i.e., playbooks, cookbooks) in S3; grabbing STS credentials to use for deployment; checking an enterprise ITSM to make sure an open ticket exists for our current deployment; and the list goes on. In each of these cases, we could continue to rely on custom scripts, or we could look toward something more general purpose to meet our needs. Orchestration tools look to fill these types of gaps in pre- and post-deployment stages, while relying on CloudFormation to manage deployments.

Sceptre

Sceptre[25] is a tool designed to address these types of gaps in overall deployment and orchestration tooling with respect to CloudFormation. Per Sceptre's about page, its motivation is stated as follows:

> *CloudFormation lacks a robust tool to deploy and manage stacks. The AWS CLI and Boto3 both provide some functionality, but neither offer the chaining of one stack's outputs to another's parameters or easy support for working with role assumes or in multiple accounts, all of which are common tasks when deploying infrastructure.*
>
> *Sceptre was developed to produce a single tool which can be used to deploy any and all CloudFormation.*

---

[25]Sceptre. https://sceptre.cloudreach.com/latest/about.html

Sceptre utilizes a conventions-based framework to provide cascading configurations, and the ability to manage separate CloudFormation stacks that logically belong together using a notion Sceptre refers to as a StackGroup.[26]

In my opinion, the most powerful and compelling aspect of Sceptre comes through the use of hooks.[27] These provide integration points for custom logic in the context of Sceptre's CLI commands and subcommands. Going back to our previous discussion about pre-deployment actions such as landing Lambda code in an S3 bucket, validating or registering a ticket in an ITSM system, or whatever the case, Sceptre provides a clean, elegant facility for implementing this type of logic by authoring custom Python classes. Authoring a custom hook involves adding to a specified directory a Python class of the form shown in Listing 2-7.

Listing 2-7. Sceptre Hook Python Class Boilerplate

```
from sceptre.hooks import Hook

class CustomHook(Hook):

    def __init__(self, *args, **kwargs):
        super(CustomHook, self).__init__(*args, **kwargs)

    def run(self):
        """

        run is the method called by Sceptre. It should carry
        out the work
        intended by this hook.
```

---

[26]Sceptre StackGroup Config. https://sceptre.cloudreach.com/latest/docs/
stack_group_config.html

[27]Sceptre Hooks. https://sceptre.cloudreach.com/latest/docs/hooks.html

```
self.argument is available from the base class and
contains the
argument defined in the Sceptre config file (see the
following)

The following attributes may be available from the base
class:
self.stack_config  (A dict of data from <stack_name>.
yaml)
self.stack.stack_group_config  (A dict of data from
config.yaml)
self.connection_manager (A connection_manager)
"""

print(self.argument)
```

Sceptre utilizes YAML to create declarative templates to define deployments. These templates reference CloudFormation templates as well as other metadata, such as configuration data. Hooks are also referenced from these templates, as seen in Listing 2-8.

Listing 2-8. Example Sceptre Stack Config File (References Custom Hook Defined in Listing 2-7)

```
template_path: <...>
hooks:
  before_create:
    - !custom_hook <argument> # The argument is accessible via
      self.argument
```

In addition to the powerful features just discussed, the use of Sceptre's orchestration capabilities can be coupled with some of the previously mentioned DSL tools, namely, Troposphere. It also integrates with the Python-based Jinja2[28] templating engine. These impressive features merit consideration for your next project in lieu of bespoke orchestration tooling.

Other Representatives

Just as we saw with the DSL tools, there is a pretty considerable ecosystem of these types of tools. Some have features that Sceptre do not, and vice versa. If you are in the market for an effective orchestration tool for CloudFormation and you have requirements Sceptre doesn't meet, check out some of the tools in the Appendix.

Tools Not Based on CloudFormation

Terraform

Terraform[29] currently has a strong position in the infrastructure world where third-party tools are used. Terraform does not rely on CloudFormation as a provisioning mechanism; instead, it relies on the AWS SDK (Golang, as Terraform itself is written in Golang) for its underlying interactions with the AWS API layer. Terraform has its own built-in state management mechanism for mapping desired state (represented by code) to actual state (actual EC2 instances, S3 buckets, etc.). Terraform describes its state mechanism as follows:[30]

---

[28]Jinja2. http://jinja.pocoo.org/docs/2.10/

[29]Terraform. www.terraform.io/

[30]Terraform – Purpose of Terraform State. www.terraform.io/docs/state/purpose.html

*Terraform requires some sort of database to map
Terraform config to the real world. When you have a
resource "aws_instance" "foo" in your configuration,
Terraform uses this map to know that instance
i-abcd1234 is represented by that resource.*

*For some providers like AWS, Terraform could
theoretically use something like AWS tags. Early
prototypes of Terraform actually had no state files
and used this method. However, we quickly ran into
problems. The first major issue was a simple one: not
all resources support tags, and not all cloud providers
support tags.*

*Therefore, for mapping configuration to resources in
the real world, Terraform uses its own state structure.*

Terraform uses a custom DSL – called HCL (short for "HashiCorp
Configuration Language") for authoring its templates. HCL is a superset of
JSON. An example HCL file is shown in Listing 2-9.[31]

Listing 2-9. Terraform HCL Example

```
resource "aws_instance" "w1_instance" {
  instance_type = "t2.nano"
  vpc_security_group_ids = [ "${aws_security_group.w1_security_
  group.id}" ]
  associate_public_ip_address = true
  user_data = "${file("../../shared/user-data.txt")}"
```

---

[31]Smartling Terraform Examples Repo. https://raw.githubusercontent.com/
Smartling/aws-terraform-workshops/master/answers/w1/ec2.tf

```
tags {
  Name = "w1-myinstance"
}

ami = "ami-cb2305a1"
availability_zone = "us-east-1c"

# This is fake VPC subnet ID, please put real one to make
this config work
subnet_id = "subnet-1111111"
}
```

Terraform relies upon complex built-in logic to figure out dependencies and uses that logic when creating, updating, and removing resources.

What Does Terraform Offer?

While some third-party tools intrinsically trust CloudFormation as a safe, reliable way to manage AWS resources, there are some aspects of Terraform that are stark points of contrast relative to CloudFormation, such as

- *State Visibility.* As we just mentioned, Terraform utilizes its own state-tracking mechanism. This offers us the ability to quickly and easily look at the state of our deployment, to detect drift (though CloudFormation also offers this functionality as of recently[32]).

- *State Manipulation.* Though better left to more advanced users, Terraform provides interfaces through which to manipulate resources managed by state.

---

[32]CloudFormation - Drift Detection. https://aws.amazon.com/blogs/aws/new-cloudformation-drift-detection/

Perhaps an EC2 instance was unintentionally removed by someone through the console – it is a relatively trivial task to remove that resource from Terraform's state file, usually with no negative consequences moving forward. The options to deal with this scenario in CloudFormation are less palatable – ranging from deleting the entire stack and reprovisioning it to trying to "trick" the engine[33] into coming back into sync. This is an extremely powerful and differentiating feature of Terraform, but it is also crucially important to understand what state means to Terraform and how Terraform represents state before attempting to manipulate it (we will also discuss some ways to safeguard yourself while manipulating state in Chapter 4).

- ***Interoperability.*** Much to the same point made previously with regard to Serverless, while the focus of this book is on AWS, I would do any reader of this book a grave disservice to ignore the notion that we interact with other service providers – perhaps Fastly[34] for CDN, or maybe DNSimple[35] or Infoblox[36] for DNS management – to manage the entirety of our application ecosystems. While conceptually we can address these needs with custom resources within CloudFormation or perhaps a tool like Sceptre to fetch

---

[33]AWS Support Knowledge Center. "How do I update an AWS CloudFormation stack that's failing because of a resource that I manually deleted?". https://aws.amazon.com/premiumsupport/knowledge-center/failing-stack-updates-deleted/

[34]Fastly. www.fastly.com

[35]DNSimple. https://dnsimple.com

[36]Infoblox. www.infoblox.com/

information before we deploy our stacks, what if we could use the same tool to manage our interaction with all of these service providers in the same way? To be brief, Terraform provides that functionality. Out-of-the-box, it supports a plethora of service providers[37] (with a robust ecosystem of community-provided provider plugins[38]).

- **Extensibility.** Building upon the previous point, it is also possible to write your own plugins to work with services for which a provider plugin isn't already available.

- **Built-In Orchestration Capabilities.** Our pre-deployment needs don't go away simply because we choose a different toolchain. However, choices in tooling can mitigate the need for additional tools altogether. For instance, in the case of our simple Lambda packaging setup for Sceptre, we could actually accomplish the same functionality without third-party tools using Terraform's archive_file data source[39] and null_resource with local-exec provisioner.[40]

---

[37]Terraform Providers. www.terraform.io/docs/providers/

[38]Terraform Community Providers. www.terraform.io/docs/providers/type/community-index.html

[39]Terraform – archive_file Data Source. www.terraform.io/docs/providers/archive/d/archive_file.html

[40]Terraform – null_resource Resource. www.terraform.io/docs/providers/null/resource.html

- *Open Source.* Terraform exists under the Mozilla Public
License (MPL). While it may be a moot point to some to
want to use an open source tool to interact with closed-
source cloud service provider backends, Terraform itself
is an open source tool, whereas CloudFormation is not (to
be fair, this is a bit of an apples-to-oranges comparison).

Pulumi

Pulumi[41] is an interesting tool that has shown up in industry circles as of
late. It is in many ways analogous to the AWS CDK, providing a higher-
level programming language abstraction over runtimes that manage
API-driven infrastructure deployments (e.g., CloudFormation in the
case of the CDK). Based on Pulumi's documentation,[42] Pulumi's runtime
wraps Terraform providers to provide API-level interactions with service
providers. Developers, however, can ignore this low-level plumbing, ditch
HashiCorp Configuration Language (HCL), and stick with authoring
infrastructure using object-oriented or component-oriented application
designs to create reusable software components for defining infrastructure
in Golang, JavaScript (or TypeScript, or any language that can be transpiled
to JavaScript for that matter), or Python.

Pulumi also provides its own web-backed service for managing state
(something that HashiCorp has recently begun to offer and also a topic we
will dive deep into in Chapter 4) and a CLI to scaffold projects and manage
deployments. While I haven't yet had the chance to manage a production
deployment with Pulumi, I am looking forward to rolling up our sleeves
and getting some hands-on experience with Pulumi in Chapter 6 later in
this book.

---

[41]Pulumi. www.pulumi.com/

[42]Pulumi – Integration with Terraform. https://pulumi.io/reference/vs/
terraform/#integration-with-terraform

Non-declarative Tooling

So what makes a tool declarative? Is it simply the use of YAML or JSON and an underlying engine to provision resources? In short, the answer is no. Working back from our own attempt to derive some sort of bespoke tooling in Chapter 1, we could have easily adapted our tooling to read in from a JSON or YAML template before we introduced some sort of state-tracking mechanism (though our state-tracking mechanism was service-specific and not very robust). The point I'm trying to make here though is that what makes the tooling declarative is that your code represents a desired state which the tooling is able to track against current state. While a state-tracking mechanism doesn't have to be a local file or database (i.e., for a limited set of AWS services, we could perhaps rely on resource tags), the fact stands that the tool is declarative when it is able to reconcile a desired outcome against a current reality. Ansible's ec2 module demonstrates this lack of true declarative behavior, and we'll take a more in-depth look at how it fails to meet the definition in the chapter dealing with these types of tools.

Conclusion

As we wrap up this chapter, I hope you have an appreciation for the vastness of the horizon as we survey the current infrastructure automation landscape. If you didn't make a point of doing so during the chapter, please have a look at the Appendix – while we have covered general tooling types, there is a vast ecosystem of tools in each class (and even some that address multiple types of concerns) available to you. If you have strong preferences toward programming languages, have a look at some of those language-specific tools, or maybe even kick the wheels on Terraform to see if it's worth investing an evening or two to better understand how these tools work and the time you can potentially save yourself in the long run by reducing development of bespoke tooling to address some of the boilerplate concerns in this rapidly evolving space.

53

CHAPTER 3

CloudFormation In-Depth

Though there are no definitive numbers on the percentage of AWS users that rely on infrastructure-as-code tooling, or how those users would decompose into a "CloudFormation vs. everything else" categorization, a general survey of AWS-related jobs on LinkedIn or elsewhere should be a pretty good indicator that CloudFormation has yet to be supplanted by third-party tools. Especially among businesses with AWS Support contracts, one of the most compelling arguments in favor of its adoption is that it is a native offering from AWS, and it falls under the purview of AWS Support.

In this chapter, we will work through the following concepts:

- ***Template Anatomy.*** What a basic template looks like

- ***Deployment.*** How to manage stacks using the CLI

- ***Custom Resources.*** What they are, when you might need to use one, and how to create them

- ***Advanced Intrinsic Functions and Macros.*** How to use these and scenarios in which you might want to use them

© Bradley Campbell 2020
B. Campbell, *The Definitive Guide to AWS Infrastructure Automation*,
https://doi.org/10.1007/978-1-4842-5398-4_3

- **Nested Stacks.** Benefits of nested stacks and how to build with them

- **Stack Sets.** Benefits of Stack Sets and tradeoffs in relation to nested stacks (and other CloudFormation functionality)

Template Anatomy

Templates can be written in JSON or YAML. I would recommend writing any new templates you create in YAML as they are much easier to work with. As you work more and more with CloudFormation, you will likely come across legacy templates authored in JSON. In such cases, you will find it helpful to have a tool like cfn-flip[1] in your toolbox; in the meantime, though, we're going to put that in our back pocket and move on with creating resources from a template we'll create ourselves.

Listing 3-1. ec2_instance_template.yml

```
AWSTemplateFormatVersion: '2010-09-09'
Description: |
  Creates an EC2 instance with a security group.
  Based on AWS sample template
"EC2InstanceWithSecurityGroupSample",
      which is available at https://amzn.to/2WdaX2i.

Parameters:
  KeyName:
    Description: Name of an existing EC2 KeyPair to enable
    access to the instance
```

---

[1]aws-cfn-template-flip. https://github.com/awslabs/aws-cfn-template-flip

```
  Type: String
  Default: "
  ConstraintDescription: must be a string.

OperatingSystem:
  Description: Chosen operating system
  Type: String
  Default: AmazonLinux2
  AllowedValues:
    - AmazonLinux2
    - Windows2016Base

InstanceType:
  Description: EC2 instance type
  Type: String
  Default: t2.small
  AllowedValues:
    - t2.nano
    - t2.micro
    - t2.small
    - t2.medium
    - m4.large
    - m4.xlarge
  ConstraintDescription: must be a valid EC2 instance type.

PublicLocation:
  Description: The IP address range that can be used to
  connect to the EC2 instances
  Type: String
  MinLength: '9'
  MaxLength: '18'
  Default: '0.0.0.0/0'
```

```
      AllowedPattern: (\d{1,3})\.(\d{1,3})\.(\d{1,3})\.(\d{1,3})/
      (\d{1,2})
      ConstraintDescription: must be a valid IP CIDR range of the
      form x.x.x.x/x.
Conditions:
  HasKeypair: !Not [ !Equals [ !Ref KeyName, " ]]
Mappings:
  Global:
    ConnectPortByOs:
      Windows2016Base: 3389
      AmazonLinux2: 22
  AmiByOs:
    us-east-1:
      Windows2016Base: ami-06bee8e1000e44ca4
      AmazonLinux2: ami-0c6b1d09930fac512
    us-west-2:
      Windows2016Base: ami-07f35a597a32e470d
      AmazonLinux2: ami-0cb72367e98845d43
Resources:
  EC2Instance:
    Type: "AWS::EC2::Instance"
    Properties:
      InstanceType: !Ref 'InstanceType'
      SecurityGroups:
        - !Ref 'InstanceSg'
      KeyName: !If [ 'HasKeypair', !Ref KeyName, !Ref
      "AWS::NoValue" ]
      ImageId: !FindInMap
        - 'AmiByOs'
        - !Ref "AWS::Region"
        - !Ref 'OperatingSystem'
```

```
InstanceSg:
  Type: "AWS::EC2::SecurityGroup"
  Properties:
    GroupDescription: Enable public access via OS-specific port
    SecurityGroupIngress:
      - IpProtocol: tcp
        FromPort: !FindInMap
          - 'Global'
          - 'ConnectPortByOs'
          - !Ref 'OperatingSystem'
        ToPort: !FindInMap
          - 'Global'
          - 'ConnectPortByOs'
          - !Ref 'OperatingSystem'
        CidrIp: !Ref 'PublicLocation'
Outputs:
  InstanceId:
    Description: InstanceId of the EC2 instance
    Value: !Ref 'EC2Instance'
  AZ:
    Description: AZ of the EC2 instance
    Value: !GetAtt 'EC2Instance.AvailabilityZone'
  PublicDNS:
    Description: Public DNSName of the EC2 instance
    Value: !GetAtt 'EC2Instance.PublicDnsName'
  PublicIP:
    Description: Public IP address of the EC2 instance
    Value: !GetAtt 'EC2Instance.PublicIp'
```

Have a look at this template for a few moments. You'll see the following top-level sections:

- AWSTemplateFormatVersion

- Description

- Parameters

- Conditions

- Mappings

- Resources

- Outputs

AWSTemplateFormatVersion

This section is optional. Per AWS docs,[2] if this field isn't specified, the latest version is assumed (which, as of the time of this writing, can only be "2010-09-09"). If used, this field can currently only accept a string literal value.

It is a good idea to include this field as it future-proofs your template to a degree. Suppose AWS introduces a newer version which includes breaking changes (e.g., the behavior of an intrinsic function changes or support for an intrinsic function used in your template is dropped altogether), it is reasonable to assume that a deprecation period would follow for the older template format version. Your templates would continue to function under the older template format version until they could be refactored against the specifications for the newer template format version.

---

[2]https://docs.aws.amazon.com/AWSCloudFormation/latest/UserGuide/
format-version-structure.html

Description

This section is also optional. It must follow the AWSTemplateFormat
Version section (if that section is used). The section supports 1024 bytes
and must be a string literal as well.

Parameters

Believe it or not, parameters are optional. Of course, the scenario that
creates this possibility is that all values are hard-coded in the resource
definitions themselves. That said, don't be surprised if you see this
"optional" section in every template example you encounter throughout
the rest of this book. For the sake of completeness, the full properties
reference for a given parameter is available in AWS docs;[3] my goal
here, though, is to walk you through those properties that are most
indispensible, how to leverage them effectively, and to provide some
personal context around why I see limited usefulness in the others. Let's
look at the **OperatingSystem** parameter for starters. Here, we've got

- *Description.* Optional, but I propose you treat it as
  though it's not. I suppose you can create sufficiently
  long parameter names as to clearly identify the purpose
  of the parameter, but short parameter names help
  you with modularity further, passing values between
  contexts (e.g., the use of a wrapper script or something
  like Sceptre). You have 4,000 characters for your
  description, but I would recommend keeping it under
  80 if it is possible.

---

[3]https://docs.aws.amazon.com/AWSCloudFormation/latest/UserGuide/
parameters-section-structure.html

- *Type.* Required. CloudFormation has support for an interesting variety of types, and you'll need to provide this information in your CloudFormation template.

- *AllowedValues.* Optional. If your input value can easily be constrained to an acceptable list of values, then I would highly recommend using this property to catch bad inputs.

- *Default.* Optional. This is another property I strongly recommend the use of whenever possible.

Looking at the other parameters, let's look at some of the other properties we see in the template:

- *MinLength/Value.* Optional. Dictates minimum length of any value passed as this parameter. I use this sparingly (this and **MaxLength** can also be ignored and captured in an effective regular expression using **AllowedPattern** if desired).

- *MaxLength/Value.* Optional. Dictates maximum length of any value passed as this parameter. I use this sparingly (this and **MinLength** can also be ignored and captured in an effective regular expression using **AllowedPattern** if desired).

- *AllowedPattern.* Optional. Allows you to define a regular expression to validate parameter value inputs. I do not use this frequently (see the "Points of Extended Consideration" section for more info).

- *ConstraintDescription.* Optional. If a constraint is broken by a value passed as a parameter, this message is displayed by the console to give the user a detailed description of the constraint that was flouted. I do not use this property frequently.

- *NoEcho.* Optional. This one is interesting; it masks the value passed to the parameter in the CloudFormation console. While this can provide some level of protection, keep in mind if you're using CloudFormation to seed this same value as an environment variable on a Lambda function, the value is exposed.

Points of Extended Consideration

- *Type.* Be careful of being overzealous in defining parameters using AWS-specific parameter types. If you are using these types, you'll find yourself unable to specify empty values (see the **KeyName** parameter in Listing 3-1); in this case, we were able to use a Condition (e.g., **HasKeyPair**) to conditionally supply the name of the key pair for the **EC2Instance** resource, nulling the parameter out entirely in the event that an actual value wasn't actually provided (e.g., the **!Ref "AWS::NoValue"** being passed in the second condition of the **!If** statement on the **EC2Instance**'s **KeyName** property).

  Another potential pitfall of specifying complex types is in the context of nested stacks. Though we have yet to discuss nested stacks, nested stacks aren't capable of receiving **List<>** parameter types.

  Generally speaking, I have found that it is better to work with more generic types. While it is true that some of the more specific types have interesting and compelling use cases, just remember that if you are working with nested stack implementations or need to heavily rely on conditional logic in your templates, some of these more complex types could potentially cause issues that may leave you between a rock and a hard place further down the road.

- *AllowedPattern.* I love regular expressions. Truly, I do. I would strongly caution you to use them sparingly, however. For instance, in the **PublicLocation** parameter in Listing 3-1, we see the regular expression **(\d{1,3})\.(\d{1,3})\.(\d{1,3})\.(\d{1,3})/(\d{1,2})**; while this is a good regular expression that accurately identifies any valid IPv4 address, consider another value which would be successfully validated by this regular expression: 500.000.0.505/99. This is certainly not a valid IPv4 address and yet is valid in this case. While extremely powerful, they are not a silver bullet – you will often find that coming up with a valid expression for your use case takes a fair amount of time. Additionally, there are frequently unconsidered edge cases (as demonstrated here) that effectively defeat the regex's intent as a validation mechanism.

Conditions

Conditions are optional. My estimation would be that I end up with conditions in about 70% of my templates. In my usage, conditions generally end up falling into one of two categories: those that define whether the stack defined by the template is being deployed in a production or nonproduction environment and those that serve as a trigger for nulling nullable properties on resources based on the values of parameters passed to the stack. Much less frequently, the creation of some specific resource will be contingent on multiple parameter values, and I will map these into a condition specific to that singular resource, though these types of scenarios have been rare in my experience.

Let's have a look at the condition defined in our template from Listing 3-1. We have the condition defined as

```
HasKeypair: !Not [ !Equals [ !Ref KeyName, " ]]
```

Starting from the innermost expression, the **!Equals** … expression evaluates whether the **KeyName** parameter is equal to an empty string or not. That result is then negated. Reading this literally, it could be interpreted as "the value of the **KeyName** parameter is not equal to an empty string."

Mappings

The mappings section is optional. Mappings are stores of predefined values. Keys, intermediate keys, and values of mappings must be string literals; mapping values can also be lists of string literals. For instance, either of the following examples would be a valid mapping.

Listing 3-2. AMI Mapping

```
AmiByOs:
  us-east-1:
    Windows2016Base: ami-06bee8e1000e44ca4
    AmazonLinux2: ami-0c6b1d09930fac512
  us-west-2:
    Windows2016Base: ami-07f35a597a32e470d
    AmazonLinux2: ami-0cb72367e98845d43
```

Listing 3-3. AMI Mapping with Lists

```
AmiByOs:
  us-east-1:
    ValidAMIs:
      - ami-06bee8e1000e44ca4
      - ami-0c6b1d09930fac512
```

```
us-west-2:
  ValidAMIs:
    - ami-07f35a597a32e470d
    - ami-0cb72367e98845d43
```

Mappings must contain a top-level and mid-level key. The **!FindInMap** (or **Fn::FindInMap**) function is used in templates to access mapping values. This function accepts a list as an argument, as seen in Listing 3-1.

```
FromPort: !FindInMap
  - 'Global'
  - 'ConnectPortByOs'
  - !Ref 'OperatingSystem'
```

```
The alternative one-liner YAML list syntax can also be used,
yielding
```

```
FromPort: !FindInMap [ 'Global', 'ConnectPortByOs', !Ref
'OperatingSystem' ]
```

Regional Values

It is not unusual to see maps with intermediate keys that correspond to AWS regions. Well-crafted templates are designed to accommodate multiple AWS regions. Many of the example templates created by AWS accommodate nearly every AWS region, leading to extremely long mappings. Region-specific values can correspond to values such as VPC IDs, subnet IDs, security group IDs, AMI IDs, and so on. You can see one such mapping in Listing 3-2 (which references Listing 3-1). Throughout several years of building solutions to handle deployments to multiple regions, it is rare to see the need for more than two or three regions (one to two primary regions and a failover/DR region). For deployments modeling internationally available SaaS products, you might need to support more regions. Regardless of the number of regions, the model looks the same: build up the map with region-specific keys and appropriate values, and look them up with **!FindInMap**, using the **"AWS::Region"** pseudo-parameter, as demonstrated in passing an AMI ID when setting up our EC2 instance in Listing 3-1.

```
ImageId: !FindInMap
  - 'AmiByOs'
  - !Ref "AWS::Region"
  - !Ref 'OperatingSystem'
```

Pseudo-parameters are parameters that aren't really parameters.[4] They are predefined values made available in templates by the CloudFormation runtime. Despite the fact that they are not defined by you as the user, they are referenced the same way as any other parameter – that is, they can be referenced with the **!Ref** function for use in string substitutions using the **!Sub** function.

Resources

Given that the entire reason that CloudFormation exists is to manage the lifecycle of resources on your behalf, it probably goes without saying that this section is required. Resource definitions vary depending on the type of resource. Given AWS' extensive documentation on all supported resource types, there's no need to try to cover each supported resource here. Instead, here we'll focus on some of the resource independent properties defined for each resource.

---

[4]https://docs.aws.amazon.com/AWSCloudFormation/latest/UserGuide/pseudo-parameter-reference.html

Identifier

There is no "Identifier" parameter, per se. There identifier is the YAML key for the resource. Referring back to Listing 3-1, resource identifiers are **EC2Instance** and **InstanceSg**. The only constraints with the identifier are that they must be[5]

- Unique within the template

- Alphanumeric (A-Za-z0-9)

This field is required.

Type

The "Type" parameter specifies the type of resource being used. A list of available resource types, grouped by service, is available on AWS' documentation site.[6] This attribute is required.

Condition

The "Condition" parameter is optional. It is only necessary in situations where you want to conditionally create a resource. Typically, I use resource-level conditions when using the same templates to provision resources between production and nonproduction environments. For example, perhaps you want to create an Aurora cluster with your templates. For test environments, you decide that a single-node cluster is adequate for app-testing purposes while also keeping costs down with a single node. For production deployments, however, you want a multinode

---

[5]https://docs.aws.amazon.com/AWSCloudFormation/latest/UserGuide/resources-section-structure.html

[6]https://docs.aws.amazon.com/AWSCloudFormation/latest/UserGuide/aws-template-resource-type-ref.html

cluster for purposes of availability and performance (e.g., you can use one endpoint as read-only). In Listing 3-4, we see an example (nonfunctioning) template that demonstrates this concept.

Listing 3-4. Example Template with Conditional Resources

```
...

Parameters:

    Environment:
        Description: Application environment
        Default: test
        AllowedValues:
            - test
            - prod
...
Conditions:

    ProdEnv: !Equals [ !Ref Environment, 'prod' ]

...
Resources:

    DbCluster:
        Type: "AWS::RDS::DBCluster"
        Properties:

            ...

    DbInstance1:
        Type: "AWS::RDS::DBInstance"
        Properties:

            ...

            DBClusterIdentifier: !Ref DbCluster
```

```
DbInstance2:
    Condition: ProdEnv
    Type: "AWS::RDS::DBInstance"
    Properties:
        ...
        DBClusterIdentifier: !Ref DbCluster
```

...

In the preceding example template, we have a stripped-down, nonfunctional template that has a few elements. We accept a parameter called "Environment"; this parameter can either have a value of "test" or "prod", and it would describe the type of environment the template is being used by an operator to build. Also, notice that we use the safer (at least from a cost perspective) default value of "test".

Let's assume for the sake of example, however, that we set the value of the "Environment" parameter to "prod" and provision our template. The ProdEnv condition would evaluate to true. In the context of resource-level conditions, using this condition directly would cause the resource to be created (had we explicitly passed the "test" value for the parameter or passed no value, allowing its default value of "test" to be instead used, the condition would be false and no resource created). Knowing this, as we see in Listing 3-4, the resource "DbInstance2" would be created on the basis of the resource-level condition.

Properties

The "Properties" attribute is a map of resource-specific attributes. This section is required for every resource you define in the template and will itself have attributes that are required and not required. Attributes defined in properties can themselves be simple types like string and numeric values but can also be lists or even more complex types like hashes or lists of hashes or hashes of hashes. The "Properties" section will always be resource-specific, and AWS' documentation is the canonical reference for attributes for each supported resource type. The left navigation pane of the AWS Resource and Property Types Reference[7] contains collapsible fieldsets for each type, expanding down to individual elements within the supported properties for each type of resource, as shown in Figure 3-1.

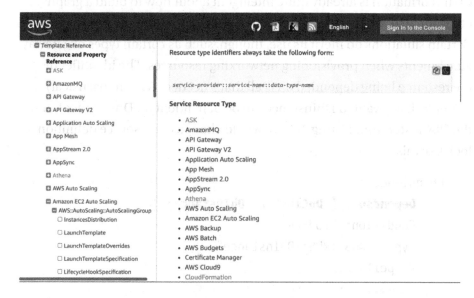

Figure 3-1. *AWS Resource and Property Types Reference Page*

It's a great idea to keep this page open on a separate monitor or device while working on CloudFormation templates, as you will reference it frequently during your work.

---

[7]https://docs.aws.amazon.com/AWSCloudFormation/latest/UserGuide/aws-template-resource-type-ref.html

Other Parameters

There are a handful of other top-level resource parameters that, while not encountered often, are worth being aware of as you build your templates.

DependsOn

CloudFormation is already quite intelligent about how to build a graph of resource interdependencies before actually provisioning resources. Certain situations do merit its use, though, such as certain types of gateway attachments when provisioning networking resources. The identifier of the resource being depended on is all that's needed. As a (nonsensical) example, if we wanted DbInstance2 to be dependent on DbInstance1 and the DbCluster from Listing 3-4, we would change the resource definition to look like this:

```
DbInstance2:
    DependsOn: [ DbCluster, DbInstance1 ]
    Condition: ProdEnv
    Type: "AWS::RDS::DBInstance"
    Properties:
        ...
        DBClusterIdentifier: !Ref DbCluster
```

Unless you determine that this attribute is strictly needed, I would use this attribute sparingly. Needlessly declaring dependencies can create unintended consequences, especially during subsequent updates where new resources are added or existing resources are taken away.

CreationPolicy/UpdatePolicy

Each of these types of attributes works in concert with updates to provisioning EC2 instances (whether standalone or as part of an autoscaling group). Configuration management logic built into your templates calls the cfn-signal helper when their work is done, signaling either success or failure back to the CloudFormation runtime, which assesses whether the resource was created successfully or not based on the values set forth in the Creation/UpdatePolicy section of the resource definition.

UpdateReplacePolicy/DeletePolicy

Often, you will see these attributes specified on resources that are data-oriented. For instance, CloudFormation actually will not let you delete an S3 bucket if the bucket is not empty before deleting the stack which manages it. Often, you will see "DeletionPolicy: Retain" set on S3 buckets, allowing the stack (and all of its other resources) to be deleted without errors. For services that support snapshotting (e.g., RDS databases, EBS volumes, Elasticache clusters), the DeletePolicy can be set to a value of "snapshot," telling CloudFormation not to proceed with destroying the resource until a final snapshot of the resource is taken. This is a great "safeguard-in-depth" toward protecting your data, should a stack be accidentally or maliciously deleted that contains critical data resources, as your snapshot will still exist once the stack is destroyed.

Deployment

While we have already mentioned entire standalone frameworks and tools dedicated to managing the burgeoning deployment needs of more complex stacks, here we're going to take a step back from that for a moment and focus solely on the AWS-provided mechanisms for deployment, the web console and the CLI.

Web Console

With a template that is under 460KB in size, you can directly upload the template to the console. If you don't have a template of your own or just want to play around with CloudFormation, you can use one of AWS' sample templates. After uploading your template, the console displays an S3-based HTTP URL to show where your template has been uploaded. In Figure 3-2, I've uploaded a copy of the template defined in Listing 3-1.

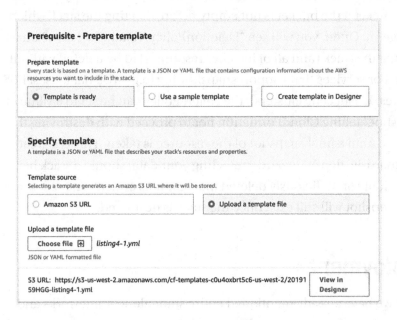

Figure 3-2. *CloudFormation Console After Uploading Template*

Moving on to the next screen, you'll see a set of inputs. The first input asks for a stack name – though not captured in Figure 3-3, call it *web-demo*. Below that, you'll see a set of inputs for parameters.

Specify stack details

Stack name

Stack name

Enter a stack name

Stack name can include letters (A-Z and a-z), numbers (0-9), and dashes (-).

Parameters

Parameters are defined in your template and allow you to input custom values when you create or update a stack.

InstanceType
EC2 instance type

t2.small   ▼

KeyName
Name of an existing EC2 KeyPair to enable access to the instance

OperatingSystem
Chosen operating system

AmazonLinux2   ▼

PublicLocation
The IP address range that can be used to connect to the EC2 instances

0.0.0.0/0

Figure 3-3. *Stack Details Input Form*

If you look at the Parameters section, you'll notice some interesting things going on, and they directly correlate to the Parameters section of our template. First, have a look at the values that are prepopulated; if you look at the values, you'll notice they are the same as the DefaultValue attribute on each parameter. Also, notice the form elements that display the name and descriptions for each input; once again, you'll notice that these directly correlate to the template.

Looking at InstanceType and OperatingSystem, you'll notice that they are dropdown form elements. At this point, you can probably guess what's hiding behind that element when clicked on, but for the sake of driving the point home, we'll go ahead and click on it just to see what's there in Figure 3-4.

75

Parameters

Parameters are defined in your template and allow you to input custom values when you create or update a stack.

InstanceType
EC2 instance type

t2.small	▼
t2.nano	
t2.micro	
t2.small	
t2.medium	
m4.large	
m4.xlarge	

Figure 3-4. *Parameter Dropdown Corresponding to AllowedValues List*

As you likely guessed, these are the values in our AllowedValues list for the InstanceType parameter.

For now, you can move the remaining screens using the "Next" button at the bottom of each screen. When you reach the Review screen, you can click the "Create stack" button, which will create your stack. CloudFormation dutifully creates the resources you request; and with that, you've created your first stack from the CloudFormation web console.

Command-Line Interface

While the web console is convenient for one-off stack builds, it poses some limitations as you progress in terms of efficiency, flexibility, and process maturity. Let's break these down one-by-one:

- ***Efficiency.*** Logging into the console takes significant time and effort relative to the use of the CLI. Even obtaining STS credentials for one-time usage takes a limited amount of time relative to authenticating to the console. What's more, wrapping automation around scripted interactions is much easier than trying to automate complex web interactions.

- *Flexibility.* If you want to integrate with enterprise change management systems, check out credentials from a third-party service or API; you'll find it somewhat more challenging to perform these actions in an automated fashion if you are strictly deploying from the web console. Simply stated, the use of the CLI (or custom app built with an SDK) gives you much more flexibility, particularly within the contexts of integration with other systems and task automation.

- *Process Maturity.* As we begin to look at concepts such as CI/CD, automated infrastructure testing, and automated deployments, we will have to turn to the CLI (or SDK-based apps) to enable these more advanced processes.

Deployment

So what does a deployment from the console actually look like? Let's find out! First though, you'll need to make sure you have an account setup[8] and the AWS CLI properly installed.[9] With those tasks complete, navigate to the folder where you have a template saved corresponding to Listing 3-1. Assuming you have everything setup correctly, a basic deployment looks like in Figure 3-5.

---

[8]https://docs.aws.amazon.com/comprehend/latest/dg/setting-up.html
[9]https://docs.aws.amazon.com/cli/latest/userguide/cli-chap-install.html

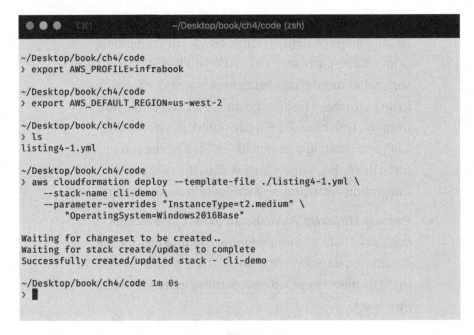

```
~/Desktop/book/ch4/code (zsh)

~/Desktop/book/ch4/code
> export AWS_PROFILE=infrabook

~/Desktop/book/ch4/code
> export AWS_DEFAULT_REGION=us-west-2

~/Desktop/book/ch4/code
> ls
listing4-1.yml

~/Desktop/book/ch4/code
> aws cloudformation deploy --template-file ./listing4-1.yml \
    --stack-name cli-demo \
    --parameter-overrides "InstanceType=t2.medium" \
        "OperatingSystem=Windows2016Base"

Waiting for changeset to be created..
Waiting for stack create/update to complete
Successfully created/updated stack - cli-demo

~/Desktop/book/ch4/code 1m 0s
>
```

Figure 3-5. *CloudFormation Stack Deployment from CLI*

Breaking these down:

- ***export AWS_PROFILE=....*** Here I am setting an
  environment variable that the AWS CLI looks for that
  represents an entry in my AWS credentials file.[10] In
  my case, I am using a separate account solely for the
  purposes of writing this book, and the name of the
  section heading referring to these credentials in my
  credentials and config files is "infrabook".

---

[10]https://docs.aws.amazon.com/cli/latest/userguide/cli-configure-
files.html

- *export AWS_DEFAULT_REGION=....* Here I am setting
  an environment variable that the AWS CLI looks for
  as a default region for any AWS CLI command (any
  command can override this by using the **--region** flag),
  in this case, us-west-2 (Oregon).

- *ls.* Here I am showing the name of my local file, as it
  helps establish a bit of context for the command that
  directly follows.

- *aws cloudformation deploy ....* Here we do the heavy
  lifting of deploying the stack, telling the CLI where our
  template file is located on our local disk, what name
  to assign to the stack, and any parameters we wish to
  override. I have overridden the default instance type
  and operating system. One thing I really like about the
  deploy command is that it works regardless of whether
  you're provisioning a new stack or updating an existing
  one. Until it was introduced, you had to build wrapper
  scripts that could dynamically handle either scenario
  by listing existing stacks and determining whether to
  run a create command if the stack didn't already exist
  or to update the stack with an update command if the
  stack did exist.

Now that the stack is deployed, let's jump into the console and see
how things look from there. Finding the stack in the console, we see
that the stack is indeed provisioned with our overridden parameters in
Figure 3-6.

Figure 3-6. *cli-demo Stack CloudFormation Console*

Now that you know the basic mechanics of deploying a template from the command line, let's look at a few other things we can do with CloudFormation from the CLI.

Listing Stacks

Figure 3-7 shows my console after running an **aws cloudformation list-stacks** command.

```
 ● ● ●                      ~/Desktop/book/ch4/code (zsh)
           }
        },
        {
            "StackId": "arn:aws:cloudformation:us-west-2:521416197183:stack/demo
/e5afbe20-8601-11e9-9c19-0ade61d04ee6",
            "StackName": "demo",
            "TemplateDescription": "Creates an EC2 instance with a security grou
p.\nTemplate EC2InstanceWithSecurityGroupSample: Create an Amazon EC2 instance r
unning the Amazon Linux AMI. The AMI is chosen based on the region in which the
stack is run. This example creates an EC2 security group for the instance to giv
e you SSH access. **WARNING** This template creates an Amazon EC2 instance. You
will be billed for the AWS resources used if you create a stack from this templa
te.",
            "CreationTime": "2019-06-03T13:17:11.881Z",
            "DeletionTime": "2019-06-03T13:33:26.372Z",
            "StackStatus": "DELETE_COMPLETE",
            "DriftInformation": {
                "StackDriftStatus": "NOT_CHECKED"
            }
        }
    ]
}
~/Desktop/book/ch4/code
> █
```

Figure 3-7. *AWS CloudFormation List-Stacks Output*

There's a lot of output – so much, in fact that there's really nothing
of use here. It is apparent that I have a lot of deleted stacks that are
consuming terminal buffer. As it turns out, the CLI gives us facilities to
do extensive manipulation of the data returned by CLI calls as shown in
Figure 3-8.

```
 ● ● ●                      ~/Desktop/book/ch4/code (zsh)

~/Desktop/book/ch4/code
> aws cloudformation list-stacks --output table \
    --stack-status-filter "CREATE_COMPLETE" "CREATE_IN_PROGRESS" \
    --query 'StackSummaries[*].[StackName,StackStatus]'
--- --- --- --- --- --- --- --- --- ---
|             ListStacks             |
+--- --- --- ---+--- --- --- --- ---+
|  web-demo |   CREATE_COMPLETE  |
|  cli-demo |   CREATE_COMPLETE  |
+--- --- --- ---+--- --- --- --- ---+
```

Figure 3-8. *Transformed List-Stacks Output*

Much better! The **--output**[11] and **--query**[12] flags are available regardless of the command. The **--stack-status-filter** flag is specific to this operation; it allows you to zero in on the stacks you want to look at, by status. As we're only concerned with stacks that were just created, we're looking here at those that are still being created or were being created. Each CLI command is well-documented[13] and contains information on all flags, their effect on the command, and their accepted values.

Deleting Stacks

Stacks are easily destroyed from the CLI as well. Let's tear down the **cli-demo** stack.

```
~/Desktop/book/ch4/code
> aws cloudformation delete-stack --stack-name cli-demo

~/Desktop/book/ch4/code
> echo $?
0
```

Figure 3-9. *Delete Stack*

The delete stack command returns a 0 exit code when the call is acknowledged at the API layer – a 0 exit code does not imply success of the actual stack deletion. Determining the actual success or failure of the delete

---

[11]https://docs.aws.amazon.com/cli/latest/userguide/cli-usage-output.html#cli-usage-output-format

[12]https://docs.aws.amazon.com/cli/latest/userguide/cli-usage-output.html#cli-usage-output-filter

[13]https://docs.aws.amazon.com/cli/latest/reference/cloudformation/index.html

operation can only be determined by using a stack waiter.[14] The **deploy** command (ref. Figure 3-1) already incorporates a waiter, so there's no need to use a separate wait command if you're using the deploy command.

Protecting Stacks

Stacks often contain mission-critical resources. While some AWS resources offer resource-level protections (e.g., EC2 instances offer termination protection), there is no universal, resource-agnostic mechanism by which to protect resources. CloudFormation gives us the ability to protect all resources allocated by the stack by protecting the stack itself. Let's set up protection on the *web-demo* stack we created earlier.

```
~/Desktop/book/ch4/code
> aws cloudformation update-termination-protection \
>     --enable-termination-protection \
>     --stack-name web-demo
{
    "StackId": "arn:aws:cloudformation:us-west-2:            :stack/web-demo/23a
62fd0-8a3e-11e9-a173-067bdfc711c4"
}
```

Figure 3-10. *Enabling Stack Termination Protection*

Figure 3-11 shows what happens when attempting to delete a stack from the CLI that has termination protection enabled.

---

[14]https://docs.aws.amazon.com/cli/latest/reference/cloudformation/
   wait/stack-delete-complete.html

```
~/Desktop/book/ch4/code
> aws cloudformation delete-stack --stack-name web-demo

An error occurred (ValidationError) when calling the DeleteStack operation: Stac
k [web-demo] cannot be deleted while TerminationProtection is enabled
```

Figure 3-11. *Deleting a Stack with Termination Protection Enabled*

Figure 3-12 shows what happens when attempting to delete a stack from the web console with termination protection enabled.

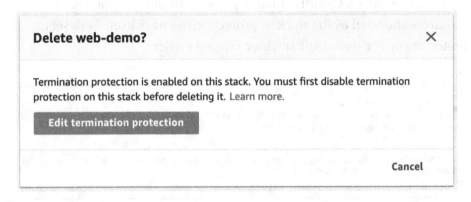

Figure 3-12. *Deleting a Stack with Termination Protection Enabled*

Custom Resources

If CloudFormation resources are the bricks in the wall, custom resources are the mortar that holds them together. A common task in building templates is hunting down values (albeit through use of the console or CLI commands) for things like subnet IDs, security group IDs, and AMI IDs. In our example template in Listing 3-1, you'll notice that I hunted these values down for two separate regions and prepopulated the templates with the values. This is limiting in two ways: first, it constrains us to deploying in only the regions where I am willing to first find the value for the correct AMI and add the corresponding value to a subkey corresponding to the region; second, AMIs are frequently refreshed with security and maintenance patches. Automating the mundane task of looking up these values reduces the burden on operators to keep templates up to date. Binx. io has a great blog post on using a custom resource for this very common use case,[15] along with a production-ready implementation of the function[16] and a great example of how to leverage this function in your template.[17]

Listing 3-5. cfn-ami-provider Implemented in Template

```
AMI:
  Type: Custom::AMI
  Properties:
    Filters:
      name: 'amzn-ami-2017.09.a-amazon-ecs-optimized'
    ServiceToken: !Sub 'arn:aws:lambda:${AWS::Region}:${AWS::
    AccountId}:function:binxio-cfn-ami-provider'

Instance:
  Type: AWS:EC2::Instance
  EC2Instance:
      Type: AWS::EC2::Instance
      Properties:
          ImageId: !Ref AMI
```

This is useful, but seeing it in the context of our original model template from Listing 3-1 might help drive the point home a bit. We see this in Listing 3-6. The changes from the original template are bolded for reference as you look over the listing.

---

[15]https://binx.io/blog/2018/04/22/keeping-your-amis-up-to-date-in-aws-cloudformation/

[16]https://github.com/binxio/cfn-ami-provider

[17]https://github.com/binxio/cfn-ami-provider/blob/master/README.md#how-do-get-the-ami-id-by-name

Listing 3-6. Original Chapter Template with Custom Resources for AMI IDs

```
AWSTemplateFormatVersion: '2010-09-09'
Description: |
  Creates an EC2 instance with a security group.
  Based on AWS sample template "EC2InstanceWithSecurityGroup
  Sample", which is available at https://amzn.to/2WdaX2i.

Parameters:
  KeyName:
    Description: Name of an existing EC2 KeyPair to enable
    access to the instance
    Type: String
    Default: "
    ConstraintDescription: must be a string.

  OperatingSystem:
    Description: Chosen operating system
    Type: String
    Default: AmazonLinux2
    AllowedValues:
      - AmazonLinux2
      - Windows2016Base

  InstanceType:
    Description: EC2 instance type
    Type: String
    Default: t2.small
    AllowedValues:
      - t2.nano
      - t2.micro
      - t2.small
```

```
    - t2.medium
    - m4.large
    - m4.xlarge
  ConstraintDescription: must be a valid EC2 instance type.
PublicLocation:
  Description: The IP address range that can be used to
  connect to the EC2 instances
  Type: String
  MinLength: '9'
  MaxLength: '18'
  Default: '0.0.0.0/0'
  AllowedPattern: (\d{1,3})\.(\d{1,3})\.(\d{1,3})\.(\d{1,3})/
  (\d{1,2})
  ConstraintDescription: must be a valid IP CIDR range of the
  form x.x.x.x/x.

Conditions:
  HasKeypair: !Not [ !Equals [ !Ref KeyName, " ]]

Mappings:
  Global:
    ConnectPortByOs:
      Windows2016Base: 3389
      AmazonLinux2: 22
    AmiSearchString:
      AmazonLinux2: 'amzn2-ami-hvm-2.0.20190508-x86_64-gp2'
      Windows2016Base: 'Windows_Server-2016-English-Full-
      Base-2019.05.15'

Resources:
  AMI:
    Type: "Custom::AMI"
```

```
    Properties:
      Filters:
        name: !FindInMap [ 'Global', 'AmiSearchString', !Ref
        OperatingSystem ]
        ServiceToken: !Sub 'arn:aws:lambda:${AWS::Region}:${AWS::
        AccountId}:function:binxio-cfn-ami-provider'

EC2Instance:
  Type: "AWS::EC2::Instance"
  Properties:
    InstanceType: !Ref 'InstanceType'
    SecurityGroups:
      - !Ref 'InstanceSg'
    KeyName: !If [ 'HasKeypair', !Ref KeyName, !Ref
    "AWS::NoValue" ]
    ImageId: !Ref AMI

InstanceSg:
  Type: "AWS::EC2::SecurityGroup"
  Properties:
    GroupDescription: Enable public access via OS-specific port
    SecurityGroupIngress:
      - IpProtocol: tcp
        FromPort: !FindInMap
          - 'Global'
          - 'ConnectPortByOs'
          - !Ref 'OperatingSystem'
        ToPort: !FindInMap
          - 'Global'
          - 'ConnectPortByOs'
          - !Ref 'OperatingSystem'
        CidrIp: !Ref 'PublicLocation'
```

```
Outputs:
  AmiId:
    Description: Dynamically-chosen AMI ID
    Value: !Ref AMI

  InstanceId:
    Description: InstanceId of the EC2 instance
    Value: !Ref EC2Instance

  AZ:
    Description: AZ of the EC2 instance
    Value: !GetAtt 'EC2Instance.AvailabilityZone'

  PublicDNS:
    Description: Public DNSName of the EC2 instance
    Value: !GetAtt 'EC2Instance.PublicDnsName'

  PublicIP:
    Description: Public IP address of the EC2 instance
    Value: !GetAtt 'EC2Instance.PublicIp'
```

Let's deploy this and see what happens!

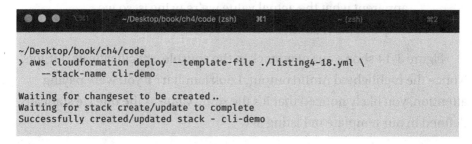

Figure 3-13. *Deploying Updated Template*

Our stack has been deployed successfully, so let's talk about the changes that we made so that we can understand what's going on:

- *Mappings.Global.AmiSearchString.* We replace the old region-based lookup utilizing hard-coded AMI IDs with a name-based string that the custom resource can use to dynamically grab the correct AMI ID by using the ec2 describe-images API call. The **most important thing** that needs to be called out here is the way the lookup is incorporated; the existing parameter maintains any compatibility with existing automation/scripts that may invoke the template.

- *Resources.AMI.* This is the invocation of our custom resource. Depending on the search string passed (which is now derived from our mapping), the proper AMI ID is returned by this resource.

- *Resources.EC2Instance.Properties.ImageId.* Here we pass in the AMI ID retrieved by the custom resource.

- *Ouputs.AmiId.* Since we're dynamically grabbing the AMI ID from the custom resource, it's not readily apparent what the actual value we're using is, so we output it for visibility.

Figure 3-14 shows our new stack in the console, specifically its outputs. Notice the highlighted AmiId output. Look familiar? If you were paying attention, you likely noticed that it's the same value as the one we statically defined in our template in Listing 3-1.

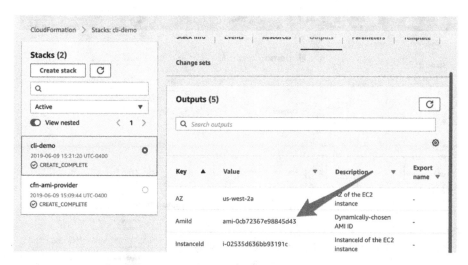

Figure 3-14. *Outputs Tab in CloudFormation Console*

As one last accentuation of the point of dynamic enablement, let's see what happens if we decide we want to begin to operate out of a new AWS region; "us-east-2" will do. In Figure 3-15, we set the target region and deploy the stack.

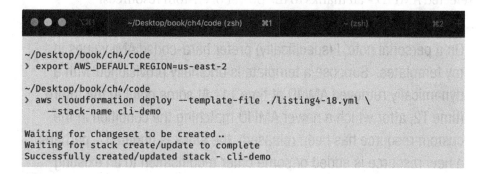

Figure 3-15. *Building in us-east-2*

Next step: check the console, which we do in Figure 3-16.

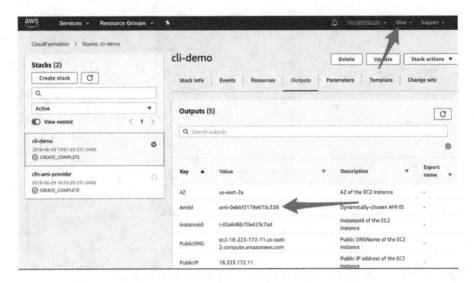

Figure 3-16. *CloudFormation Console in us-east-2*

The callouts in the figure emphasize the points I'd like to call out here: namely, that we deployed a new region (Ohio) with no additional changes needed to our template. The second callout shows our dynamically selected AMI ID – all thanks to the power of custom resources!

On a personal note, I (specifically) prefer hard-coded AMI values in my templates. Suppose a template is originally provisioned with a dynamically retrieved AMI ID at time T1. At some point in the future (time T2, after which a newer AMI ID matching the condition in the custom resource has been released), the stack is updated – perhaps a new resource is added or some other modification to an existing resource is made. You will be quite surprised to notice the EC2 instance tied to the EC2Instance logical identifier will be destroyed and created anew. Why? The ImageId attribute of the EC2::Instance resource requires the instance to be re-created;[18] obviously, this could have at best unintended and quite possibly disastrous consequences if unforeseen and unplanned for. While this is a very specific case relative to the EC2 ImageId, it's representative of a class of unintended consequences that runtime automation can cause when the implications of its use are not fully understood.

Advanced Intrinsic Functions and Macros
Fn::Transform and AWS::Serverless

The AWS::Serverless transform is a CloudFormation-level interaction for the AWS SAM. As we have an entire chapter that includes SAM, we'll defer discussion until that chapter.

Fn::Transform and AWS::Include

The AWS::Include transform is a method to reference static content separate from the current template to be included in the current template at runtime. As I alluded to previously, I am generally cautious of too much automation in my templates. I find that the use of the include transform is a good balance between heavy runtime automation and the desire for flexibility and some level of dynamic content.

Listing 3-7 shows how we can use the include transform to dynamically pull in mappings at runtime. Listing 3-7 is an adaptation of Listing 3-1.

---

[18]https://docs.aws.amazon.com/AWSCloudFormation/latest/UserGuide/aws-properties-ec2-instance.html#cfn-ec2-instance-imageid

Listing 3-7. Template with Mapping Transform

```
AWSTemplateFormatVersion: '2010-09-09'
Description: |
  Creates an EC2 instance with a security group.
  Based on AWS sample template
"EC2InstanceWithSecurityGroupSample",
      which is available at https://amzn.to/2WdaX2i.

Parameters:
  StagingBucket:
    Description: Bucket where templates are staged
    Type: String

  Environment:
    Description: Application environment
    Type: String
    Default: test
    AllowedValues:
      - test
      - prod

  OperatingSystem:
    Description: Chosen operating system
    Type: String
    Default: AmazonLinux2
    AllowedValues:
      - AmazonLinux2
      - Windows2016Base

  InstanceType:
    Description: EC2 instance type
    Type: String
    Default: t2.small
```

```
AllowedValues:
  - t2.nano
  - t2.micro
  - t2.small
  - t2.medium
  - m4.large
  - m4.xlarge
ConstraintDescription: must be a valid EC2 instance type.

PublicLocation:
  Description: The IP address range that can be used to
  connect to the EC2 instances
  Type: String
  MinLength: '9'
  MaxLength: '18'
  Default: '0.0.0.0/0'
  AllowedPattern: (\d{1,3})\.(\d{1,3})\.(\d{1,3})\.(\d{1,3})/
  (\d{1,2})
  ConstraintDescription: must be a valid IP CIDR range of the
  form x.x.x.x/x.

Mappings:
  'Fn::Transform':
  Name: 'AWS::Include'
  Parameters:
    Location: !Sub "s3://${StagingBucket}/
    mappings/${Environment}.yml"
  Global:
  ConnectPortByOs:
    Windows2016Base: 3389
    AmazonLinux2: 22
```

```yaml
Resources:
  EC2Instance:
    Type: "AWS::EC2::Instance"
    Properties:
      InstanceType: !Ref 'InstanceType'
      SecurityGroups:
        - !Ref 'InstanceSg'
      KeyName: !FindInMap [ 'Keypair', !Ref "AWS::Region",
      'Name' ]
      ImageId: !FindInMap [ 'AmiByOs', !Ref "AWS::Region",
      !Ref OperatingSystem ]

  InstanceSg:
    Type: "AWS::EC2::SecurityGroup"
    Properties:
      GroupDescription: Enable public access via OS-specific
      port
      SecurityGroupIngress:
        - IpProtocol: tcp
          FromPort: !FindInMap
            - 'Global'
            - 'ConnectPortByOs'
            - !Ref 'OperatingSystem'
          ToPort: !FindInMap
            - 'Global'
            - 'ConnectPortByOs'
            - !Ref 'OperatingSystem'
          CidrIp: !Ref 'PublicLocation'

Outputs:
  InstanceId:
    Description: InstanceId of the EC2 instance
    Value: !Ref EC2Instance
```

```
AZ:
  Description: AZ of the EC2 instance
  Value: !GetAtt 'EC2Instance.AvailabilityZone'

PublicDNS:
  Description: Public DNSName of the EC2 instance
  Value: !GetAtt 'EC2Instance.PublicDnsName'

PublicIP:
  Description: Public IP address of the EC2 instance
  Value: !GetAtt 'EC2Instance.PublicIp'
```

Listings 3-8 and 3-9 show the contents of *mappings/test.yml* and *mappings/prod.yml*, respectively.

Listing 3-8. mappings/test.yml

```
---
AmiByOs:
  us-east-1:
    Windows2016Base: ami-06bee8e1000e44ca4
    AmazonLinux2: ami-0c6b1d09930fac512
  us-west-2:
    Windows2016Base: ami-07f35a597a32e470d
    AmazonLinux2: ami-0cb72367e98845d43
Keypair:
  us-east-1:
    Name: ec2-key-test-ue1
  us-west-2:
    Name: ec2-key-test-uw2
```

Listing 3-9. mappings/prod.yml

```
---
AmiByOs:
  us-east-1:
    Windows2016Base: ami-06bee8e1000e44ca4
    AmazonLinux2: ami-0c6b1d09930fac512
  us-west-2:
    Windows2016Base: ami-07f35a597a32e470d
    AmazonLinux2: ami-0cb72367e98845d43
Keypair:
  us-east-1:
    Name: ec2-key-prod-ue1
  us-west-2:
    Name: ec2-key-prod-uw2
```

Figure 3-17 shows the directory structure locally of these three files. Figure 3-18 shows how the files were deployed to a staging bucket and the CLI invocation used to successfully build the stack detailed in Listing 3-7.

```
~/Desktop/book/ch4/code
> tree
.
├── listing4-1.yml
├── listing4-18.yml
├── listing4-23.yml
├── listing4-24.yml
└── mappings
    ├── prod.yml
    └── test.yml

1 directory, 6 files
```

Figure 3-17. *tree Output*

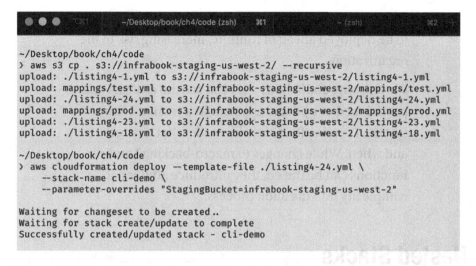

```
~/Desktop/book/ch4/code
> aws s3 cp . s3://infrabook-staging-us-west-2/ --recursive
upload: ./listing4-1.yml to s3://infrabook-staging-us-west-2/listing4-1.yml
upload: mappings/test.yml to s3://infrabook-staging-us-west-2/mappings/test.yml
upload: ./listing4-24.yml to s3://infrabook-staging-us-west-2/listing4-24.yml
upload: mappings/prod.yml to s3://infrabook-staging-us-west-2/mappings/prod.yml
upload: ./listing4-23.yml to s3://infrabook-staging-us-west-2/listing4-23.yml
upload: ./listing4-18.yml to s3://infrabook-staging-us-west-2/listing4-18.yml

~/Desktop/book/ch4/code
> aws cloudformation deploy --template-file ./listing4-24.yml \
    --stack-name cli-demo \
    --parameter-overrides "StagingBucket=infrabook-staging-us-west-2"

Waiting for changeset to be created..
Waiting for stack create/update to complete
Successfully created/updated stack - cli-demo
```

Figure 3-18. *Stack Staging and Deployment*

While this demo only demonstrates differential EC2 Keypair names,
mappings can be vastly different between environments – as environments
can represent different VPCs, custom AMIs built by a custom AMI-building
pipeline, even different AWS accounts altogether.

Macros

I considered omitting any discussion of macros as they provide a facility
to delegate extensive logic to provisioning at runtime without a clear
understanding of what the outcome will be. Even with transform/
includes that are for resources and mappings, those template segments
are predefined, visible, known quantities ahead of runtime. Suffice to say,
macros do a few things that I am not a fan of, including

- Creating language-specific bindings to what are
  supposed to be programming language-agnostic
  declarative templates.

- Diminishing visibility and "knowability" of what's going to be deployed ahead of runtime, increasing risk to the organization.

- Diminishing auditability – If I can see the artifacts that provisioned or updated a system in a version control system, I can in effect see who made what changes and when. While changes to macro-backing Lambda functions can be traced, they introduce additional complexity into the audit process.

Nested Stacks

Nested stacks are one of my favorite CloudFormation features. They provide a mechanism for modularity and reusability of infrastructure components, all of which are features worthy of advocation. As common components are used, battle-tested, and iterated, they become better, refined, and more robust. While perhaps a bit contrived, we can demonstrate a nested stack with a bit of imaginative context. Let us suppose that the single EC2 instance deployed in our template from Listing 3-1 represents an instance that houses an application. That application represents a SaaS-based offering; each instance deployed correlates to a customer. To keep revenue calculations simple, we deploy a single instance per customer, as this limits the blast radius of instance failure and helps to keep client data separated (in reality, there would be many more considerations here – we're just keeping this simple to demonstrate the nested stacks concept). Hence, our unit of repeatability in this case is the EC2 instance and dedicated security group, as we give clients the ability to restrict traffic to their instance of our application to a set of given public IPs.

Listing 3-10 demonstrates the template that models the child stack – that is, the part of our deployments that we want abstracted and repeatable.

Listing 3-10. Child Stack with EC2 Instance and Security Group

```
AWSTemplateFormatVersion: '2010-09-09'
Description: |
  Creates an EC2 instance with a security group.
  Based on AWS sample template "EC2InstanceWithSecurity
  GroupSample",
      which is available at https://amzn.to/2WdaX2i.

Parameters:
  CustomMappingsPrefix:
    Description: Customer-specific mappings prefix/folder
    Type: String
    Default: default

  StagingBucket:
    Description: Bucket where templates are staged
    Type: String

  Environment:
    Description: Application environment
    Type: String
    Default: test
    AllowedValues:
      - test
      - prod

  OperatingSystem:
    Description: Chosen operating system
    Type: String
    Default: AmazonLinux2
    AllowedValues:
      - AmazonLinux2
      - Windows2016Base
```

```
  InstanceType:
    Description: EC2 instance type
    Type: String
    Default: t2.small
    AllowedValues:
      - t2.nano
      - t2.micro
      - t2.small
      - t2.medium
      - m4.large
      - m4.xlarge
    ConstraintDescription: must be a valid EC2 instance type.

  PublicLocation:
    Description: The IP address range that can be used to
    connect to the EC2 instances
    Type: String
    MinLength: '9'
    MaxLength: '18'
    Default: '0.0.0.0/0'
    AllowedPattern: (\d{1,3})\.(\d{1,3})\.(\d{1,3})\.(\d{1,3})/
    (\d{1,2})
    ConstraintDescription: must be a valid IP CIDR range of the
    form x.x.x.x/x.

Mappings:
  'Fn::Transform':
    Name: 'AWS::Include'
    Parameters:
      Location: !Sub "s3://${StagingBucket}/nested_stack_demo/
      mappings/${CustomMappingsPrefix}/${Environment}.yml"
```

```
Global:
  ConnectPortByOs:
    Windows2016Base: 3389
    AmazonLinux2: 22

Resources:
  EC2Instance:
    Type: "AWS::EC2::Instance"
    Properties:
      InstanceType: !Ref 'InstanceType'
      SecurityGroups:
        - !Ref 'InstanceSg'
      KeyName: !FindInMap [ 'Keypair', !Ref "AWS::Region",
      'Name' ]
      ImageId: !FindInMap [ 'AmiByOs', !Ref "AWS::Region", !Ref
      OperatingSystem ]

  InstanceSg:
    Type: "AWS::EC2::SecurityGroup"
    Properties:
      GroupDescription: Enable public access via OS-specific port
      SecurityGroupIngress:
        - IpProtocol: tcp
          FromPort: !FindInMap
            - 'Global'
            - 'ConnectPortByOs'
            - !Ref 'OperatingSystem'
          ToPort: !FindInMap
            - 'Global'
            - 'ConnectPortByOs'
            - !Ref 'OperatingSystem'
          CidrIp: !Ref 'PublicLocation'
```

```
Outputs:
  InstanceId:
    Description: InstanceId of the EC2 instance
    Value: !Ref EC2Instance

  AZ:
    Description: AZ of the EC2 instance
    Value: !GetAtt 'EC2Instance.AvailabilityZone'

  PublicDNS:
    Description: Public DNSName of the EC2 instance
    Value: !GetAtt 'EC2Instance.PublicDnsName'

  PublicIP:
    Description: Public IP address of the EC2 instance
    Value: !GetAtt 'EC2Instance.PublicIp'
```

Let's quickly talk about the differences between what we see in Listing 3-10 and Listing 3-7. For the most part, the template remains the same, with the exception of the **CustomMappingsPrefix** parameter. This parameter is used to provide a facility to "override" mapping values from a default set of mappings. Given your understanding of parameters, it should be clear that mappings will be ingested from a "default" prefix in S3, unless a customer-specific prefix is passed as a parameter.

In Listing 3-11, we see the top-level (or "parent") stack, which invokes multiple instances of the single template defined in Listing 3-10. The files under *mappings/default* directory are identical to those found in Listings 3-7 and 3-8, so I won't relist them here. Listings 3-12 and 3-13 display the contents of *mappings/CustomerA/test.yml* and *mappings/ CustomerA/prod.yml*, respectively.

Listing 3-11. Parent Stack

```
AWSTemplateFormatVersion: '2010-09-09'
Description: |
  Demo parent stack for nested stack demonstration.
Parameters:
  StagingBucket:
    Description: Bucket where templates are staged
    Type: String

  Environment:
    Description: Application environment
    Type: String
    Default: test
    AllowedValues:
      - test
      - prod
Mappings:
  Global:
    Tags:
      App: MyAwesomeApp
      CostCenter: IT
Conditions:
  Prod: !Equals [ !Ref Environment, 'prod' ]
Resources:
  CustomerA:
    Type: "AWS::CloudFormation::Stack"
    Properties:
      TemplateURL: !Sub "https://s3.amazonaws.com/${Staging
      Bucket}/nested_stack_demo/listing3-16.yml"
```

```yaml
    Parameters:
      CustomMappingsPrefix: CustomerA
      StagingBucket: !Ref StagingBucket
      Environment: !Ref Environment
      InstanceType: t2.medium
    Tags:
      - Key: Customer
        Value: CustomerA
      - Key: Environment
        Value: !Ref Environment
      - Key: App
        Value: !FindInMap [ 'Global', 'Tags', 'App' ]
      - Key: CostCenter
        Value: !FindInMap [ 'Global', 'Tags', 'CostCenter' ]
  CustomerB:
    Type: "AWS::CloudFormation::Stack"
    Properties:
      TemplateURL: !Sub "https://s3.amazonaws.
      com/${StagingBucket}/nested_stack_demo/listing3-16.yml"
      Parameters:
        StagingBucket: !Ref StagingBucket
        Environment: !Ref Environment
        InstanceType: t2.small
        OperatingSystem: Windows2016Base
        PublicLocation: '1.2.3.4/32'
      Tags:
        - Key: Customer
          Value: CustomerB
        - Key: Environment
          Value: !Ref Environment
        - Key: App
          Value: !FindInMap [ 'Global', 'Tags', 'App' ]
```

```
      - Key: CostCenter
        Value: !FindInMap [ 'Global', 'Tags', 'CostCenter' ]
  CustomerC:
    Type: "AWS::CloudFormation::Stack"
    Condition: Prod
    Properties:
      TemplateURL: !Sub "https://s3.amazonaws.com/${Staging
      Bucket}/nested_stack_demo/listing3-16.yml"
      Parameters:
        StagingBucket: !Ref StagingBucket
        Environment: !Ref Environment
        InstanceType: t2.large
      Tags:
        - Key: Customer
          Value: CustomerC
        - Key: Environment
          Value: !Ref Environment
        - Key: App
          Value: !FindInMap [ 'Global', 'Tags', 'App' ]
        - Key: CostCenter
          Value: !FindInMap [ 'Global', 'Tags', 'CostCenter' ]
```

Listing 3-12. mappings/CustomerA/test.yml

```
---
AmiByOs:
  us-east-1:
    Windows2016Base: ami-06bee8e1000e44ca4
    AmazonLinux2: ami-0c6b1d09930fac512
  us-west-2:
    Windows2016Base: ami-07f35a597a32e470d
    AmazonLinux2: ami-0cb72367e98845d43
```

```
Keypair:
  us-east-1:
    Name: ec2-key-custa-test-ue1
  us-west-2:
    Name: ec2-key-custa-test-uw2
```

Listing 3-13. mappings/CustomerA/prod.yml

```
---
AmiByOs:
  us-east-1:
    Windows2016Base: ami-06bee8e1000e44ca4
    AmazonLinux2: ami-0c6b1d09930fac512
  us-west-2:
    Windows2016Base: ami-07f35a597a32e470d
    AmazonLinux2: ami-0cb72367e98845d43
Keypair:
  us-east-1:
    Name: ec2-key-custa-prod-ue1
  us-west-2:
    Name: ec2-key-custa-prod-uw2
```

Let's break things down starting from Listing 3-11. Since the parent stack is essentially a contextual wrapper, the parameters needed can be pared down from a standalone template (i.e., the earlier examples from this chapter). CloudFormation only needs to know what S3 bucket to go look in for the templates representing the nested stacks and, for the sake of the resources in the children stacks, whether or not this is a prod or test environment. We pass both of these resources into the top-level stack at the time of deployment, and we also pass them to the child stacks (defined by Listing 3-10) via parameters. Let's see what it might look like to actually deploy this solution from the CLI; with some observable results in place, we will then talk through what we see. Figure 3-19 shows what our local

directory structure looks like. Figures 3-20 and 3-21 demonstrate how we
stage the CloudFormation artifacts in S3 and how we deploy the parent
stack from the CLI, respectively.

```
~/Desktop/book/ch4/code/nested_stack_demo
> tree
.
├── listing4-29.yml
├── listing4-30.yml
└── mappings
    ├── CustomerA
    │   ├── prod.yml
    │   └── test.yml
    └── default
        ├── prod.yml
        └── test.yml

3 directories, 6 files
```

Figure 3-19. *Local Directory Structure*

```
~/Desktop/book/ch4/code/nested_stack_demo
> aws s3 cp . s3://infrabook-staging-us-west-2/nested_stack_demo/ --recursive
upload: mappings/CustomerA/test.yml to s3://infrabook-staging-us-west-2/nested_s
tack_demo/mappings/CustomerA/test.yml
upload: mappings/default/prod.yml to s3://infrabook-staging-us-west-2/nested_sta
ck_demo/mappings/default/prod.yml
upload: mappings/CustomerA/prod.yml to s3://infrabook-staging-us-west-2/nested_s
tack_demo/mappings/CustomerA/prod.yml
upload: ./listing4-30.yml to s3://infrabook-staging-us-west-2/nested_stack_demo/
listing4-30.yml
upload: mappings/default/test.yml to s3://infrabook-staging-us-west-2/nested_sta
ck_demo/mappings/default/test.yml
upload: ./listing4-29.yml to s3://infrabook-staging-us-west-2/nested_stack_demo/
listing4-29.yml
```

Figure 3-20. *Staging CloudFormation Artifacts in S3*

```
~/Desktop/book/ch4/code/nested_stack_demo
> aws cloudformation deploy --template-file ./listing4-30.yml \
    --stack-name nested-stack-demo \
    --capabilities CAPABILITY_AUTO_EXPAND \
    --parameter-overrides "StagingBucket=infrabook-staging-us-west-2"

Waiting for changeset to be created..
Waiting for stack create/update to complete
Successfully created/updated stack - nested-stack-demo
```

Figure 3-21. *Parent Stack Deployment*

With the exception of the added **--capabilities CAPABILITY_AUTO_EXPAND** flag in Figure 3-21 and the additional objects in our file hierarchy, this isn't significantly different from what was deployed in our include transform demonstration. The CAPABILITY_AUTO_EXPAND is essentially us telling CloudFormation that we're OK with the engine deploying resources that are not strictly defined in the template that we're deploying. Let's have a look at what's now deployed in the console to further our discussion.

Figure 3-22. *Parent Stack Resources*

As expected, the resources provisioned by our parent stack are indeed CloudFormation stacks in their own right. If you're wondering why there is no CustomerC stack, notice the **Condition** attribute on the **CustomerC** resource in Listing 3-11. As we didn't override the **Environment** parameter when creating the parent stack in Figure 3-21, the default value of "test" was used for this parameter. As that value sets the Prod Condition to false, the condition on the CustomerC resource evaluates to false, and so the resource isn't provisioned.

Moving onto the **CustomerA** stack, notice that we populated the **CustomMappingsPrefix** parameter in the parent template (Listing 3-11), overriding the "default" value in the child stack. Looking at the mapping include transform in the child template (Listing 3-10), you will notice that setting this value to anything besides "default" will grab mappings from a corollary prefix from the bucket set by the **StagingBucket** parameter.

On each stack, we also created a set of tags to help identify our stacks. Not only are the actual stacks themselves tagged in the CloudFormation console, but the resources created by these stacks are tagged as well. Figure 3-23 shows the EC2 console. Both instances displayed are instances created through these nested stacks. The figure shows the instance from the CustomerA stack selected. In the figure, you can see the wide array of tags applied to the resource, including those that are applied to the stack itself in our templates.

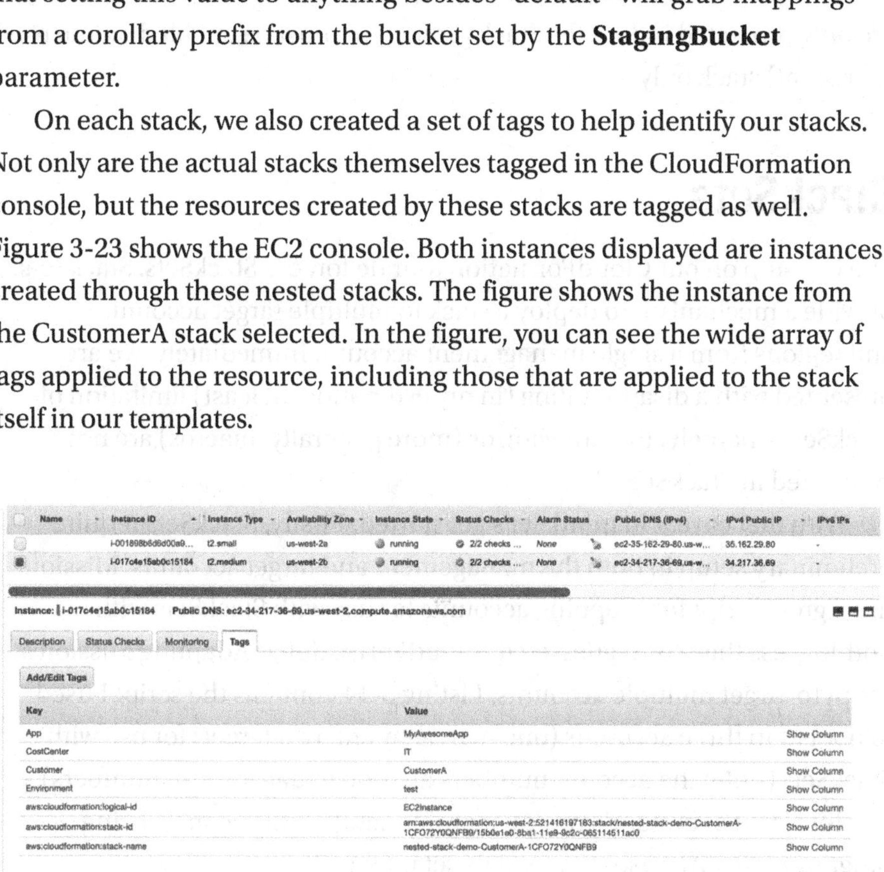

Figure 3-23. *EC2 Console*

Per AWS' docs, "[a]ll stack-level tags, including automatically created tags, are propagated to resources that AWS CloudFormation supports. Currently, tags are not propagated to Amazon EBS volumes that are created from block device mappings."[19]

Nested stacks can be protected using stack protection. However, they are only protected indirectly. Stack protection must be enabled on the root (or parent) stack only.

StackSets

The last stop on our CloudFormation tour de force is StackSets. StackSets provide a mechanism to deploy a stack to multiple target accounts and regions from a single management account. Immediately, we are presented with a disappointing (in my estimation, at least) limitation of StackSets – namely, that transforms (more generally, macros) are not supported in StackSets.[20]

With that caveat in mind, let's get started. Firstly, StackSets require preliminary setup in both the management and target accounts. Mission has a great script for prepping accounts for use with StackSets with nothing less than? You guessed it: CloudFormation.[21] Adapting Mission's script to target multiple accounts, Listing 3-14 contains the script I used to bootstrap three accounts (one management, two target) for use with StackSets (note: the account numbers are not actual account numbers). The local CLI commands rely on a profile setup with accompanying programmatic IAM user credentials set up locally.

---

[19]https://docs.aws.amazon.com/AWSCloudFormation/latest/UserGuide/aws-properties-resource-tags.html

[20]https://docs.aws.amazon.com/AWSCloudFormation/latest/UserGuide/stacksets-limitations.html

[21]https://github.com/reliam/cloudformation-stacksets-demo

Listing 3-14. StackSet Bootstrapping Script

```bash
#!/bin/bash

ADMIN_STACK_URL="https://s3.amazonaws.com/
cloudformation-stackset-sample-templates-us-east-1/
AWSCloudFormationStackSetAdministrationRole.yml"
ADMIN_STACK_NAME="stackset-admin"
TGT_STACK_URL="https://s3.amazonaws.com/
cloudformation-stackset-sample-templates-us-east-1/
AWSCloudFormationStackSetExecutionRole.yml"
TGT_STACK_NAME="stackset-execution"
MGMT_ACCT="111111111111"
MGMT_PROFILE="infrabook"
TGT_ACCTS=("000000000001" "000000000002")
TGT_PROFILES=("infrabook-org1" "infrabook-org2")
DEFAULT_REGION="us-west-2"

echo "Creating managment stack in management account \
"${MGMT_ACCT}\""
aws cloudformation create-stack \
    --template-url "${ADMIN_STACK_URL}" \
    --stack-name "${ADMIN_STACK_NAME}" \
    --region "${DEFAULT_REGION}" \
    --profile "${MGMT_PROFILE}" \
    --capabilities CAPABILITY_NAMED_IAM

i=0
for acct in "${TGT_ACCTS[@]}"
do
    echo "Creating target stack in target account \"${acct}\""
    aws cloudformation create-stack \
        --template-url "${TGT_STACK_URL}" \
```

```
        --stack-name "${TGT_STACK_NAME}" \
        --region ${DEFAULT_REGION} \
        --capabilities CAPABILITY_NAMED_IAM \
        --profile "${TGT_PROFILES[i]}" \
        --parameters ParameterKey=AdministratorAccountId,Parame
        terValue=${MGMT_ACCT}
    i=$((i + 1))
done
```

Now that the management and execution stacks have been allocated, we can create stack set instances in the target accounts. The process is as follows:

- Firstly, a StackSet is created in the management account.

- Actual stacks are deployed to the target accounts in any number of target regions. Stack instances are associated with the StackSet in the management account.

Listing 3-16 shows the stack template that we'll be deploying to our target accounts via our StackSet. This template will look very familiar at this point; the main difference between this instance and Listing 3-1 is that the **KeyName** parameter has been removed, as stacks deployed via StackSets fail with empty parameters.

Listing 3-15. StackSet Deployment Stack

```
AWSTemplateFormatVersion: '2010-09-09'
Description: |
  Creates an EC2 instance with a security group.
  Based on AWS sample template
"EC2InstanceWithSecurityGroupSample",
      which is available at https://amzn.to/2WdaX2i.
```

```
Parameters:
  OperatingSystem:
    Description: Chosen operating system
    Type: String
    Default: AmazonLinux2
    AllowedValues:
      - AmazonLinux2
      - Windows2016Base

  InstanceType:
    Description: EC2 instance type
    Type: String
    Default: t2.small
    AllowedValues:
      - t2.nano
      - t2.micro
      - t2.small
      - t2.medium
      - m4.large
      - m4.xlarge
    ConstraintDescription: must be a valid EC2 instance type.

  PublicLocation:
    Description: The IP address range that can be used to
    connect to the EC2 instances
    Type: String
    MinLength: '9'
    MaxLength: '18'
    Default: '0.0.0.0/0'
    AllowedPattern: (\d{1,3})\.(\d{1,3})\.(\d{1,3})\.(\d{1,3})/
    (\d{1,2})
    ConstraintDescription: must be a valid IP CIDR range of the
    form x.x.x.x/x.
```

```
Mappings:
  Global:
    ConnectPortByOs:
      Windows2016Base: 3389
      AmazonLinux2: 22
  AmiByOs:
    us-east-1:
      Windows2016Base: ami-06bee8e1000e44ca4
      AmazonLinux2: ami-0c6b1d09930fac512
    us-west-2:
      Windows2016Base: ami-07f35a597a32e470d
      AmazonLinux2: ami-0cb72367e98845d43

Resources:
  EC2Instance:
    Type: "AWS::EC2::Instance"
    Properties:
      InstanceType: !Ref 'InstanceType'
      SecurityGroups:
        - !Ref 'InstanceSg'
      ImageId: !FindInMap
        - 'AmiByOs'
        - !Ref "AWS::Region"
        - !Ref 'OperatingSystem'

  InstanceSg:
    Type: "AWS::EC2::SecurityGroup"
    Properties:
      GroupDescription: Enable public access via OS-specific port
      SecurityGroupIngress:
        - IpProtocol: tcp
          FromPort: !FindInMap
            - 'Global'
```

```
          - 'ConnectPortByOs'
          - !Ref 'OperatingSystem'
       ToPort: !FindInMap
          - 'Global'
          - 'ConnectPortByOs'
          - !Ref 'OperatingSystem'
       CidrIp: !Ref 'PublicLocation'
Outputs:
  InstanceId:
    Description: InstanceId of the EC2 instance
    Value: !Ref 'EC2Instance'

  AZ:
    Description: AZ of the EC2 instance
    Value: !GetAtt 'EC2Instance.AvailabilityZone'

  PublicDNS:
    Description: Public DNSName of the EC2 instance
    Value: !GetAtt 'EC2Instance.PublicDnsName'

  PublicIP:
    Description: Public IP address of the EC2 instance
    Value: !GetAtt 'EC2Instance.PublicIp'
```

Listing 3-16 is the script we'll use to deploy our StackSet and target stack deployments.

Listing 3-16. StackSet Deployment Script

```
#!/bin/bash

ADMIN_STACK_URL="https://s3.amazonaws.com/
cloudformation-stackset-sample-templates-us-east-1/
AWSCloudFormationStackSetAdministrationRole.yml"
ADMIN_STACK_NAME="stackset-admin"
```

117

```
TGT_STACK_URL="https://s3.amazonaws.com/
cloudformation-stackset-sample-templates-us-east-1/
AWSCloudFormationStackSetExecutionRole.yml"
TGT_STACK_NAME="stackset-execution"
MGMT_ACCT="111111111111"
MGMT_PROFILE="infrabook"
TGT_ACCTS=("000000000001" "000000000002")
TGT_PROFILES=("infrabook-org1" "infrabook-org2")
DEFAULT_REGION="us-west-2"
TPLT="listing3-39"

echo "Creating stack set in management account \"${MGMT_ACCT}\""
aws cloudformation create-stack-set \
    --profile "${MGMT_PROFILE}" \
    --template-body "file://${TPLT}.yml" \
    --stack-set-name "${TPLT}" \
    --region "${DEFAULT_REGION}" \
    --capabilities CAPABILITY_NAMED_IAM

i=0
for acct in "${TGT_ACCTS[@]}"
do
    echo "Deploying to target account \"${acct}\""
    aws cloudformation create-stack-instances \
        --profile "${MGMT_PROFILE}" \
        --stack-set-name "${TPLT}" \
        --accounts "${acct}" \
        --regions "us-east-1" "us-west-2" \
        --region "${DEFAULT_REGION}"
    i=$((i + 1))
```

```
if [[ "${i}" -lt "${#TGT_ACCTS[@]}" ]]; then
    sleep 300
fi
done
```

Figure 3-24 is the output of running the deployment script via CLI.

```
~/Desktop/book/ch4/code/stackset_demo
> ./listing4-40.sh
Creating stack set in management account "          7183"
{
    "StackSetId": "listing4-39:c19567f0-1c74-499e-a5de-9a40c0bde411"
}
Deploying to target account "        5309"
{
    "OperationId": "4e91e831-24e3-472b-884b-2027c56d7e57"
}
Deploying to target account "        9628"
{
    "OperationId": "b1a06c4d-4b43-476e-b1d9-943f03b304c5"
}
```

Figure 3-24. *Deployment Script Output*

Figure 3-25 displays the CloudFormation StackSet console; it displays references to the stacks deployed to the target accounts. As referenced, the StackSet itself is but a container in the management account which allocates a template to any number of target accounts and regions.

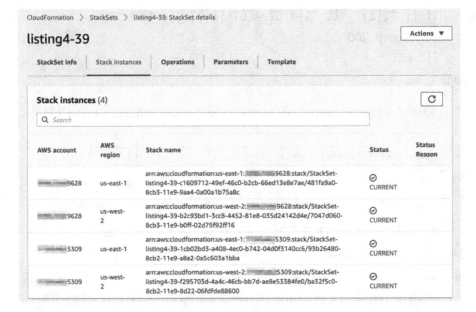

Figure 3-25. *CloudFormation StackSet Console*

Figure 3-26 shows the CloudFormation console in one of the target accounts. As you would expect, you see the deployed CloudFormation stack (along with the stackset-execution stack).

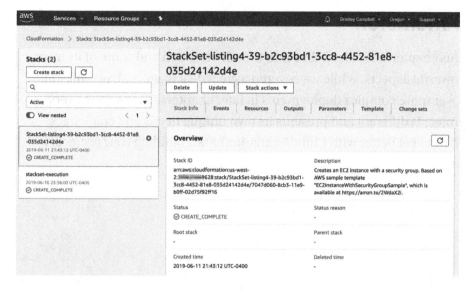

Figure 3-26. *CloudFormation Console in Target Account*

Discussion

StackSets are essentially a multiaccount, multiregional orchestration mechanism for CloudFormation stacks. With the administrative power of AWS Organizations, there are other options for managing deployments to multiaccount hierarchies. Using alternative mechanisms such as continuous deployment servers tied to organizational roles, deployments can be orchestrated to any number of target accounts using role assumption, standard IAM credentials, or STS credentials and standard CLI tooling. Using an alternative methodology like this, we can reclaim some of the more powerful features of CloudFormation such as include transforms. If you have no need of these more powerful aspects of CloudFormation and no desire to maintain the necessary infrastructure and tooling to maintain your own deployment solution, then StackSets are a viable alternative.

Conclusion

This chapter was a deep dive into CloudFormation and some of its more powerful aspects. While we covered a great deal of ground, we will still cover more complex deployments in later chapters. The byline? Every project is different and presents its own unique needs and challenges. Want to get better with CloudFormation? Start building your projects with it today!

CHAPTER 4

Terraform In-Depth

Now that we have a solid understanding of CloudFormation, we'll take a look at the third-party ecosystem. When it comes to third-party tools, the tool you will most frequently encounter – for now – will be Terraform. Even if you currently are or plan to manage your AWS deployments solely via CloudFormation, it's worth having a good working knowledge of Terraform. Key points of differentiation with respect to CloudFormation include: a much more robust modularization mechanism than nested stacks; the ability to bring existing resources under active management using an "import" command that interrogates the resource and creates an entry in Terraform's state management "database" for that resource (though you do have to write matching code for the resource); a powerful DSL with support for flow control with for loops (as of Terraform v0.12) and pseudo for-like functionality with its *count* parameters that any resource can utilize; first-class support for data-gathering operations (e.g., getting a list of subnet IDs based on a tag to deploy an EC2 instance into) as opposed to the need to author a custom resource; interfaces that support authoring local scripts as opposed to having to deploy custom resource Lambdas for other operations that aren't specifically supported by a resource or data source; and, lastly, the capability to manage services that form other parts of your toolchain, like GitHub repositories, databases within a database server, database users, and loads of other services.

© Bradley Campbell 2020
B. Campbell, *The Definitive Guide to AWS Infrastructure Automation*,
https://doi.org/10.1007/978-1-4842-5398-4_4

In this chapter, we will work through the following concepts:

- **Code Anatomy.** Structure of basic code. Terraform provides generous flexibility in how you structure code, in contrast to CloudFormation.

- **Variable Values.** Variable values can be stored and passed to the runtime in various ways.

- **Locals.** As an extension to Terraform's concept of variables, locals are a module-scoped variable. Additionally, locals are able to evaluate expressions that standard variables are unable to evaluate, making them very useful as intermediate value stores.

- **Remote State.** Remote state provides a variety of methods for storing the "database" Terraform uses to keep track of your deployments and infrastructure.

- **Modules.** Modules provide a method of reuse and abstraction for Terraform resources. Modules are designed with the flexibility to be hosted remote in centralized repositories such as S3 buckets or Git repositories and can be referenced and sourced from these centralized sources, making their collaborative use and development simple.

- **Providers.** Providers are the interfaces to resource-providing APIs – most notably in this case, AWS. They implement logic that assists in dependency mapping between resources and implement the actual provider APIs that translate DSL to actual resources in the target environment.

- *Pinning*. Pinning provides a way to ensure that the same versions of any binaries involved in provisioning your infrastructure fall within certain version constraints. This provides a consistent way to interact with your codebase. Pinning provides a way to ensure that your Terraform code and state are kept compatible in multiuser environments.

Code Anatomy

Terraform code is authored in a custom DSL called HCL (short for "HashiCorp Language"). While Terraform also accepts native JSON, I have yet to see any usage of Terraform that utilizes JSON in 5+ years of usage of the tool. Keeping in line with our CloudFormation examples, let's have a look at the same EC2 instance authored in Listing 4-1, except written for Terraform.

Listing 4-1. ec2_instance.tf

```
# All Terraform code needs a provider to work
provider "aws" {}

# This provides an analogue to the ${AWS::Region} pseudo-
variable
# in CloudFormation.
data "aws_region" "current" {}

# These correspond to 3-1 Parameters
variable "key_name" {
  type = "string"
  description = "Name of an existing EC2 KeyPair to enable
  access to the instance"
  default = ""
}
```

```
variable "operating_system" {
  type = "string"
  description = "Chosen operating system"
  default = "AmazonLinux2"
}

variable "instance_type" {
  type = "string"
  description = "EC2 instance type"
  default = "t2.small"
}

variable "public_location" {
  type = "string"
  description = "The IP address range that can be used to
connect to the EC2 instances"
  default = "0.0.0.0/0"
}

# These correspond to 3-1 Mappings
variable "connect_port_by_os" {
  type = "map"
  description = "Port mappings for operating systems"
  default = {
    Windows2016Base = "3389"
    AmazonLinux2 = "22"
  }
}

variable "ami_by_region_os" {
  type = "map"
  description = "AMI ID by region and OS"
  default = {
```

```
    us-east-1 = {
      Windows2016Base = "ami-06bee8e1000e44ca4"
      AmazonLinux2 = "ami-0c6b1d09930fac512"
    }
    us-west-2 = {
      Windows2016Base = "ami-07f35a597a32e470d"
      AmazonLinux2 = "ami-0cb72367e98845d43"
    }
  }
}

resource "aws_security_group" "public_os_access" {
  name        = "public_os_access"
  description = "Enable public access via OS-specific port"

  ingress {
    from_port   = "${lookup(var.connect_port_by_os, var.
                  operating_system)}"
    to_port     = "${lookup(var.connect_port_by_os, var.
                  operating_system)}"
    protocol    = "tcp"
    cidr_blocks = ["${var.public_location}"]
  }
}

resource "aws_instance" "public_instance" {
  instance_type = "${var.instance_type}"
  key_name = "${var.key_name}"
  ami = "${lookup(var.ami_by_region_os[data.aws_region.current.
  name], var.operating_system)}"
  vpc_security_group_ids = ["${aws_security_group.public_os_
access.id}"]
}
```

```
output "instance_id" {
  value = "${aws_instance.public_instance.id}"
}

output "az" {
  value = "${aws_instance.public_instance.availability_zone}"
}

output "public_dns" {
  value = "${aws_instance.public_instance.public_dns}"
}

output "public_ip" {
  value = "${aws_instance.public_instance.public_ip}"
}
```

Unlike the CloudFormation template from Listing 3-1, you'll see that Terraform code is structured a bit differently. First, Terraform code does not enforce a strict hierarchy or organization of a functional body of code the way that CloudFormation does. While Listing 4-1 is organized in such a way that similar element types (i.e., "variable," "resource," "output") are grouped together, this isn't a necessary requirement for the code to actually work. Nevertheless, as there are several distinct types of elements here, let's walk through them briefly:

- Provider

- Data

- Variable

- Resource

- Output

Provider

The provider indicates to Terraform the platform or service that the Terraform runtime will be operating against. Providers provide the abstraction layer between Terraform's configuration language and the management of resources within the service itself. In the context of AWS, this will mean things like S3 buckets, EC2 instances, Route53 records, and so on. The provider block must be declared, though it can have varying degrees of configuration.

Data

The "data" elements are called data sources. Data sources are not required, though the flexibility and power they bring to Terraform means that, practically speaking, you will see them in all but the most basic of implementations. Data sources provide a mechanism to gather data from the provider. In our example from Listing 4-1, I used a data source to get the AWS region Terraform was currently being used with. Since this data source is able to use context directly from the provider, it doesn't require any additional arguments/parameters to function correctly. Other data sources – for example, a data source meant to provide information about AMIs – accept parameters that allow the data source to filter down to a specific value (or set of values) to be used elsewhere in your codebase.

Variables

Variables provide the means by which you will parametrize your deployments. They are not strictly required for Terraform to work, but I would desecrate any pull request that ever came to me for approval that used hard-coded values in lieu of variables. While we're talking about variables, it's worth talking about CloudFormation a bit. By way of comparison, it's obvious that Terraform's variables are analogous to CloudFormation's parameters. What may be less obvious is that Terraform's variables also cover the features provided by CloudFormation's mapping constructs. Take a look at the "connect_port_by_os" and "ami_by_region_os" variables in Listing 3-1 – they are both defined as a "map"-type variable; this type of variable gives you the ability to create a hierarchy of values within a single variable. As you look at the variables, you will notice a common set of attributes for each, all of which are optional:

- *Description.* Self-explanatory and will definitely create a better overall experience for end users and consumers of your code and modules.

- *Type.* While not required, I (and the Terraform developers) strongly urge you to set this attribute appropriately, especially if you're going to be using a type besides a basic string. If no type constraint is set, then a value of any type is accepted.[1]

- *Default.* This allows you to set a default value in the variable's **definition**. Terraform has a mechanism whereby multiple avenues to define variable values are provided with a set of built-in precedences that allow you to define defaults in other ways, aside from the variable's definition.

These are all of the attributes supported by Terraform. I have always been a bit disappointed personally that Terraform doesn't support the many facets of input validation that CloudFormation supports with Parameters. At this time, there aren't really any great third-party

---

[1] www.terraform.io/docs/configuration/variables.html#type-constraints

solutions to the problem, either; if you're looking for a great open source contribution opportunity, coming up with a good tool for this would definitely fill a gap in the Terraform toolchain.

Resources

In a similar vein to CloudFormation, Resources are the essential "unit of work" in a Terraform-defined deployment. Since resources obviously correspond to any number of different kinds of AWS resource, the parameters will be reflective of that particular class of resource. There are, however, "meta-arguments" that Terraform makes available for all resources. It is worth taking a look at these in Listing 4-1.

count

In my experience, you will use none of these meta-arguments more frequently than the *count* meta-argument. As you might suspect from its name, this meta-argument gives you access to a powerful logic not available in CloudFormation. While the argument can accept a literal value, embedded ternary (if-else) logic can be passed to this argument to create or not create the resource under certain conditions, or to even create a certain number of this resource (even with advanced if-else logic).

depends_on

Very similar to CloudFormation's DependsOn attribute, this argument allows you to specifically define dependencies between resources. Use this with care, as often it is not necessary. As Terraform's docs state:

> *Terraform analyses any expressions within a resource block to find references to other objects, and treats those references as implicit ordering requirements when creating, updating, or destroying resources.*

> *Since most resources with behavioral dependencies on other resources also refer to those resources' data, it's usually not necessary to manually specify dependencies between resources.*
>
> *However, some dependencies cannot be recognized implicitly in configuration. For example, if Terraform must manage access control policies and take actions that require those policies to be present, there is a hidden dependency between the access policy and a resource whose creation depends on it. In these rare cases, the depends_on meta-argument can explicitly specify a dependency.*[2]

lifecycle

This argument allows you to control (and perhaps override) how Terraform deals with the lifecycle of resources it manages, specifically when updating or destroying resources. It allows you to keep a resource even if a destroy command is successfully executed. It also gives you a mechanism for carrying out blue/green deployments by using the *create_before_destroy* argument with an autoscaling group (see Terraform's docs[3] for a specific treatment of this topic).

---

[2]`www.terraform.io/docs/configuration/resources.html#resource-dependencies`

[3]`www.terraform.io/docs/providers/aws/r/launch_configuration.html#using-with-autoscaling-groups`

provider

Within a single set of configuration files/deployment, Terraform gives you the ability to use more than a single provider. Since providers are limited in scope to a single AWS region, multiple providers give you the flexibility to essentially define and build a multiregional deployment within a single configuration. Consider a situation where an application provides for a real-time replica in a secondary region, such a deployment might be modeled and built in a manner resembling Listing 4-2.

Listing 4-2. Multiregional Deployment

```
# default configuration
provider "aws" {
  region = "us-east-1"
}
# alternative, aliased configuration
provider "aws" {
  alias  = "uw2"
  region = "us-west-2"
}

resource "aws_instance" "primary" {
  # ...
}

resource "aws_instance" "failover" {
  provider = aws.uw2

  # ...
}
```

provisioner and connection

Terraform provides a mechanism to configure resources after they have been provisioned using the provider API – namely, EC2 instances. Provisioner and connection allow you to remotely connect to these resources and issue commands to them in order to fully configure the instances with needed software and configuration.

Code Layout and Structure

Terraform differs greatly in the meaning of files relative to a single deployment with respect to CloudFormation. With CloudFormation, a single file represented a single deployment, with additional files corresponding to snippets, nested stacks, or perhaps mapping files. Nonetheless, generally a single file corresponds to a single deployment with CloudFormation. Terraform functions significantly differently in this regard. With Terraform, the runtime looks for every ∗.tf file in the local directory and evaluates a composite of those files as a whole. Relative to Listing 4-1, we could easily have split that code across a few separate files and arrive at the same result from Terraform's perspective.

Let's suppose for a moment that Listing 4-1 comprises the entirety of our deployment. Our code directory then would look like what we see in Listing 4-3.

Listing 4-3. Local Directory Listing

```
$ tree -I 'setup'
.
└── ec2_instance.tf

0 directories, 1 file
```

Listing 4-1 could easily be refactored into multiple files. Listings 4-4, 4-5, 4-6, and 4-7 demonstrate a refactored Listing 4-1. Let's suppose for a moment that Listing 4-1 comprises the entirety of our deployment. Our code directory then would look like what we see in Listing 4-8. As the filenames and their contents certainly make things easier to find from a code maintenance perspective, the code contained in Listing 4-3 and Listing 4-8 are equivalent from Terraform's perspective.

Listing 4-4. provider.tf

```
# All Terraform code needs a provider to work
provider "aws" {}
```

Listing 4-5. variables.tf

```
# These correspond to 3-1 Parameters
variable "key_name" {
  type = "string"
  description = "Name of an existing EC2 KeyPair to enable
access to the instance"
  default = ""
}

variable "operating_system" {
  type = "string"
  description = "Chosen operating system"
  default = "AmazonLinux2"
}

variable "instance_type" {
  type = "string"
  description = "EC2 instance type"
  default = "t2.small"
}
```

```
variable "public_location" {
  type = "string"
  description = "The IP address range that can be used to
connect to the EC2 instances"
  default = "0.0.0.0/0"
}

# These correspond to 3-1 Mappings
variable "connect_port_by_os" {
  type = "map"
  description = "Port mappings for operating systems"
  default = {
    Windows2016Base = "3389"
    AmazonLinux2 = "22"
  }
}

variable "ami_by_region_os" {
  type = "map"
  description = "AMI ID by region and OS"
  default = {
    us-east-1 = {
      Windows2016Base = "ami-06bee8e1000e44ca4"
      AmazonLinux2 = "ami-0c6b1d09930fac512"
    }
    us-west-2 = {
      Windows2016Base = "ami-07f35a597a32e470d"
      AmazonLinux2 = "ami-0cb72367e98845d43"
    }
  }
}
```

Listing 4-6. resources.tf

```
# This provides an analogue to the ${AWS::...} pseudo-variables
# in CloudFormation.
data "aws_region" "current" {}

resource "aws_security_group" "public_os_access" {
  name        = "public_os_access"
  description = "Enable public access via OS-specific port"

  ingress {
    from_port   = "${lookup(var.connect_port_by_os, var.
                  operating_system)}"
    to_port     = "${lookup(var.connect_port_by_os, var.
                  operating_system)}"
    protocol    = "tcp"
    cidr_blocks = ["${var.public_location}"]
  }
}

resource "aws_instance" "public_instance" {
  instance_type = "${var.instance_type}"
  key_name = "${var.key_name}"
  ami = "${lookup(var.ami_by_region_os[data.aws_region.current.
  name], var.operating_system)}"
  vpc_security_group_ids = ["${aws_security_group.public_os_
  access.id}"]
}
```

Listing 4-7. outputs.tf

```
output "instance_id" {
  value = "${aws_instance.public_instance.id}"
}
```

```
output "az" {
  value = "${aws_instance.public_instance.availability_zone}"
}

output "public_dns" {
  value = "${aws_instance.public_instance.public_dns}"
}

output "public_ip" {
  value = "${aws_instance.public_instance.public_ip}"
}
```

Listing 4-8. Directory contents.

```
$ tree
.
├── outputs.tf
├── provider.tf
├── resources.tf
└── variables.tf

0 directories, 4 files
```

Variable Values

Terraform allows you to pass variable values through multiple avenues. It is important to understand these mechanisms to understand how to effectively leverage the tool. Before diving deep into precedence mechanisms for variables, let's take a look at how we actually deploy with Terraform to appreciate its mechanisms for variable-value handling.

terraform.tfvars

.tfvars files are files in the deployment directory ending with the .tfvars suffix. By default, Terraform will look for a file name terraform.tfvars without any explicit instruction on the command line. .tfvars files look a bit different from a .tf file. Considering our example deployment modeled in either Listing 4-1 or Listings 4-4 through 4-7, what might a tfvars file look like? Listing 4-9 shows a file that sets values for the variables defined in the deployment that will override the defaults set in the actual variable declarations.

Listing 4-9. terraform.tfvars

```
operating_system = "Windows2016Base"
instance_type = "t2.medium"
public_location = "1.2.3.4/32"
```

Variables in Context of Deployment

Deployment from the root directory of a project can be as simple as running two commands: "terraform init" and "terraform apply". This presumes that your local environment is populated with variables that are capable of authenticating to an AWS account (e.g., AWS_PROFILE or AWS_ACCESS_KEY_ID/AWS_SECRET_ACCESS_KEY[4]). Listings 4-10 and 4-11 demonstrate the outcome of running these two commands in a directory that contains files from Listings 4-1 and 4-9.

---

[4]https://docs.aws.amazon.com/cli/latest/userguide/cli-configure-profiles.html

Listing 4-10. terraform init

```
$ terraform init

Initializing the backend...

Initializing provider plugins...
```

The following providers do not have any version constraints in configuration, so the latest version was installed.

To prevent automatic upgrades to new major versions that may contain breaking changes, it is recommended to add version = "..." constraints to the corresponding provider blocks in configuration, with the constraint strings suggested below.

```
* provider.aws: version = "~> 2.19"
```

Terraform has been successfully initialized!

You may now begin working with Terraform. Try running "terraform plan" to see any changes that are required for your infrastructure. All Terraform commands should now work.

If you ever set or change modules or backend configuration for Terraform, rerun this command to reinitialize your working directory. If you forget, other commands will detect it and remind you to do so if necessary.

Listing 4-11. terraform apply

```
$ terraform apply
data.aws_region.current: Refreshing state...
```

An execution plan has been generated and is shown in the following.
Resource actions are indicated with the following symbols:
```
  + create
```

Terraform will perform the following actions:

```
  # aws_instance.public_instance will be created
  + resource "aws_instance" "public_instance" {
      + ami                            = "ami-06bee8e1000e44ca4"
      + arn                            = (known after apply)
      + associate_public_ip_address    = (known after apply)
      + availability_zone              = (known after apply)
      + cpu_core_count                 = (known after apply)
      + cpu_threads_per_core           = (known after apply)
      + get_password_data              = false
      + host_id                        = (known after apply)
      + id                             = (known after apply)
      + instance_state                 = (known after apply)
      + instance_type                  = "t2.medium"
      + ipv6_address_count             = (known after apply)
      + ipv6_addresses                 = (known after apply)
      + key_name                       = (known after apply)
      + network_interface_id           = (known after apply)
      + password_data                  = (known after apply)
      + placement_group                = (known after apply)
      + primary_network_interface_id   = (known after apply)
      + private_dns                    = (known after apply)
      + private_ip                     = (known after apply)
      + public_dns                     = (known after apply)
      + public_ip                      = (known after apply)
      + security_groups                = (known after apply)
      + source_dest_check              = true
      + subnet_id                      = (known after apply)
      + tenancy                        = (known after apply)
      + volume_tags                    = (known after apply)
      + vpc_security_group_ids         = (known after apply)
```

```
    + ebs_block_device {
        + delete_on_termination = (known after apply)
        + device_name           = (known after apply)
        + encrypted             = (known after apply)
        + iops                  = (known after apply)
        + snapshot_id           = (known after apply)
        + volume_id             = (known after apply)
        + volume_size           = (known after apply)
        + volume_type           = (known after apply)
      }

    + ephemeral_block_device {
        + device_name  = (known after apply)
        + no_device    = (known after apply)
        + virtual_name = (known after apply)
      }

    + network_interface {
        + delete_on_termination = (known after apply)
        + device_index          = (known after apply)
        + network_interface_id  = (known after apply)
      }

    + root_block_device {
        + delete_on_termination = (known after apply)
        + iops                  = (known after apply)
        + volume_id             = (known after apply)
        + volume_size           = (known after apply)
        + volume_type           = (known after apply)
      }
  }
```

```
# aws_security_group.public_os_access will be created
+ resource "aws_security_group" "public_os_access" {
    + arn                      = (known after apply)
    + description              = "Enable public access via OS-
                                 specific port"
    + egress                   = (known after apply)
    + id                       = (known after apply)
    + ingress                  = [
        + {
            + cidr_blocks       = [
                + "1.2.3.4/32",
              ]
            + description       = ""
            + from_port         = 3389
            + ipv6_cidr_blocks  = []
            + prefix_list_ids   = []
            + protocol          = "tcp"
            + security_groups   = []
            + self              = false
            + to_port           = 3389
          },
      ]
    + name                     = "public_os_access"
    + owner_id                 = (known after apply)
    + revoke_rules_on_delete   = false
    + vpc_id                   = (known after apply)
  }

Plan: 2 to add, 0 to change, 0 to destroy.
```

```
Do you want to perform these actions?
  Terraform will perform the actions described earlier.
  Only 'yes' will be accepted to approve.

  Enter a value: yes

aws_security_group.public_os_access: Creating...
aws_security_group.public_os_access: Creation complete after 3s
[id=sg-02866422c43f574bc]
aws_instance.public_instance: Creating...
aws_instance.public_instance: Still creating... [10s elapsed]
aws_instance.public_instance: Still creating... [20s elapsed]
aws_instance.public_instance: Still creating... [30s elapsed]
aws_instance.public_instance: Creation complete after 36s
[id=i-08c5be452e877d7ed]

Apply complete! Resources: 2 added, 0 changed, 0 destroyed.

Outputs:

az = us-east-1d
instance_id = i-08c5be452e877d7ed
public_dns = ec2-3-87-212-18.compute-1.amazonaws.com
public_ip = 3.87.212.18
```

Lastly, Listing 4-12 shows the outputs defined in Listing 4-1. This is the last bit of output from the "terraform apply" command.

Listing 4-12. Terraform Apply – Outputs

```
Outputs:

az = us-east-1d
instance_id = i-08c5be452e877d7ed
public_dns = ec2-3-87-212-18.compute-1.amazonaws.com
public_ip = 3.87.212.18
```

If you observe Listing 4-11, you'll notice that the "ami" parameter is the same as our Windows2016Base AMI ID specified in the "ami_by_region_os" map variable in Listing 4-1. Despite our "AmazonLinux2" variable default for OS, we now have a Windows AMI being passed as an argument by virtue of the fact that the value is specified in our terraform.tfvars file.

With an understanding of how the terraform.tfvars file works, what else can we do with tfvars files? Thankfully, Terraform's mechanism for utilization of tfvars files is actually much more powerful than simply possessing an awareness of using values from a local terraform.tfvars file. Let's have a look at how we might leverage tfvars files in a more flexible, powerful way and what we'll need to do from the CLI to exploit this mechanism.

Advanced tfvars Files Usage

To take advantage of the flexibility and power of AWS in offering multiple regions for our infrastructure builds, let's consider how it might reshape our configuration files to more effectively accommodate additional regions using tfvars files. If we were to model a single application deployment across multiple regions limited to the concept of a single tfvars file, we end up copying the main configuration files to a second directory and populating a terraform.tfvars accordingly. Let's look for a way to keep our code a bit DRYer by exploiting a commonsense approach to using tfvars files (with a small example). Listing 4-13 (an adaptation of Listing 4-1) is a self-contained configuration file that creates a security group and an EC2 instance. You'll note that the "ami_by_region_os" map variable is no longer present; instead, we have replaced it with generic "windows_ami" and "linux_ami" string variables.

Listing 4-13. app.tf

```
provider "aws" {}

variable "instance_type" {
  type = "string"
  description = "EC2 instance type"
  default = "t2.small"
}

variable "public_location" {
  type = "string"
  description = "The IP address range that can be used to
  connect to the EC2 instances"
  default = "0.0.0.0/0"
}

variable "connect_port" {
  type = "map"
  default = {
    windows = "3389"
    linux = "22"
  }
}

variable "os_type" {
  type = "string"
  description = "windows|linux"
  default = "linux"
}

variable "windows_ami" {
  type = "string"
  description = "Windows AMI"
```

```
  default = ""
}

variable "linux_ami" {
  type = "string"
  description = "Linux AMI"
  default = ""
}

resource "aws_security_group" "public_os_access" {
  name        = "public_os_access"
  description = "Enable public access via OS-specific port"

  ingress {
    from_port   = "${lookup(var.connect_port, var.os_type)}"
    to_port     = "${lookup(var.connect_port, var.os_type)}"
    protocol    = "tcp"
    cidr_blocks = ["${var.public_location}"]
  }
}

resource "aws_instance" "public_instance" {
  instance_type = "${var.instance_type}"
  ami = "${var.os_type == "windows" ? var.windows_ami :
  var.linux_ami}"
  vpc_security_group_ids = ["${aws_security_group.public_
  os_access.id}"]
}

output "instance_id" {
  value = "${aws_instance.public_instance.id}"
}
```

```
output "az" {
  value = "${aws_instance.public_instance.availability_zone}"
}

output "public_dns" {
  value = "${aws_instance.public_instance.public_dns}"
}

output "public_ip" {
  value = "${aws_instance.public_instance.public_ip}"
}
```

While the map variable we used in Listing 4-1 to serve as a region-specific index of AMIs (see Note 4-1) was useful in the context of that example, it begins to become cumbersome if we desire to scale it horizontally or vertically (ok, this sounds weird in the context of a variable, right?). This is demonstrated as follows.

Listing 4-14. Scaling ami_by_region_os Vertically

```
variable "ami_by_region_os" {
  type = "map"
  description = "AMI ID by region and OS"
  default = {
    qa = {
      us-east-1 = {
        Windows2016Base = "ami-..."
        AmazonLinux2 = "ami-..."
      }
      us-west-2 = {
        Windows2016Base = "ami-..."
        AmazonLinux2 = "ami-..."
      }
    }
```

```
stg = {
  us-east-1 = {
    Windows2016Base = "ami-..."
    AmazonLinux2 = "ami-..."
  }
  us-west-2 = {
    Windows2016Base = "ami-..."
    AmazonLinux2 = "ami-..."
  }
}
prod = {
  us-east-1 = {
    Windows2016Base = "ami-..."
    AmazonLinux2 = "ami-..."
  }
  us-west-2 = {
    Windows2016Base = "ami-..."
    AmazonLinux2 = "ami-..."
  }
}
  }
}
```

You'll notice in Listing 4-14 that I've added an additional dimension that correlates to different deployment environments (e.g., qa/stg/prod). While it is useful to be able to add arbitrary dimensions to maps like this, they make "consumer" code more complex and logic harder to follow. Consider the line of code in our example from 4-1 that selects the ami for the EC2 instance resource:

```
ami = "${lookup(var.ami_by_region_os[data.aws_region.current.
name], var.operating_system)}"
```

Even in that form, it's not the simplest thing to wrap your head around. Every dimension added to the variable has to be accounted for here. Additionally, we now need another variable (e.g., "deploy_env") to account for the deployment environment, so we end up with

```
ami = "${lookup(lookup(var.ami_by_region_os[var.deploy_env],
data.aws_region.current.name), var.operating_system)}"
```

or alternatively

```
ami = "${var.ami_by_region_os[var.deploy_env][data.aws_region.
current.name][var.operating_system]}"
```

While the second form is certainly more readable, it's still cumbersome. In the case of our original ami_by_region_os variable, we can also consider the case of scaling the variable horizontally, as in Listing 4-15.

Listing 4-15. Scaling ami_by_region_os Horizontally

```
variable "ami_by_region_os" {
  type = "map"
  description = "AMI ID by region and OS"
  default = {
    us-east-1 = {
      Windows2016Base = "ami-06bee8e1000e44ca4"
      AmazonLinux2 = "ami-0c6b1d09930fac512"
    }
    us-east-2 = {
      Windows2016Base = "ami-..."
      AmazonLinux2 = "ami-..."
    }
    us-west-2 = {
      Windows2016Base = "ami-07f35a597a32e470d"
      AmazonLinux2 = "ami-0cb72367e98845d43"
    }
```

```
    eu-west-1 = {
      Windows2016Base = "ami-..."
      AmazonLinux2 = "ami-..."
    }
    ap-southeast-1 = {
      Windows2016Base = "ami-..."
      AmazonLinux2 = "ami-..."
    }
  }
}
```

This sort of expansion to accommodate multiple regions is not uncommon as services/products grow their user bases. While this accomplishes the goal of maintaining region-specific configurations, it's error-prone and requires direct manipulation of configuration code to accommodate the change. Tfvars files and handling them from the CLI interface make it possible to arrive at a more flexible and easily extensible solution. Working from Listing 4-13 as a base, let's consider a directory structure like the one in Listing 4-16.

Listing 4-16. Directory Listing

```
$ tree -I 'setup'
.
├── app.tf
├── prod
│   ├── us-east-1.tfvars
│   └── us-west-2.tfvars
└── qa
    ├── us-east-1.tfvars
    └── us-west-2.tfvars

2 directories, 5 files
```

Using directory-based structures corresponding to environments and regions shown in Listing 4-16 along with the configuration code design in Listing 4-13, we now have a flexible design that allows us to onboard new environments and regions by simply adding a new tfvars file to an appropriate directory. It's pretty simple to incorporate this from the command line via several methods. For these examples, we will use Terraform's "plan" command,[5] which shows us what Terraform would do in the event that we were running an "apply" command (which actually effects changes, whereas "plan" does not). Let's plan a production deployment in us-east-1:

```
$ terraform plan -var-file=prod/us-east-1.tfvars
```

As you'll notice, we are telling Terraform to use the us-east-1.tfvars file in the production directory to specify parameter values specified in that file. Listing 4-17 shows the contents of the prod/us-east-1.tfvars file.

Listing 4-17. Contents of prod/us-east-1.tfvars

```
windows_ami = "ami-06bee8e1000e44ca4"
linux_ami = "ami-0c6b1d09930fac512"
```

In the context of designating which particular tfvars file to use from the shell, there are different ways to do so, which you may want to utilize in specific contexts. Earlier, we explicitly passed these values to the plan command. However, maybe we want to create a shell script to handle the entire Terraform deployment process for us (note: while this is a working script, it is a naïve implementation [i.e., this is for illustrative purposes only; don't use it for instance to manage a production deployment]).

---

[5] www.terraform.io/docs/commands/plan.html

Listing 4-18. Deployment script (tf_deploy.sh)

```
#!/bin/bash

type terraform >/dev/null 2>&1 || { echo >&2 "terraform is
required, but not installed.  Aborting."; exit 1; }

if [[ -z "${DEPLOY_ENV}" ]]; then
    echo "Please set the \$DEPLOY_ENV variable prior to
    running this script."
    exit 1
fi

if [[ -z "${DEPLOY_REGION}" ]]; then
    echo "Please set the \$DEPLOY_REGION variable prior to
    running this script."
    exit 1
fi

echo -e "Preparing ${DEPLOY_ENV} deployment in region ${DEPLOY_
REGION}.\n"

###
# Add custom pre-deployment logic here -- e.g. create a ticket
in a release tracking system, send a message to a release
channel via Slack, etc.
#

terraform init
terraform plan -var-file="${DEPLOY_ENV}/${DEPLOY_REGION}.
tfvars" -detailed-exitcode
PLAN_STATUS=$?
```

```
# PLAN_STATUS will be 0 if this is a new deployment, 2 if we
are updating
# an existing deployment where changes will be made.
# PLAN_STATUS will be 1 in case of a failure of the plan command.
if [[ "${PLAN_STATUS}" -ne "1" ]]; then
        echo "Plan succeeded.  Proceeding to apply."
else
        echo "Plan failed.  Aborting."
        exit 1
fi

terraform apply -var-file="${DEPLOY_ENV}/${DEPLOY_REGION}.
tfvars" -auto-approve
```

As mentioned previously, this script is functional and will deploy
assuming the DEPLOY_ENV and DEPLOY_REGION variables are set in the
environment with valid values prior to running this script. From a shell,
this would look something like

```
$ export DEPLOY_ENV=prod
$ export DEPLOY_REGION=us-east-1
$ ./tf_deploy.sh
```

Why wrap the deployment logic in a script like this? As you'll see in
the preceding code, at a bare minimum, you need to run the init and
apply commands to deploy with Terraform. However, it is certainly
plausible that you might want to perform additional actions around your
deployments (as noted in the comments in the preceding script). Often,
these sorts of actions wrap deployment logic in separate steps or stages
in a continuous deployment pipeline. On the flip side of that argument,
though, sometimes it is convenient to have a script like this that can be run
from an administrator's local laptop in the event that a CI/CD server is not
available; the script itself as written is still usable from within the context of
many different CI/CD servers.

WHAT ABOUT WORKSPACES?

Workspaces[6] is a feature that allows a Terraform user to use the same configuration files to deploy separate environments, or "workspaces." While the concept is useful and is argued for since the mechanism is built directly into the Terraform runtime, its use of the same backend[7] for all supported workspaces is problematic. In practice, a development and production environment will likely be partitioned into separate resources (e.g., separate S3 buckets at a minimum, more likely separate accounts) with separate access patterns, compliance needs, and so on, making uniform access to a backend to store metadata related to a development, QA, staging, and production environment problematic. Additionally, even with workspaces, multiple Terraform commands must be run to provision infrastructure described by a set of a configuration files, so the concept of using an orchestration script like the one we used in Listing 4-18 would still be applicable. So, despite the advertised benefits of workspaces, I see the use of the feature being highly problematic in real-world scenarios. So, while I am giving visibility to the feature in this sidebar for the sake of those readers who want to look more in-depth at the feature and see if it fits their own use cases, this book won't cover the feature any further than this sidebar.

Let's look at a different type of resource to consider our next point of consideration regarding tfvars files. Listing 4-19 contains a resource definition for a Cloudwatch alarm.

---

[6]www.terraform.io/docs/state/workspaces.html
[7]www.terraform.io/docs/backends/

Listing 4-19. cw_alarm.tf

```
provider "aws" {}

variable "threshold_percentage" {
  type = "string"
  description = "Percentage (integer) over which alarm is
  triggered"
}

resource "aws_cloudwatch_metric_alarm" "infrabook" {
  alarm_name                = "aws-infrabook-ec2"
  comparison_operator       = "GreaterThanOrEqualToThreshold"
  evaluation_periods        = "2"
  metric_name               = "CPUUtilization"
  namespace                 = "AWS/EC2"
  period                    = "120"
  statistic                 = "Average"
  threshold                 = "${var.threshold_percentage}"
  alarm_description         = "This metric monitors ec2 cpu
utilization"
  insufficient_data_actions = []
}
```

In the same directory, we'll create a terraform.tfvars files for our defaults.

Listing 4-20. terraform.tfvars

```
threshold_percentage = "95"
```

Now, by default, the Cloudwatch alarm will have a 95% CPU utilization threshold. Generally speaking, that should be ok, but maybe we would like a bit more of a cushion in our staging environment.

Listing 4-21. stg.tfvars

```
threshold_percentage = "85"
```

We can take advantage of our new staging configuration from the CLI like so:

```
$ terraform [plan|apply] -var-file=stg.tfvars
```

Since, as discussed previously, Terraform will automatically consider terraform.tfvars, we should expect to see the threshold percentage set to 85 in our plan.

Listing 4-22. Plan Output

```
$ terraform plan -var-file=stg.tfvars
Refreshing Terraform state in-memory prior to plan...
The refreshed state will be used to calculate this plan, but
will not be
persisted to local or remote state storage.

------------------------------------------------------------------

An execution plan has been generated and is shown in the
following.
Resource actions are indicated with the following symbols:
  + create

Terraform will perform the following actions:

  # aws_cloudwatch_metric_alarm.infrabook will be created
  + resource "aws_cloudwatch_metric_alarm" "infrabook" {
      + actions_enabled                   = true
      + alarm_description                 = "This metric
                                            monitors
                                            ec2 cpu
                                            utilization"
```

```
    + alarm_name                                  = "aws-infrabook-
                                                    ec2"
    + arn                                         = (known after
                                                    apply)
    + comparison_operator                         = "Greater
                                                    ThanOr
                                                    EqualTo
                                                    Threshold"
    + evaluate_low_sample_count_percentiles = (known after
                                                    apply)
    + evaluation_periods                          = 2
    + id                                          = (known after
                                                    apply)
    + metric_name                                 = "CPU
                                                    Utilization"
    + namespace                                   = "AWS/EC2"
    + period                                      = 120
    + statistic                                   = "Average"
    + threshold                                   = 85
    + treat_missing_data                          = "missing"
  }
```

Plan: 1 to add, 0 to change, 0 to destroy.

As expected, our plan indicates the threshold will be set to 85. To bring this concept home, let's consider that an 85% threshold, while effective for a staging environment, may not be appropriate for our production environment. The SRE team advises a threshold of 70% for this alarm. We accommodate their request in Listing 4-23.

Listing 4-23. prod.tfvars

```
threshold_percentage = "70"
```

Although there's only one parameter to be considered here, let's look at how to override our staging parameters with our production parameters, which we see in Listing 4-24.

Listing 4-24. plan Command with Staging and Prod tfvars files

```
$ terraform plan -var-file=stg.tfvars -var-file=prod.tfvars
Refreshing Terraform state in-memory prior to plan...
The refreshed state will be used to calculate this plan, but
will not be
persisted to local or remote state storage.

------------------------------------------------------------

An execution plan has been generated and is shown in the
following example.
Resource actions are indicated with the following symbols:
  + create

Terraform will perform the following actions:

  # aws_cloudwatch_metric_alarm.infrabook will be created
  + resource "aws_cloudwatch_metric_alarm" "infrabook" {
      + actions_enabled                = true
      + alarm_description              = "This metric
                                         monitors
                                         ec2 cpu
                                         utilization"
      + alarm_name                     = "aws-infrabook-
                                         ec2"
```

```
        + arn                                        = (known after
                                                       apply)
        + comparison_operator                        = "Greater
                                                       ThanOr
                                                       EqualTo
                                                       Threshold"
        + evaluate_low_sample_count_percentiles = (known after
          apply)
        + evaluation_periods                         = 2
        + id                                         = (known after
                                                       apply)
        + metric_name                                = "CPU
                                                       Utilization"
        + namespace                                  = "AWS/EC2"
        + period                                     = 120
        + statistic                                  = "Average"
        + threshold                                  = 70
        + treat_missing_data                         = "missing"
    }

Plan: 1 to add, 0 to change, 0 to destroy.

------------------------------------------------------------------
Note: You didn't specify an "-out" parameter to save this plan,
so Terraform
can't guarantee that exactly these actions will be performed if
"terraform apply" is subsequently run.
```

As you perhaps suspected, our threshold is now 70% as specified by the prod.tfvars file listed in Listing 4-23. While specifying the prod.tfvars file directly after specifying the stg.tfvars file is a bit contrived, it does demonstrate the fact that Terraform uses the value in the last-specified tfvars file, if more than one is specified and more than one of the files contain a value for the given parameter. Listing 4-25 shows how the solution looks if we incorporate the idea of a region-specific tfvars file that is meant to override a global file.

Listing 4-25. Directory Listing

```
$ tree -I 'setup'
.
├── app.tf
├── prod
│   ├── globals.tfvars
│   ├── us-east-1.tfvars
│   └── us-west-2.tfvars
└── qa
    ├── globals.tfvars
    ├── us-east-1.tfvars
    └── us-west-2.tfvars

2 directories, 7 files
```

In this case, the usefulness of the override mechanism perhaps becomes clearer. Tying this together with our deployment script, we would end up with a set of terraform plan/apply commands in the deployment script that might look something like this:

```
terraform [plan|apply] -var-file="${DEPLOY_ENV}/globals.tfvars" \
    -var-file="${DEPLOY_ENV}/${DEPLOY_REGION}.tfvars"
```

The globals files would contain region-agnostic names – things like IAM role names, universal resource name prefixes, database usernames, metric thresholds, and so on. Should there be any desire to override one of these values with a region-specific value, it would be placed in the region-specific file (and thus override the value in the globals.tfvars file).

Runtime Variable Values

Now that you have an understanding of the possibilities of tfvars files, let's talk about a few other mechanisms Terraform has for ingesting variable values. These methods can (and should) be considered as an accompaniment to our previous discussion of how to use tfvars files.

Environment Variables

Terraform will accept a value for any declared variable set in the environment with the TF_VAR_ prefix. As an example, based on our previous Cloudwatch alarm example, let's set the threshold_percentage variable with an environment – this would assume that there are no tfvars files alongside the cw_alarm.tf file found in Listing 4-19. We see how this works in Listing 4-26.

Listing 4-26. Using Environment Variable for Plan

```
$ export TF_VAR_threshold_percentage="65"
$ terraform init
$ terraform plan
Refreshing Terraform state in-memory prior to plan...
The refreshed state will be used to calculate this plan, but
will not be
persisted to local or remote state storage.

------------------------------------------------------------

An execution plan has been generated and is shown in the
following.
Resource actions are indicated with the following symbols:
  + create
```

Terraform will perform the following actions:

```
  # aws_cloudwatch_metric_alarm.infrabook will be created
  + resource "aws_cloudwatch_metric_alarm" "infrabook" {
      + actions_enabled                         = true run
      + alarm_description                       = "This metric
                                                  monitors
                                                  ec2 cpu
                                                  utilization"
      + alarm_name                              = "aws-infrabook-
                                                  ec2"
      + arn                                     = (known after
                                                  apply)
      + comparison_operator                     = "Greater
                                                  ThanOr
                                                  EqualTo
                                                  Threshold"
      + evaluate_low_sample_count_percentiles   = (known after
        apply)
      + evaluation_periods                      = 2
      + id                                      = (known after
                                                  apply)
      + metric_name                             = "CPU
                                                  Utilization"
      + namespace                               = "AWS/EC2"
      + period                                  = 120
      + statistic                               = "Average"
      + threshold                               = 65
      + treat_missing_data                      = "missing"
    }
```

```
Plan: 1 to add, 0 to change, 0 to destroy.
```

```
Note: You didn't specify an "-out" parameter to save this plan,
so Terraform can't guarantee that exactly these actions will be
performed if "terraform apply" is subsequently.
```

CLI Variables

If tfvars files are used, those values will override anything set via an
environment variable. The bolded threshold parameter confirms that
Terraform leveraged our environment variable to set the value of the
threshold_percentage variable. Terraform can also accept a variable
value as a parameter directly through CLI invocation. In this case, the
value taking precedence is the last one passed on the command line.
This is demonstrated, in the context of Listing 4-24, as follows.

Listing 4-27. cw_alarm.tf with tfvars files and Explicit Value

```
$ terraform plan -var-file=stg.tfvars -var-file=prod.tfvars
-var="threshold_percentage=55"
Refreshing Terraform state in-memory prior to plan...
The refreshed state will be used to calculate this plan, but
will not be
persisted to local or remote state storage.
```

```
An execution plan has been generated and is shown in the
following.
Resource actions are indicated with the following symbols:
  + create
```

Terraform will perform the following actions:

```
# aws_cloudwatch_metric_alarm.infrabook will be created
+ resource "aws_cloudwatch_metric_alarm" "infrabook" {
    + actions_enabled                           = true
    + alarm_description                         = "This metric
                                                  monitors
                                                  ec2 cpu
                                                  utilization"
    + alarm_name                                = "aws-infrabook-
                                                  ec2"
    + arn                                       = (known after
                                                  apply)
    + comparison_operator                       = "Greater
                                                  ThanOr
                                                  EqualTo
                                                  Threshold"
    + evaluate_low_sample_count_percentiles = (known after
      apply)
    + evaluation_periods                        = 2
    + id                                        = (known after
                                                  apply)
    + metric_name                               = "CPU
                                                  Utilization"
    + namespace                                 = "AWS/EC2"
    + period                                    = 120
    + statistic                                 = "Average"
    + threshold                                 = 55
    + treat_missing_data                        = "missing"
  }
```

```
Plan: 1 to add, 0 to change, 0 to destroy.

---------------------------------------------------------------

Note: You didn't specify an "-out" parameter to save this plan,
so Terraform can't guarantee that exactly these actions will be
performed if "terraform apply" is subsequently run.
```

As you'll notice from Listing 4-27, the threshold parameter is 55, as dictated by the literal value passed in to the plan command. Since this value comes *after* the declaration of the tfvars files, it overrides the value set in either of the stg.tfvars or prod.tfvars files. In any case, tfvars files and literal var values passed with the -var flag will override a value set via an environment variable. It is useful, however, to know that these mechanisms are available to you. The -var mechanism if often useful for overriding values in CI/CD pipelines, where you may want to set a tag value to distinguish a set of resources as having been created by a CI/CD tool for purposes of inspection, enumeration, or testing.

Modules, Locals, Remote State, Providers, and Pinning

There is a lot to cover here, but we'll start first with modules. Terraform's modules are one of its most powerful features, giving you the ability to abstract common infrastructure elements into a distinct "unit of work" – versionable, reusable, and easily parametrized. Let's imagine for a moment that you work for a SaaS provider whose product comprises a pretty basic architecture: each deployment consists of an elastic load balancer (ELB) fronting an app hosted on an EC2 instance, a backend RDS instance, a Route 53 entry that creates a customer-specific ALIAS record for the ELB, and the necessary security groups to set all this up securely.

Modules

The Module Itself

Modules put the full power of Terraform on display. Before we truly dig into modules, the directory listing in Listing 4-28 will be a central point of reference throughout the following discussion, so it may be helpful to bookmark this page, as you'll refer to it frequently for the next few pages of discussion.

Listing 4-28. Module-Based Directory Listing

```
$ tree -I '*.tfstate*' --dirsfirst
.
├── modules
│   └── app
│       ├── main.tf
│       ├── outputs.tf
│       ├── userdata.sh
│       └── variables.tf
├── prod
│   ├── globals.tfvars
│   └── us-east-1.tfvars
├── deployments.tf
├── outputs.tf
├── provider.tf
└── variables.tf

3 directories, 10 files
```

This directory listing doesn't look altogether alien from anything we've seen previously. The main difference you see here is the *modules/app* directory and its contents. These files contain the supporting elements and resources mentioned in the introduction to this section. Let's have a look at the files:

Listing 4-29. modules/app/variables.tf

```
locals {
  instance_type = {
    small = "t2.micro"
    medium = "t2.medium"
    large = "t2.large"
  }

  db_instance_class = {
    small = "db.t3.micro"
    medium = "db.t3.medium"
    large = "db.t3.large"
  }

  db_storage = {
    small = 25
    medium = 50
    large = 100
  }

  elb_zone_id = {
    us-east-1 = "Z35SXDOTRQ7X7K"
    us-east-2 = "Z3AADJGX6KTTL2"
    us-west-2 = "Z1H1FL5HABSF5"
  }
}
```

```
variable "acm_cert_arn" {
  description = "ARN of ACM certificate"
  type = string
}

variable "customer_type" {
  description = "Customer designation (small|medium|large)"
  type = string
  default = "small"
}

variable "customer_name" {
  description = "Customer name"
  type = string
}

variable "environment" {
  type = string
  description = "Deployment environment"
}

variable "public_subnets" {
  description = "Public subnet IDs"
  type = list(string)
}

variable "private_subnets" {
  description = "Private subnet IDs"
  type = list(string)
}

variable "db_subnet_group_name" {
  description = "RDS subnet group name"
  type = string
}
```

```
variable "vpc_id" {
  description = "VPC ID"
  type = string
}

variable "zone_id" {
  type = string
  description = "Route53 Zone ID"
}

variable "zone_suffix" {
  type = string
  description = "Route53 Zone Suffix"
}
```

The variables you see in Listing 4-29 shouldn't be anything new, as we've previously talked about variables previously. You will notice the locals block, however, which is new (bolded in the Listing for clarity). See the "Locals" sidebar for a more in-depth discussion of locals. Back on the subject of variables, a key point about modules is that *variables form the external interface to your module*. If you're familiar at all with the concept of abstraction in traditional software engineering, you can think of variables much in the same way you think of function arguments: that is, think very carefully about the interfaces you provide to your modules. Strive to keep them generic, allowing you (as a module maintainer) the flexibility to change the underlying implementation as needed and desired without changing the interface as much as is in your power to do so. Following a semantic versioning paradigm[8] for our modules (which we'll talk about more later), changing variables on a module should trigger a major version increment, as this would represent a backward-incompatible change to the module's API.

---

[8]https://semver.org/

LOCALS

Locals are similar to variables in that they store values that can be used as arguments to various types of resources and data providers; a few key points of differentiation between the two to keep in mind are as follows:

- Unlike variables, the values assigned in a local can contain logic (variable assignments can only be static values).

- Locals are intended to be encapsulated to the context of a module, essentially forming an internal interface. As Terraform's docs say, "[u]se local values only in moderation, in situations where a single value or result is used in many places and that value is likely to be changed in future. The ability to easily change the value in a central place is the key advantage of local values."[9]

While most of the variable values are self-documenting in what types of values they expect from the caller, it's worth talking through the values in the locals block a bit so that you have an understanding of what they're actually doing in our code:

- ***instance_type.*** One of the arguments to our module represents a classification of customer scale – for example, will this customer's SaaS app receive a small, medium, or large amount of traffic? According to that estimation, we provision an EC2 instance of appropriate size.

---

[9]www.terraform.io/docs/configuration/locals.html#when-to-use-local-values

- ***db_instance_class.*** This value follows the same logic
  as "instance_type", except applies to an RDS instance
  instead of an EC2 instance.

- ***db_storage.*** This value follows the same logic as its two
  predecessors but relates to RDS database storage.

- ***elb_zone_id.*** This value map is something you'll need
  whenever you are creating DNS ALIAS records (a
  Route53 implementation-specific type of A record) to
  the public DNS name of an AWS load balancer. ELB
  DNS names belong to an AWS-owned Route53 zone
  and are region-specific.[10] Route53 needs this zone ID to
  properly create the DNS record in the AWS-owned zone
  on your behalf.

Next, let's have a look at the **main.tf** file (Listing 4-30), which contains
all of our data sources and resources.

Listing 4-30. modules/app/main.tf

```
data "aws_region" "current" {}

resource "aws_security_group" "public" {
  name        = "${var.customer_name}-public"
  description = "Allow inbound web traffic"
  vpc_id = "${var.vpc_id}"

  ingress {
    from_port   = 443
    to_port     = 443
    protocol    = "tcp"
    cidr_blocks = ["0.0.0.0/0"]
  }
```

---

[10]https://docs.aws.amazon.com/general/latest/gr/rande.html#elb_region

```
  ingress {
    from_port   = 80
    to_port     = 80
    protocol    = "tcp"
    cidr_blocks = ["0.0.0.0/0"]
  }

  egress {
    from_port       = 0
    to_port         = 0
    protocol        = "-1"
    cidr_blocks     = ["0.0.0.0/0"]
  }

  tags = {
    Name = "${var.customer_name}-public"
    Customer = "${var.customer_name}"
    Environment = "${var.environment}"
  }
}
resource "aws_security_group" "app" {
  name        = "${var.customer_name}-app"
  description = "Allow traffic from ELB"
  vpc_id = "${var.vpc_id}"

  ingress {
    from_port   = 80
    to_port     = 80
    protocol    = "tcp"
    security_groups = ["${aws_security_group.public.id}"]
  }

  egress {
    from_port       = 0
    to_port         = 0
```

```
      protocol        = "-1"
      cidr_blocks     = ["0.0.0.0/0"]
   }

   tags = {
     Name = "${var.customer_name}-app"
     Customer = "${var.customer_name}"
     Environment = "${var.environment}"
   }
}

resource "aws_security_group" "data" {
   name         = "${var.customer_name}-data"
   description = "Allow inbound data traffic"
   vpc_id = "${var.vpc_id}"

   ingress {
     from_port    = 3306
     to_port      = 3306
     protocol     = "tcp"
     security_groups = ["${aws_security_group.app.id}"]
   }

   egress {
     from_port       = 0
     to_port         = 0
     protocol        = "-1"
     cidr_blocks     = ["0.0.0.0/0"]
   }

   tags = {
     Name = "${var.customer_name}-data"
     Customer = "${var.customer_name}"
     Environment = "${var.environment}"
   }
}
```

```
data "aws_ami" "amazon-linux-2" {
  most_recent = true
  owners = ["amazon"]

  filter {
    name   = "owner-alias"
    values = ["amazon"]
  }

  filter {
    name   = "name"
    values = ["amzn2-ami-hvm*"]
  }

  filter {
    name = "architecture"
    values = ["x86_64"]
  }
}

resource "aws_instance" "app" {
  ami            = "${data.aws_ami.amazon-linux-2.id}"
  instance_type = "${lookup(local.instance_type, var.customer_
  type)}"
  vpc_security_group_ids = ["${aws_security_group.app.id}"]
  subnet_id = "${element(var.private_subnets, 1)}"
  user_data = "${file("${path.module}/userdata.sh")}"

  tags = {
    Name = "${var.customer_name}-app"
    Designation = "${var.customer_type}"
    Customer = "${var.customer_name}"
    Environment = "${var.environment}"
  }
}
```

```
resource "aws_elb" "public" {
  name = "${lower(var.customer_name)}-elb"
  subnets = "${var.public_subnets}"
  security_groups = ["${aws_security_group.public.id}"]

  listener {
    instance_port     = 80
    instance_protocol = "http"
    lb_port           = 80
    lb_protocol       = "http"
  }

  listener {
    instance_port      = 80
    instance_protocol  = "http"
    lb_port            = 443
    lb_protocol        = "https"
    ssl_certificate_id = "${var.acm_cert_arn}"
  }

  health_check {
    healthy_threshold   = 2
    unhealthy_threshold = 2
    timeout             = 3
    target              = "HTTP:80/"
    interval            = 30
  }

  instances                   = ["${aws_instance.app.id}"]
  cross_zone_load_balancing   = true
  idle_timeout                = 400
  connection_draining         = true
  connection_draining_timeout = 400
```

```
  tags = {
    Name = "${lower(var.customer_name)}-elb"
    Customer = "${var.customer_name}"
    Environment = "${var.environment}"
  }
}

resource "aws_db_instance" "db" {
  depends_on           = ["aws_security_group.data"]
  identifier           = "${lower(var.customer_name)}"
  allocated_storage    = "${lookup(local.db_storage, var.
                          customer_type)}"
  engine               = "mysql"
  engine_version       = "5.7"
  instance_class       = "${lookup(local.db_instance_class, var.
                          customer_type)}"
  name                 = "AppDb"
  username             = "admin"
  password             = "changeme123"
  vpc_security_group_ids = ["${aws_security_group.data.id}"]
  db_subnet_group_name = "${var.db_subnet_group_name}"
  skip_final_snapshot  = true

  tags = {
    Name = "${var.customer_name}-db"
    Designation = "${var.customer_type}"
    Customer = "${var.customer_name}"
    Environment = "${var.environment}"
  }
}

resource "aws_route53_record" "elb_alias" {
  zone_id = "${var.zone_id}"
  name    = "${lower(var.customer_name)}.${var.zone_suffix}"
  type    = "A"
```

```
  alias {
    name                     = "${aws_elb.public.dns_name}"
    zone_id                  = "${lookup(local.elb_zone_id, data.
                                aws_region.current.name)}"
    evaluate_target_health = false
  }
}
```

As the main point of this book isn't to model robust, production-worthy architectures but rather to look at how we orchestrate the deployment of such architectures, I'm not going to spend a great amount of energy here talking about the architecture. Essentially, we are grabbing the most recent AWS Linux 2 AMI and creating an EC2 instance with it. That EC2 instance lives in its own security group; the EC2 instance's security group allows traffic inbound on port 80 (HTTP port) from another security group (and only from this security group) that encapsulates a public-facing load balancer, which can accept traffic from anyone on ports 80 and 443. We also have an RDS instance in a separate security group that allows incoming traffic on port 3306 (MySQL's typical port) only from the security group that our EC2 instance resides in. While not apparent at this stage, each of these resources (EC2 instance, load balancer, RDS instance) will be deployed into separate groups of subnets: the EC2 instance and RDS instance will go into "private" subnets (i.e., subnets that use a NAT gateway to allow outbound traffic), while the load balancer will go into "public" subnets (subnets with an Internet gateway attached through which all traffic is routed by default). Subnet choices are up to the implementer, though, so these resources don't necessarily have to end up with such a network disposition (though they will in this example). We create our Route53 DNS alias as our final resource; it is also worth noting that we are using an ACM certificate on the HTTPS interface to our load balancer; while I could use a data provider to grab the certificate ARN, I wanted to put the ARN in a tfvars file as an example to reinforce our environment/region tfvars pattern discussed previously.Let's next have a

look at the userdata script our EC2 instance will use to bootstrap itself in
Listing 4-31.

Listing 4-31. modules/app/userdata.sh

```
#!/bin/bash

set -xe

amazon-linux-extras install nginx1.12
systemctl start nginx
```

This will likely be the simplest userdata script you ever see in your
career; we're installing Nginx and starting it with systemd. If you have
provisioned database-backed software architectures and products and
have at this point noticed that we are not actually deploying any software
that leverages the database, you are correct. I could have written some
elaborate userdata script to pull down Wordpress and do a bunch of
magic with sed, awk, and grep to configure a connection to our database,
but that's not central to the theme of this example, so I'll leave that as
an exercise to you, the reader (besides, we might end up disagreeing on
whether Chef, Ansible, SaltStack, or shell scripts is the best way to tackle
this task). The point of the database here is to demonstrate an archetype of
a somewhat common real-world architecture, even if all of the constituent
parts of that architecture aren't "production-ready" (and to that point,
you wouldn't deploy this in a production scenario, so please don't try
to use this as such – you would want to consider autoscaling-based
architectures, instance size choices based on an assessment tool, etc.),
merely illustrative. As you manage multiple deployments, having insight
into certain attributes of the infrastructure is critical. You will want to easily
describe values like database DNS names, IP addresses, and perhaps even
original input values to leverage those values within other automation
tooling. Terraform's outputs allow you to do this. Outputs are defined at the

module level and can be "bubbled up" to the top-level directory (which technically comprises a module, sometimes called the "root module"). Let's have a look at the app module's outputs file.

Listing 4-32. modules/app/outputs.tf

```
output "elb_dns" {
  value = "${aws_elb.public.dns_name}"
}

output "dns" {
  value = "${aws_route53_record.elb_alias.name}"
}

output "db_endpoint" {
  value = "${aws_db_instance.db.endpoint}"
}
```

As alluded to, I'm exporting a few values in Listing 4-32 that represent the main points of connectivity. The "elb_dns" and "dns" outputs actually point to the same public interface of the load balancer; however, the "dns" value won't throw a warning in a browser since we have an ACM cert issued against the DNS name the ELB is ALIASed to attached via Route53 record. Lastly, we export the database endpoint; this could be a helpful value for a DBA or DevOps engineer who has some responsibility for post-provisioning setup and configuration.

Calling a Module

Now that we have a working module created, how do we use it? Let's have a look at the code in the top-level directory.

Listing 4-33. provider.tf

```
provider "aws" {}
```

While Listing 4-33 is quite barebones for the moment, there is a lot of power yet to be explored here. But for now, we'll leave it as is, knowing that it serves as an indicator to Terraform that we're managing resources on AWS. Next up, Listing 4-34, which contains our variables.

Listing 4-34. variables.tf

```
variable "environment" {
  type = string
  description = "Deployment environment (qa|stg|prod)"
  default = "qa"
}

variable "zone_id" {
  type = string
  description = "Route53 Zone ID"
}

variable "zone_suffix" {
  type = string
  description = "Route53 Zone Suffix"
}

variable "acm_cert_arn" {
  type = string
  description = "ACM Cert ARN"
}
```

We capture the environment of our application deployment, some info regarding our Route53 hosted zone, and ARN of the ACM cert we want to attach to the HTTPS port of the load balancer. Moving on to Listing 4-35, we get to the crux of our deployment.

181

Listing 4-35. deployments.tf

```
data "aws_vpc" "vpc" {
  filter {
    name = "tag:Environment"
    values = [
      "${var.environment}"
    ]
  }
}

data "aws_subnet_ids" "public" {
  vpc_id = "${data.aws_vpc.vpc.id}"

  filter {
    name = "tag:Tier"
    values = [
      "public"
    ]
  }
}

data "aws_subnet_ids" "private" {
  vpc_id = "${data.aws_vpc.vpc.id}"

  filter {
    name = "tag:Tier"
    values = [
      "private"
    ]
  }
}

data "aws_subnet_ids" "data" {
  vpc_id = "${data.aws_vpc.vpc.id}"
```

```
  filter {
    name = "tag:Tier"
    values = [
      "data"
    ]
  }
}

resource "aws_db_subnet_group" "customer" {
  name        = "customer-db-subnet-group"
  description = "Customer DB subnet group"
  subnet_ids  = "${data.aws_subnet_ids.data.ids}"
}
module "customer_a" {
  source = "./modules/app"

  acm_cert_arn = "${var.acm_cert_arn}"
  customer_type = "small"
  customer_name = "CustomerA"
  environment = "${var.environment}"
  public_subnets = "${data.aws_subnet_ids.public.ids}"
  private_subnets = "${data.aws_subnet_ids.private.ids}"
  db_subnet_group_name = "${aws_db_subnet_group.customer.name}"
  vpc_id = "${data.aws_vpc.vpc.id}"
  zone_id = "${var.zone_id}"
  zone_suffix = "${var.zone_suffix}"
}
```

We're using data providers to describe the target VPC (and its subnets) for the app. First up, we track down a VPC that matches our target deployment environment, based on our "environment" variable. We are able to use that VPC's internal AWS ID to describe the subnets in that VPC, based on a tagging strategy pre-employed on the subnets of that VPC that distinguish between public, private, and data-tier subnets. With knowledge of our subnets, we create an RDS DB subnet group. This DB subnet group can be used as a shared resource across all of invocations of the module that creates the app. The stage is now set for the grand finale: the module invocation. Notice that the *source* parameter provides a relative path to the directory containing our module code that we reviewed earlier that forms the module. From there, the arguments are fairly self-explanatory; we pass in the subnet IDs and VPC ID that we pulled via data providers, as well as the values that we got via our variables in the root module. There, in 14 lines, you have the majesty of the module. The entirety of the infrastructure defined in the modules/app/main.tf can now be deployed through these 14 simple lines of code. In Listings 4-37 and 4-36, we'll have a look at the tfvars files. The last thing we'll take a look at in Listing 4-37 before we actually deploy all of this is the outputs of our root-level module.

Listing 4-36. prod/global.tfvars

```
environment = "prod"
zone_id = "XXXXXXXXXXXXXX"    # omitted for purposes of security
zone_suffix = "infrabook.bradcod.es"
```

Listing 4-37. prod/us-east-1.tfvars

```
acm_cert_arn = "arn:aws:acm:us-east-1:XXXXXXXXXXXXX:certificat
e/148bfe01-fb45-45f4-93c3-a4612b50ff73"    # account number
omitted for purposes of security
```

Listing 4-38. outputs.tf

```
output "customer_a" {
  value = "${
    map(
```

```
      "elb_dns", "${module.customer_a.elb_dns}",
      "https", "https://${module.customer_a.dns}",
      "db_endpoint",  "${module.customer_a.db_endpoint}",
   )
  }"
}
```

Here in the root module, we're creating a single map-based output (Listing 4-38) to capture the outputs from the module.

Let's deploy it and see what happens! Our commands and their subsequent output are captured in Listing 4-39.

Listing 4-39. terraform apply and output

```
$ export AWS_PROFILE=infrabook
$ export AWS_REGION=us-east-1
$ terraform apply -var-file="prod/globals.tfvars" \
       -var-file="prod/us-east-1.tfvars" -auto-approve
module.customer_a.data.aws_region.current: Refreshing state...
data.aws_vpc.vpc: Refreshing state...
module.customer_a.data.aws_ami.amazon-linux-2: Refreshing
state...
data.aws_subnet_ids.public: Refreshing state...
data.aws_subnet_ids.data: Refreshing state...
data.aws_subnet_ids.private: Refreshing state...
aws_db_subnet_group.customer: Creating...
module.customer_a.aws_security_group.public: Creating...
aws_db_subnet_group.customer: Creation complete after 1s
[id=customer-db-subnet-group]
module.customer_a.aws_security_group.public: Creation complete
after 3s [id=sg-02925b661261422cd]
module.customer_a.aws_security_group.app: Creating...
```

```
module.customer_a.aws_security_group.app: Creation complete
after 3s [id=sg-0b3b10668b065aa68]
module.customer_a.aws_security_group.data: Creating...
module.customer_a.aws_instance.app: Creating...
module.customer_a.aws_security_group.data: Creation complete
after 4s [id=sg-01c3ea8834cb0d37b]
module.customer_a.aws_db_instance.db: Creating...
...
module.customer_a.aws_instance.app: Creation complete after 35s
[id=i-05fd3ff6815ec4454]
module.customer_a.aws_elb.public: Creating...
module.customer_a.aws_elb.public: Creation complete after 8s
[id=customera-elb]
module.customer_a.aws_route53_record.elb_alias: Creating...
...
module.customer_a.aws_route53_record.elb_alias: Creation
complete after 37s [id=XXXXXXXXXXXXXX_customera.infrabook.
bradcod.es_A]
...
module.customer_a.aws_db_instance.db: Still creating... [3m30s
elapsed]
module.customer_a.aws_db_instance.db: Creation complete after
3m37s [id=customera]

Apply complete! Resources: 8 added, 0 changed, 0 destroyed.

Outputs:

customer_a = {
  "db_endpoint" = "customera.cea6rrp34eec.us-east-1.rds.
  amazonaws.com:3306"
```

```
  "elb_dns" = "customera-elb-1833340456.us-east-1.elb.
  amazonaws.com"
  "https" = "https://customera.infrabook.bradcod.es"
}
```

We have successfully provisioned our module, seeing through the
apply output that our resources were created successfully. Lastly, we
see the "customer_a" output map that is defined in the root outputs.tf
file. As mentioned previously, these values can easily be integrated into
downstream automation by exporting the outputs as JSON, which is very
straightforward.

Listing 4-40. Outputs as JSON

```
$ terraform output -json | jq -r .
{
  "customer_a": {
    "sensitive": false,
    "type": [
      "map",
      "string"
    ],
    "value": {
      "db_endpoint": "customera.cea6rrp34eec.us-east-1.rds.
      amazonaws.com:3306",
      "elb_dns": "customera-elb-1833340456.us-east-1.elb.
      amazonaws.com",
      "https": "https://customera.infrabook.bradcod.es"
    }
  }
}
```

Calling the "output" command with the "-json" flag exports the output as JSON, which I am passing to jq as a demonstration of the fact that the output is indeed valid JSON. All of this is demonstrated in Listing 4-40. Just as a quick point of reference that our deployment was successful and as a demonstration of how you might leverage this JSON-based output in a validation script, let's test the deployment using the https output value.

Listing 4-41. Quick Test of the Deployment Using Terraform Outputs

```
$ terraform output -json | jq -r '.customer_a.value.https' |
xargs curl -Is | grep '^HTTP' | awk '{print $2}'
200
```

Here in Listing 4-41, we're grabbing the "https" output (our DNS alias), passing it to the curl executable, getting the headers of the HTTP response (the "-I" flag of curl), looking for the HTTP header in header (the grep command), and looking at the HTTP response code (the awk command). Since the response code is a 200 (which means "OK" in HTTP-land), we're good to go! Just to drive the point home, let's check things out in a browser in Figure 4-1.

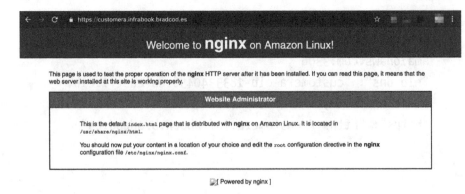

Figure 4-1. *Browser Screen Capture*

As we'd expect based on our curl test, we get a successful response in our browser when visiting the DNS name assigned to the load balancer.

Behold, the Module!

Now that you've seen a module in action, you have some appreciation for how easy it would be to onboard any new number of customers quickly and easily. Essentially, a copy and paste of the 'module "customer_a"' block of code, renamed, with proper arguments would create a new set of customer resources easily. Unfortunately, at this point in time (version 0.12.5 at the time of this writing), modules still don't support the traditional **count** and newer **for_each** looping mechanisms available on resources. For example, adding a count to our customer_a module and running a plan results in an error like the one shown in Listing 4-42.

Listing 4-42. Plan Output with Count in Module

```
$ terraform plan -var-file="prod/globals.tfvars" -var-
file="prod/us-east-1.tfvars"

Error: Reserved argument name in module block

  on deployments.tf line 51, in module "customer_a":
  51:    count = 3

The name "count" is reserved for use in a future version of
Terraform.
```

Even with this limitation, modules are still a powerful feature of Terraform, giving you the ability to encapsulate common deployment elements and logic into single, reusable units of work.

While the emphasis here has been on local module development, modules offer features that empower collaborative infrastructure development. As modules are meant to be reused, supporting centralized hosting features for distribution only makes sense. In fact, Terraform hosts a registry of vetted modules[11] authored by companies like AWS. Modules also support other methods of hosting and retrieval, one of the most universal of which is git repository hosting.[12] The source parameter in any module invocation can accept a Git URL, even with specificity for a particular branch or tag.

Providers Revisited

As we've seen, modules are an incredibly powerful construct. But, are there any features within Terraform that can potentially enhance the power of modules? As it turns out, the providers we've glossed over through our several examples actually give us a great deal of additional flexibility. As it turns out, multiple providers can exist within a single configuration. Let's alter the provider configuration in Listing 4-43:

Listing 4-43. provider.tf

```
provider "aws" {
  region = "us-east-1"
  alias  = "use1"
}
provider "aws" {
  region = "us-west-2"
  alias  = "usw2"
}
```

---

[11]https://registry.terraform.io/
[12]www.terraform.io/docs/modules/sources.html#generic-git-repository

Instead of letting the provider inherit a region from an environment variable as in previous examples, here we are hard-coding regions to a set of providers and setting an alias for each that will allow us to specifically declare it for any resources, data providers, or modules we wish to provision in that specific provider's region. This gives us the ability to perform interesting types of deployments such as multiregional applications, applications with out-of-region disaster recovery (DR) components, or complete DR analogues of our primary deployments. To demonstrate this concept, I have refactored the files in Listings 4-36, 4-37, 4-38, and 4-39, additionally adding a few files. I have also created a new module, called "dr", which lives alongside the "app" module. This module is a line-for-line copy of the main "app" module, with the exception that I have added a "-dr" component to the DNS name to differentiate the main deployment from the DR deployment. Conceptually, you can think of this as a hot backup environment, ready to be failed over to any moment in time (assuming we set up some sort of real-time sync of the main site's database to the DR site's database – once again, these examples are illustrative, so I'll leave that sort of implementation up to you if you're looking for a fun weekend challenge). Our new directory listing is shown in Listing 4-44.

Listing 4-44. Directory Listing with DR Deployment Additions

```
$ tree -I '*.tfstate*' --dirsfirst
.
├── modules
│   ├── app
│   │   ├── main.tf
│   │   ├── outputs.tf
│   │   ├── userdata.sh
│   │   └── variables.tf
│   └── dr
```

```
|              ├── main.tf
|              ├── outputs.tf
|              ├── userdata.sh
|              └── variables.tf
├── prod
|     └── globals.tfvars
├── deployments.tf
├── deployments_dr.tf
├── outputs.tf
├── provider.tf
└── variables.tf

4 directories, 14 files
```

Accordingly, the deployments.tf (Listing 4-45) and deployments_dr.tf files are refactored to account for their respective providers.

Listing 4-45. Modified deployments.tf

```
data "aws_vpc" "vpc_main" {
  provider = "aws.use1"

  filter {
    name = "tag:Environment"
    values = [
      "${var.environment}"
    ]
  }
}

data "aws_subnet_ids" "public_main" {
  vpc_id   = "${data.aws_vpc.vpc_main.id}"
  provider = "aws.use1"
```

```
  filter {
    name = "tag:Tier"
    values = [
      "public"
    ]
  }
}

...


resource "aws_db_subnet_group" "customer_main" {
  provider    = "aws.use1"
  name        = "customer-db-subnet-group"
  description = "Customer DB subnet group"
  subnet_ids  = "${data.aws_subnet_ids.data_main.ids}"
}

module "customer_a_main_site" {
  source = "./modules/app"
  providers = {
    aws = "aws.use1"
  }

  acm_cert_arn         = "${lookup(var.acm_cert_arn, "main")}"
  customer_type        = "small"
  customer_name        = "CustomerA"
  environment          = "${var.environment}"
  public_subnets       = "${data.aws_subnet_ids.public_main.ids}"
  private_subnets      = "${data.aws_subnet_ids.private_main.ids}"
  db_subnet_group_name = "${aws_db_subnet_group.customer_main.
  name}"
  vpc_id               = "${data.aws_vpc.vpc_main.id}"
```

```
  zone_id                 = "${var.zone_id}"
  zone_suffix             = "${var.zone_suffix}"
}
```

All code in deployments_dr.tf looks similar to what is shown in Listing 4-45, except the "_main" suffixes would be replaced with "_dr" suffixes and providers would be set to "aws.usw2" instead (the file is not shown here). The other main differences are the globals.tfvars file (Listing 4-46)

Listing 4-46. Modified global.tfvars

```
environment = "prod"
zone_id      = "XXXXXXXXXXXXXX"
zone_suffix = "infrabook.bradcod.es"
acm_cert_arn = {
  main = "arn:aws:acm:us-east-1:XXXXXXXXXXXX:certificate/148b
  fe01-fb45-45f4-93c3-a4612b50ff73"
  dr   = "arn:aws:acm:us-west-2:XXXXXXXXXXXX:certificate/9
         9b73163-04ea-47dd-a54c-23c201e08cdf"
}
```

and the outputs.tf file (Listing 4-47), which combines the main site and DR site outputs into a single "customer_a" object:

Listing 4-47. Modified outputs.tf

```
output "customer_a" {
  value = "${
    map(
      "main", map(
        "elb_dns", "${module.customer_a_main_site.elb_dns}",
        "https", "https://${module.customer_a_main_site.dns}",
        "db_endpoint", "${module.customer_a_main_site.db_
        endpoint}",
```

```
    ),
    "dr", map(
      "elb_dns", "${module.customer_a_dr_site.elb_dns}",
      "https", "https://${module.customer_a_dr_site.dns}",
      "db_endpoint", "${module.customer_a_dr_site.db_
      endpoint}",
    ),
  )
}"
}
```

And, the resulting deployment gives us two analogous deployments, each situated in the AWS region specified by its respective provider.

Listing 4-48. Deployment of Multiprovider Solution

```
$ terraform apply -var-file="prod/globals.tfvars"
...

An execution plan has been generated and is shown in the
following.
Resource actions are indicated with the following symbols:
  + create

...

Plan: 16 to add, 0 to change, 0 to destroy.

Do you want to perform these actions?
  Terraform will perform the actions described earlier.
  Only 'yes' will be accepted to approve.

  Enter a value: yes
```

```
aws_db_subnet_group.customer_main: Creating...
module.customer_a_main_site.aws_security_group.public:
Creating...
aws_db_subnet_group.customer_dr: Creating...
...
module.customer_a_dr_site.aws_db_instance.db: Creation complete
after 3m14s [id=customera]
module.customer_a_main_site.aws_db_instance.db: Still
creating... [3m30s elapsed]
module.customer_a_main_site.aws_db_instance.db: Creation
complete after 3m38s [id=customera]

Apply complete! Resources: 16 added, 0 changed, 0 destroyed.

Outputs:

customer_a = {
  "dr" = {
    "db_endpoint" = "customera.c3vclam6ju4y.us-west-2.rds.
    amazonaws.com:3306"
    "elb_dns" = "customera-elb-506882067.us-west-2.elb.
    amazonaws.com"
    "https" = "https://customera-dr.infrabook.bradcod.es"
  }
  "main" = {
    "db_endpoint" = "customera.cea6rrp34eec.us-east-1.rds.
    amazonaws.com:3306"
    "elb_dns" = "customera-elb-119240489.us-east-1.elb.
    amazonaws.com"
    "https" = "https://customera.infrabook.bradcod.es"
  }
}
```

From both the Terraform CLI output as well as the actual outputs shown in Listing 4-48, you can clearly see that our ELBs are both deployed to their proper AWS region (refer to the bolded elements in the outputs in Listing 4-48), further proof that our multiregional deployment worked successfully!

Remote State

Thus far, every deployment we have worked through in this chapter has used what Terraform calls "local state." That is, if you look in the directory post-deployment of any set of resources, you'll notice a file called terraform.tfstate. If you perform subsequent operations, you'll also notice tfstate.backup files in the directory. The tfstate file is a critical part of how Terraform does its magic, essentially serving as a mapping between the real-world EC2 instance IDs, S3 bucket names, IAM role ARNs, and so on, that Terraform created when it ingested your configuration code and ran the necessary operations against AWS' APIs to manage your infrastructure for you.

Terraform's docs do a great job of highlighting what remote state is, with few exceptions, and how you should be handling your state:[13]

> *When working with Terraform in a team, use of a local file makes Terraform usage complicated because each user must make sure they always have the latest state data before running Terraform and make sure that nobody else runs Terraform at the same time.*

---

[13]www.terraform.io/docs/state/remote.html

> *With remote state, Terraform writes the state data to a remote data store, which can then be shared between all members of a team. Terraform supports storing state in Terraform Enterprise, HashiCorp Consul, Amazon S3, and more.*
>
> ...
>
> *Remote state gives you more than just easier version control and safer storage. It also allows you to delegate the outputs to other teams. This allows your infrastructure to be more easily broken down into components that multiple teams can access.*
>
> *Put another way, remote state also allows teams to share infrastructure resources in a read-only way without relying on any additional configuration store.*

To reiterate the main point here, using local files is simply not a robust mechanism for statefiles. Even in scenarios where teams think they have handled this issue by managing the statefile in a git repo, all it takes is one clumsy apply against a stale, local statefile and out-of-date local code (e.g., code not yet pushed to remote that has provisioned resources and/ or a local pull hasn't yet been run), and you can watch as Terraform does its destructive magic on critical elements of your infrastructure (your resume's up to date, right?). Remote state is a mechanism to ameliorate some of those issues; in addition, you get some other perks by using S3 as a store (yes, other backends are available,[14] but this is a book about

---

[14]www.terraform.io/docs/backends/types/index.html

AWS infrastructure, so I'll be restricting this conversation to AWS-hosted backends: S3), such as KMS-backed encryption,[15] "11 9"s of durability,[16] out-of-region file replication[17] as a backup mechanism, file versioning,[18] IAM-protected file (yes, object) operations, and even MFA-only file deletion[19] if you want to go that far (and for production statefiles, this is not an unreasonable setting to enable).

How do you use remote state, then? In its simplest form, you create a terraform block somewhere in your configuration code that defines the backend, demonstrated in Listing 4-49.

Listing 4-49. Terraform Block with Backend

```
terraform {
    backend "s3" {
        bucket  = "my-state-bucket"
        key     = "prod/us-east-1/terraform.tfstate"
        region  = "us-east-1"
        encrypt = true
    }
}
```

---

[15]https://docs.aws.amazon.com/AmazonS3/latest/dev/bucket-encryption.html

[16]https://aws.amazon.com/s3/faqs/#Durability_.26_Data_Protection

[17]https://docs.aws.amazon.com/AmazonS3/latest/dev/crr.html

[18]https://docs.aws.amazon.com/AmazonS3/latest/user-guide/enable-versioning.html

[19]https://aws.amazon.com/blogs/security/securing-access-to-aws-using-mfa-part-3/

Typically, I put my "terraform" and "provider" blocks together in a file called backend.tf or provider.tf. The inner backend block even supports arguments allowing you to authenticate to a separate AWS account (or profile) than the account that you want to actually provision your infrastructure in, which is an incredibly powerful and useful feature. The *one* downside to defining your backend directly in your configuration files as in Listing 4-49 is that the values set in the terraform block must be static values – dynamic variable values cannot be used in this block. However, the backend can be set up from the CLI; to use a backend in this fashion requires what Terraform calls a partial backend – seen in Listing 4-50.

Listing 4-50. Partial Backend Configuration

```
terraform {
    backend "s3" {}
}
```

Looking back for a moment at Listing 4-18, let's revisit this line:
```
terraform init
```
Within the context of our backend configuration discussion and within the context of Listing 4-18, our script (or the command in the script, shown in Listing 4-51) can configure the backend at runtime.

Listing 4-51. Revised Init Command

```
terraform init \
    -backend=true \
    -backend-config "bucket=my-s3-state-bucket" \
    -backend-config "region=${DEPLOY_REGION}" \
    -backend-config "encrypt=true" \
    -backend-config "key=${DEPLOY_ENV}/${DEPLOY_REGION}/
    terraform.tfstate"
```

While this code makes a few assumptions about the disposition of your statefile bucket (mainly that it resides in the same region as your deployment), the purpose of this code is intended to demonstrate the concept of incorporating a partial backend with dynamic runtime configuration via CLI.

State Locking

The addition of a "dynamodb_table" parameter (and a proper DynamoDB setup in AWS) to the init command/config allows Terraform to store metadata about the state of deployment of resources in a multiuser scenario. Locking[20] is an additional layer of protection for your state and the resources it represents. If you are using Terraform in a multiuser scenario, it is worth performing the backend setup necessary to enable the use of locking.

Version Pinning

While I have often seen remote state – and to a lesser degree, locking – described in "trade literature" (read: blogs) as mechanisms that protect statefiles and the resources, I don't often see version pinning described in such terms. Terraform protects its statefiles (and hence allocated resources) by running versions checks to ensure that the statefile and the version of the tool match. If a newer version of Terraform writes to a statefile, Terraform will no longer allow older versions of the runtime to interact with that deployment.

---

[20]www.terraform.io/docs/state/locking.html

While this clearly protective measure serves an obvious benefit, it can break automated deployment systems or CI/CD systems that manage deployments for you. Imagine a situation where a CI/CD system manages deployments for you; this system currently runs version 0.12.2 of the tool. An issue arises with a deployment, and an engineer resolves the situation using her local workstation, running version 0.12.5. The statefile is now written with version 0.12.5. On the next run of the CI/CD server, it will fail. Now, we either have to update the version on the CI/CD server (perhaps cascading issues to other teams and deployments), or we do some statefile surgery to make everything copacetic. Neither of these solutions is really optimal. With a pinned version, the engineer using 0.12.5 would've gotten an error locally before the statefile was ever written, forcing her to change the pinned version, or to install 0.12.2 locally to manage the deployment (and, tools like tfenv[21] make running multiple versions side-by-side locally a pretty simple chore). Pinning the version is as simple as what we see in Listing 4-52.

Listing 4-52. Pinned Version

```
terraform {
    required_version = "= 0.12.2"
    ...
}
```

It's important to denote here the operator used in this statement. While "~> 0.12.2" is a valid configuration, its use would not have prevented the aforementioned scenario from occurring, as this statement correlates to

---

[21]https://github.com/tfutils/tfenv

"any version 0.12.2 or greater." The explicit "=" correlates to a strict equality condition, meaning that only version 0.12.2 would be allowed to interact with this configuration.

Conclusion

Terraform is an amazing piece of software. As I have stated previous times throughout this chapter, it is my assertion that it is likely the most important third-party projects in the AWS orchestration ecosystem. While AWS deployment is central to the theme of this book, Terraform's exposition of a uniform abstraction and interface over multiple service providers is a compelling selling point for organizations that want unified tooling to manage the entire lifecycle of operations over multiple facets of their IT department's operations, from onboarding developers into GitHub organizations to blue-green deployments of infrastructure. While our examples here dealt strictly with managing the entire lifecycle of a deployment – from creation to destruction – Terraform, in stark contrast to CloudFormation, permits the onboarding and ongoing management of preexisting infrastructure. Terraform also comes with a robust set of tools for managing state, which is a facet of Terraform that we didn't cover here. The fact is, even though we covered a good deal of ground here, there is still significant depth to cover on the concepts we did cover with many advanced concepts left yet unexplored. Terraform is easily a standalone subject for a 300-page book in and of itself. Despite this, what we covered here is enough to give you an introduction to the tool and to understand its capabilities and differences in implementation relative to CloudFormation. While it comes with a steeper learning curve, conquering that learning curve will give your team access to a tool capable of operating in a multiprovider or heterogeneous (e.g., on-prem + cloud) environment.

CHAPTER 5

CloudFormation-Based Tools

In Chapter 2, we looked at a variety of tools that form an ecosystem around CloudFormation. In this chapter, we'll take a look at two of these tools: Troposphere, a DSL wrapper, and Sceptre, an orchestration tool. We will discover how these tools interact with CloudFormation and how they can enhance our use of CloudFormation. Specifically, we will cover the following:

- *Troposhere*
  - *Why Troposphere?* What are the benefits of using a DSL tool like this? Are there really any tangible benefits over writing native CloudFormation templates?

  - *Getting Started.* How to install Troposphere.

  - *A Basic Exercise.* We'll begin to work out our new Troposhere muscles. This is helpful in understanding what Troposhere code looks like vis-a-vis the same resources in a CloudFormation template.

© Bradley Campbell 2020
B. Campbell, *The Definitive Guide to AWS Infrastructure Automation*,
https://doi.org/10.1007/978-1-4842-5398-4_5

- *Benefits of a Full Programming Language.* Here, we actually leverage Troposhere for what it is – a member of the Python language ecosystem. Using innate aspects of the Python language, we will show how to model an example deployment using a base class and subclasses, where the subclasses model differences for environmental contexts.

- *Sceptre*

  - *Why Sceptre?* What is Sceptre? What problems does it specifically designed to address?

  - *Getting Started.* How to install Sceptre and verify its installation.

  - *Project Setup/Hooks Demonstration.* How to build a Sceptre-based project. In this project, we address the CLI commands necessary to create a new project, deploy a project, and teardown a project. We also take a look at how to leverage Sceptre's *Hooks* feature.

Troposphere

Troposphere[1] is a tool that allows you to use Python programming to describe your infrastructure. You can generate CloudFormation code from your Python code, which you would then deploy in the manner by which you usually deploy CloudFormation templates (e.g., console, CLI, sceptre, etc.) as already explained in Chapter 3.

---

[1]Troposphere. https://github.com/cloudtools/troposphere

Why Troposphere?

As a project, Troposphere has been existence for quite some time. It is a mature project at almost seven years of age[2] with a fairly active community.[3] It provides a fairly extensive set of examples[4] for beginners. While the examples are useful for understanding the relationship between high-level CloudFormation elements (i.e., Conditions, Parameters, Resources, etc.) and the corollary Python classes in the Troposphere package, the real power of Troposphere lies in the fact that you inherit the power of the Python programming language in sum by virtue of using Troposphere. Given Troposphere's Python-based roots, we can use concepts such as classes[5] and inheritance[6] to model deployments as classes with inheritance that account for factors that might occur between development and production environments. We will explore both sets of concepts in this chapter.

Getting Started

Getting started with Troposphere is quite simple. Assuming you have a valid Python and pip in your PATH (which we will assume you do from previous chapters where we have utilized the AWS CLI), installation is as simple as running the command:

```
$ pip install troposphere
```

---

[2]Troposphere, first commit. https://github.com/cloudtools/troposphere/commit/f6d72a3e2343c26dc243bcaf7fd1886d6a485f1f

[3]Troposphere on OpenHub. www.openhub.net/p/troposphere

[4]Troposphere examples. https://troposphere.readthedocs.io/en/latest/apis/examples_toc.html

[5]Python – Classes (3.6). https://docs.python.org/3.6/tutorial/classes.html

[6]Python – Inheritance. https://realpython.com/inheritance-composition-python/

That simple command installs all of the Troposphere packages that you could potentially use as you write code to model a deployment. As we'll see in later listings, you probably won't need every class/module (and there are many of them[7]) provided by the overall package as you write your code. In code provided in this chapter, I will attempt to target the inclusion of modules from the main package so that it's clear which modules are providing which functionality.

A Basic Exercise

There is no tool to create a new project with Troposphere, as conceptually a project is nothing more than a simple Python project. To kick things off, let's quickly create a directory and set up some files. After that, let's have a look at what content these files would need to have to get a project off the ground quickly:

```
$ mkdir tropo_stack && cd tropo_stack && touch {Makefile,stack.
py,requirements.txt}
```

Note that in shells that don't support the "{}" expansion, this may be more like

```
$ mkdir tropo_stack && cd tropo_stack && touch Makefile &&
touch stack.py && touch requirements.txt
```

Regardless, you should end up with a directory called tropo_stack with contents as seen in Listing 5-1.

---

[7]Troposphere modules. https://troposphere.readthedocs.io/en/latest/apis/troposphere_toc.html

Listing 5-1. tropo_stack directory listing

```
$ tree
.
├── Makefile
├── stack.py
└── requirements.txt
```

We'll start with the requirements.txt file (Listing 5-2),[8] as this is how we will install all of our Python dependencies.

Listing 5-2. requirements.txt

```
awacs==0.9.4
awscli==1.16.179
troposphere==2.5.0
```

Assuming you have make,[9] python,[10] and pip[11] installed locally, you can use the Makefile[12] (Listing 5-3) to install the local dependencies. Before we actually install them, though, let's have a look at the Makefile.

Listing 5-3. Makefile

```
FILE_SRC ?= stack.py
FILE_OUT ?= template.yml
STACK_NAME ?= tropo-stack

.DEFAULT_TARGET: help
```

---

[8]Pip requirements file documentation. https://pip.readthedocs.io/en/1.1/requirements.html

[9]https://en.wikipedia.org/wiki/Make_(software)

[10]https://docs.python-guide.org/starting/installation/

[11]https://pip.pypa.io/en/stable/installing/

[12]www.gnu.org/software/make/manual/html_node/Simple-Makefile.html

```
.PHONY: help
help:                              ## This help.
        @grep -E '^[a-zA-Z_-]+:.*?## .*$$' $(MAKEFILE_LIST) |
        sort | awk 'BEGIN {FS = ":.*?## "}; {printf "\033[36m%-
        30s\033[0m %s\n", $$1, $$2}'

.PHONY: install_deps
install_deps:        ## Install local dependencies.
        @pip install -r requirements.txt

.PHONY: gen_cft
gen_cft:                           ## Generate CloudFormation
                                   template locally with Troposphere.
        @python $(FILE_SRC) >$(FILE_OUT)

.PHONY: deploy
deploy: gen_cft ## Run build_cft target and deploy stack from
generated template.
        @aws cloudformation deploy --stack-name $(STACK_NAME)
        --template-file ./$(FILE_OUT)

.PHONY: destroy
destroy:                           ## Destroy stack. **WARNING:
                                   DESTRUCTIVE**
     @aws cloudformation delete-stack --stack-name $(STACK_
NAME)

.PHONY: get_events
get_events:                        ## Get stack events
        @aws cloudformation describe-stack-events --stack-name
        $(STACK_NAME)
```

Simply running the command "make install_deps" will take care of everything for you; otherwise, you can run "pip install -r requirements.txt" to install everything. From here on out, I'll be working through the targets defined in the Makefile to carry out the operations relative to the tasks at hand; running the command captured in the target with proper variable substitutions will give the same result locally as well. Before we look at the stack.py file, which contains a deployment modeled in Python, have a look at Listing 3-1, as our Python deployment is the same deployment as the one that exists in that Listing; let's now have a look at stack.py.

Listing 5-4. stack.py

```
#!/usr/bin/env python

from troposphere import FindInMap, GetAtt
from troposphere import Parameter, Output, Ref, Template,
Condition, Equals, And, Or, Not, If
import troposphere.ec2 as ec2

tpl = Template()
tpl.add_version("2010-09-09")
tpl.add_description("Creates EC2 security group and instance")

params= {}
conditions = {}
mappings = {}
resources = {}

params['keyname'] = tpl.add_parameter(
        Parameter(
            "KeyName",
            Description="Name of an existing EC2 KeyPair to
            enable access to the instance",
            Type="String",
            Default="",
            ConstraintDescription="must be a string"
        )
)
```

```
params['os'] = tpl.add_parameter(
        Parameter(
                "OperatingSystem",
                Description="Chosen operating system",
                Type="String",
                Default="AmazonLinux2",
                AllowedValues=[
                        "AmazonLinux2",
                        "Windows2016Base"
                ]
        )
)

params['instance_type'] = tpl.add_parameter(
        Parameter(
                "InstanceType",
                Description="EC2 instance type",
                Type="String",
                Default="t2.small",
                AllowedValues=[
                        "t2.nano", "t2.micro", "t2.small", "t2.
                        medium",
                        "m4.large", "m4.xlarge"
                ]
        )
)

params['pub_loc'] = tpl.add_parameter(
        Parameter(
                "PublicLocation",
                Description="The IP address range that can be
                used to connect to the EC2 instances",
                Type="String",
```

```
                MinLength=9,
                MaxLength=18,
                Default="0.0.0.0/0",
                AllowedPattern="(\d{1,3})\.(\d{1,3})\.
                (\d{1,3})\.(\d{1,3})/(\d{1,2})",
                ConstraintDescription="must be a valid IP CIDR
                range of the form x.x.x.x/x"
        )
)

conditions['has_kp'] = tpl.add_condition(
        "HasKeypair",
        Not(
                Equals(Ref("KeyName"), "")
        )
)

mappings['global'] = tpl.add_mapping(
        'Global', {
                "ConnectPortByOs": {
                        "Windows2016Base": 3389,
                        "AmazonLinux2": 22,
                },
        }
)

mappings['ami_by_os'] = tpl.add_mapping(
        'AmiByOs', {
                "us-east-1": {
                        "Windows2016Base": "ami-
                        06bee8e1000e44ca4",
                        "AmazonLinux2": "ami-
                        0c6b1d09930fac512",
                },
```

```
                "us-west-2": {
                        "Windows2016Base": "ami-
                        07f35a597a32e470d",
                        "AmazonLinux2": "ami-
                        0cb72367e98845d43",
                },
        }
)

resources['sg'] = tpl.add_resource(
        ec2.SecurityGroup(
                "InstanceSg",
        GroupDescription="Enable SSH and HTTP access on the
        inbound port",
        SecurityGroupIngress=[
                ec2.SecurityGroupRule(
                        IpProtocol="tcp",
                        FromPort=FindInMap("Global",
                        "ConnectPortByOs", Ref(params['os'])),
                        ToPort=FindInMap("Global",
                        "ConnectPortByOs", Ref(params['os'])),
                        CidrIp=Ref(params['pub_loc']),
                )
        ]
        )
)

resources['ec2'] = tpl.add_resource(
        ec2.Instance(
            "Ec2Instance",
            ImageId=FindInMap("AmiByOs", Ref("AWS::Region"),
            Ref(params['os'])),
```

```
            InstanceType=Ref(params['instance_type']),
            KeyName=If(conditions['has_kp'], Ref(params
            ['keyname']), Ref("AWS::NoValue")),
            SecurityGroups=[
                Ref(resources['sg']),
            ],
        )
    )

tpl.add_output([
    Output(
        "InstanceId",
        Description="InstanceId of the EC2 instance",
        Value=Ref(resources['ec2']),
    ),
    Output(
        "AZ",
        Description="AZ of the EC2 instance",
        Value=GetAtt(resources['ec2'], "AvailabilityZone"),
    ),
    Output(
        "PublicDNS",
        Description="Public DNSName of the EC2 instance",
        Value=GetAtt(resources['ec2'], "PublicDnsName"),
    ),
    Output(
        "PublicIP",
        Description="Public IP address of the EC2 instance",
        Value=GetAtt(resources['ec2'], "PublicIp"),
    )
])

print(tpl.to_yaml())
```

Let's take a look at some of the Troposphere bits we used in Listing 5-4:

- **troposphere.FindInMap**. This is a 1:1 corollary of the CloudFormation FindInMap intrinsic function.

- **troposphere.GetAtt**. As with FindInMap, this is a reference to the CloudFormation intrinsic function.

- **troposphere.Parameter**. Models a CloudFormation Parameter element.

- **troposphere.Output**. Models a CloudFormation Output element.

- **troposphere.Ref**. A corollary to the Ref intrinsic function.

- **troposphere.Template**. An instance of a class that encapsulates the actual template. Parameters, outputs, resources, and anything else you would expect to find in an actual template are likely supported by methods of this object.

- **troposphere.Condition**. Models a CloudFormation Condition element.

- **troposphere.And, troposphere.If, troposphere.Not, troposphere.Or**. Logicals that mirror their CloudFormation intrinsic function counterparts.

- **troposphere.ec2**. Exposes a class that provides a set of methods corresponding to EC2-related services.

With a bit more understanding of the actual Troposphere package and
what we've used to model our deployment, let's now use Troposphere to
generate a CloudFormation template. Listing 5-5 uses the Makefile we
created previously to generate a CloudFormation template based on our
code in Listing 5-4.

Listing 5-5. Generated CloudFormation Template

```
$ make gen_cft && cat template.yml
AWSTemplateFormatVersion: '2010-09-09'
Conditions:
  HasKeypair: !Not
    - !Equals
      - !Ref 'KeyName'
      - ''
Description: Creates EC2 security group and instance
Mappings:
  AmiByOs:
    us-east-1:
      AmazonLinux2: ami-0c6b1d09930fac512
      Windows2016Base: ami-06bee8e1000e44ca4
    us-west-2:
      AmazonLinux2: ami-0cb72367e98845d43
      Windows2016Base: ami-07f35a597a32e470d
  Global:
    ConnectPortByOs:
      AmazonLinux2: 22
      Windows2016Base: 3389
Outputs:
  AZ:
    Description: AZ of the EC2 instance
    Value: !GetAtt 'Ec2Instance.AvailabilityZone'
```

```
  InstanceId:
    Description: InstanceId of the EC2 instance
    Value: !Ref 'Ec2Instance'
  PublicDNS:
    Description: Public DNSName of the EC2 instance
    Value: !GetAtt 'Ec2Instance.PublicDnsName'
  PublicIP:
    Description: Public IP address of the EC2 instance
    Value: !GetAtt 'Ec2Instance.PublicIp'
Parameters:
  InstanceType:
    AllowedValues:
      - t2.nano
      - t2.micro
      - t2.small
      - t2.medium
      - m4.large
      - m4.xlarge
    Default: t2.small
    Description: EC2 instance type
    Type: String
  KeyName:
    ConstraintDescription: must be a string
    Default: "
    Description: Name of an existing EC2 KeyPair to enable
    access to the instance
    Type: String
  OperatingSystem:
    AllowedValues:
      - AmazonLinux2
      - Windows2016Base
```

```
     Default: AmazonLinux2
     Description: Chosen operating system
     Type: String
   PublicLocation:
     AllowedPattern: (\d{1,3})\.(\d{1,3})\.(\d{1,3})\.(\d{1,3})/
     (\d{1,2})
     ConstraintDescription: must be a valid IP CIDR range of the
     form x.x.x.x/x
     Default: '0.0.0.0/0'
     Description: The IP address range that can be used to
     connect to the EC2 instances
     MaxLength: 18
     MinLength: 9
     Type: String
Resources:
  Ec2Instance:
    Properties:
      ImageId: !FindInMap
        - AmiByOs
        - !Ref 'AWS::Region'
        - !Ref 'OperatingSystem'
      InstanceType: !Ref 'InstanceType'
      KeyName: !If
        - HasKeypair
        - !Ref 'KeyName'
        - !Ref 'AWS::NoValue'
      SecurityGroups:
        - !Ref 'InstanceSg'
    Type: AWS::EC2::Instance
```

```
InstanceSg:
  Properties:
    GroupDescription: Enable SSH and HTTP access on the
    inbound port
    SecurityGroupIngress:
      - CidrIp: !Ref 'PublicLocation'
        FromPort: !FindInMap
          - Global
          - ConnectPortByOs
          - !Ref 'OperatingSystem'
        IpProtocol: tcp
        ToPort: !FindInMap
          - Global
          - ConnectPortByOs
          - !Ref 'OperatingSystem'
    Type: AWS::EC2::SecurityGroup
```

The generated CloudFormation template looks almost exactly like the one we saw in Listing 3-1. A "make deploy" will build your stack, while a "make destroy" will tear it down.

The Benefits of a Full Programming Language

The preceding example, while a basic demonstration of how Troposphere works, doesn't exactly provide a powerful display of the benefits of this tool (e.g., the Python-based template is larger than its YAML output). Let's now consider an example that begins to leverage some of Python's true power. The next few files implement an abstract base class[13] and two subclasses[14]

---

[13]https://docs.python.org/3/glossary.html#term-abstract-base-class
[14]https://pybit.es/python-subclasses.html

based on the original base class – while the original base class could be an abstract base class, it doesn't implement any abstract methods. We will then take a look at two inherited classes, one that models a dev environment and a prod environment. Lastly, we'll take a look at a custom script that implements an instance of each class. The first thing we'll have a look are the files in the local directory. You can create an empty directory and the files for this section by running the following command:

```
$ mkdir base_class && cd base_class && touch {BaseDeployment,
Deployments,stacks}.py
```

After that has been run, your local directory should appear as in Listing 5-6.

Listing 5-6. Directory Listing

```
$ tree
.
├── BaseDeployment.py
├── Deployments.py
└── stacks.py

0 directories, 3 files
```

Let's first look at *BaseDeployment.py* (Listing 5-7), followed by a brief discussion.

Listing 5-7. BaseDeployment.py

```
#!/usr/bin/env python

from abc import ABC, abstractmethod
import boto3
```

```python
class AbstractDeployment(ABC):

    def __init__(self, d):
        self.deployment_type = d
        super().__init__()

    def gen_template(self):
        return self.template.to_yaml()

    def dump_template(self, output_file=None):
        if output_file is None:
            output_file = f'{self.deployment_type}_template.yml'
        print(f'Generating template to {output_file}...')
        with open(f'{output_file}', 'w') as fp:
            fp.write(self.template.to_yaml())

    def build(self, client=None):
        if client is None:
            client = boto3.client('cloudformation')

        print(f'Building stack {self.deployment_type}-tropo...')
        client.create_stack(
            StackName=f'{self.deployment_type}-tropo',
            TemplateBody=self.gen_template(),
        )
```

A quick rundown of the methods in this class:

- **__init__:** Creates a new instance of the class. This method is called from each subclass to define the "deployment_type" attribute of the class.

- **gen_template:** This method generates a template object and returns it as a Python string.

- **dump_template:** This method generates a template and dumps it out to a YAML file.

- **build:** This method invokes AWS' CloudFormation API using the boto3 library to create a stack using the generated template.

Next, let's have a look at two separate classes that are derived from this base class. Listing 5-8 contains these two classes: *DevDeployment* and *ProdDeployment.*

Listing 5-8. Deployments.py

```python
#!/usr/bin/env python

from BaseDeployment import AbstractDeployment
from troposphere import FindInMap, Parameter, Output, Ref,
Template
import troposphere.ec2 as ec2

class DevDeployment(AbstractDeployment):

    def __init__(self, template=None):
        super(DevDeployment, self).__init__('dev')
        if template:
            self.template = template
        else:
            self.template = Template()
            self.template.add_version("2010-09-09")
            self.template.add_description("DevDeployment EC2
            instance")

            self.template.add_parameter(
                Parameter(
                    "Os",
```

```
                Description="Chosen operating system",
                Type="String",
                Default="AmazonLinux2",
                AllowedValues=[
                    "AmazonLinux2",
                    "Windows2016Base",
                ]
            )
        )

        self.template.add_mapping(
            'AmiByOs', {
                "us-east-1": {
                    "Windows2016Base": "ami-
                    06bee8e1000e44ca4",
                    "AmazonLinux2": "ami-
                    0c6b1d09930fac512",
                },
                "us-west-2": {
                    "Windows2016Base": "ami-
                    07f35a597a32e470d",
                    "AmazonLinux2": "ami-
                    0cb72367e98845d43",
                },
            }
        )

        self.template.add_resource(
            ec2.Instance(
                "DevEc2",
                ImageId=FindInMap("AmiByOs",
                Ref("AWS::Region"), Ref("Os")),
```

```
            InstanceType="t2.small",
        )
    )

class ProdDeployment(AbstractDeployment):

    def __init__(self, template=None):
        super(ProdDeployment, self).__init__('prod')
        if template:
            self.template = template
        else:
            self.template = Template()
            self.template.add_version("2010-09-09")
            self.template.add_description("ProdDeployment EC2
            instance")

            self.template.add_parameter(
                Parameter(
                    "Os",
                    Description="Chosen operating system",
                    Type="String",
                    Default="AmazonLinux2",
                    AllowedValues=[
                        "AmazonLinux2",
                        "Windows2016Base",
                    ]
                )
            )

            self.template.add_mapping(
            'AmiByOs', {
                "us-east-1": {
                    "Windows2016Base": "ami-
                    06bee8e1000e44ca4",
```

```
                "AmazonLinux2": "ami-
                0c6b1d09930fac512",
            },
            "us-west-2": {
                "Windows2016Base": "ami-
                07f35a597a32e470d",
                "AmazonLinux2": "ami-
                0cb72367e98845d43",
            },
        }
    )

    self.template.add_resource(
        ec2.Instance(
            "ProdEc2",
            ImageId=FindInMap("AmiByOs",
            Ref("AWS::Region"), Ref("Os")),
            InstanceType="m4.large",
        )
    )
```

To focus on the Python-oriented aspects of this, I've kept the
infrastructure quite simple; this is essentially the EC2 instance from our
first foray into Troposphere. First, I'll speak about both classes generally
and then break things down line-by-line with a focus on the bolded lines
(with the same lines being bolded in each class).

You'll notice that each class only has an __init__ method. The
other methods are inherited from the base class, meaning that both
the DevDeployment and ProdDeployment classes each implement the
gen_template, dump_template, and build methods exactly as they are
implemented in the base class. The super().__init__() method in each

subclass' __init__ method allows us to pass a description (e.g., "dev" or "prod") back to the base class' constructor; this value gets set as an attribute on the instance of the class and serves as a differentiator for stack names and output file names. Moving on line-by-line:

- ***def __init__(self, template=None).*** While each class has its own default template, advanced users could potentially create their own Template() object and pass it into the object when it's created, then leveraging the built-in class methods to do things like inspect one's template or build it.

- ***super(DevDeployment, self).__init__('dev').*** As mentioned previously, this line sets an attribute on the object by virtue of the __init__ method in the base class, determining behavior in inherited methods in the subclasses.

- ***self.template.add_description("ProdDeployment EC2 instance").*** Taking advantage of the differentiation between the two classes, we're adding custom descriptions for templates.

- ***"ProdEc2".*** Once again, taking advantage of the differentiation between the two classes and their respective templates, we can name resources accordingly.

- ***InstanceType="m4.large".*** Lastly, one of the most compelling possibilities of this sort of setup is to differentiate dev and prod deployments by parameters. Instance sizes and similar options aren't always things you want to enable access to generally speaking. Specific implementations like these enable you as an administrator to expose options you want to

> make available while hiding those you don't, which
> is something you don't really get with a vanilla
> CloudFormation implementation.

The last file we'll take a look at is stacks.py (Listing 5-9), which is a simple script in which we create new instances of each of these classes and use some of the methods.

Listing 5-9. stacks.py

```
#!/usr/bin/env

from Deployments import DevDeployment, ProdDeployment

dev = DevDeployment()
print(dev.gen_template())

prod = ProdDeployment()
prod.build()
```

Let's run it!

Listing 5-10. Output of stacks.py

```
$ python stacks.py
AWSTemplateFormatVersion: '2010-09-09'
Description: DevDeployment EC2 instance
Mappings:
  AmiByOs:
    us-east-1:
      AmazonLinux2: ami-0c6b1d09930fac512
      Windows2016Base: ami-06bee8e1000e44ca4
    us-west-2:
      AmazonLinux2: ami-0cb72367e98845d43
      Windows2016Base: ami-07f35a597a32e470d
```

```
Parameters:
  Os:
    AllowedValues:
      - AmazonLinux2
      - Windows2016Base
    Default: AmazonLinux2
    Description: Chosen operating system
    Type: String
Resources:
  DevEc2:
    Properties:
      ImageId: !FindInMap
        - AmiByOs
        - !Ref 'AWS::Region'
        - !Ref 'Os'
      InstanceType: t2.small
    Type: AWS::EC2::Instance
Building stack prod-tropo...
```

In Listing 5-10, we see the dev template, followed by a message that the prod stack is being built. So, how'd the deployment of the prod stack go (Listing 5-11)?

Listing 5-11. Describe-Stack-Events Command Output

```
$ aws cloudformation describe-stack-events --stack-name prod-
tropo
{
    "StackEvents": [
        {
            "StackId": "arn:aws:cloudformation:us-east-
            1:XXXXXXXXXXXX:stack/prod-tropo/fd0738d0-b308-11e9-
            9f8a-12c9298e4208",
```

```
        "EventId": "0a931640-b309-11e9-8775-1204ddd846a2",
        "StackName": "prod-tropo",
        "LogicalResourceId": "prod-tropo",
        "PhysicalResourceId": "arn:aws:cloudformation:us-
        east-1:XXXXXXXXXXX:stack/prod-tropo/fd0738d0-b308-
        11e9-9f8a-12c9298e4208",
        "ResourceType": "AWS::CloudFormation::Stack",
        "Timestamp": "2019-07-30T20:31:42.492Z",
        "ResourceStatus": "CREATE_COMPLETE"
    },
...
```

And there you go! A complete, functional stack built entirely using Python's class inheritance – how cool is that?!? While this demonstration focuses strictly around class inheritance, there are an abundance of features that make the argument for using something like Troposphere very compelling: the possibility of integrating with other systems via Python libs and SDKs, advanced control constructs, looping, and so on, all are very compelling reasons to consider the use of something like Troposphere as you model your infrastructure with code.

Sceptre

Hearkening back to our previous discussion of tooling in Chapter 2, Sceptre comes from a class of tools that perform orchestration functions.

Why Sceptre?

While CloudFormation is in itself an orchestrator of AWS resources, there is a good deal of bespoke tooling that generally gets wrapped around it on "the ends" – pre- and post-deployment. Sceptre has an elegant hook-based mechanism[15] for dealing with this common problem. It also gives you the ability to use outputs of stacks parameter inputs to other stacks through a mechanism known as resolvers.[16]

Getting Started

As with Troposphere, there is very little to do in the way of installing dependencies. With Python and pip installed, a *pip install sceptre* will give you everything you need to get going. Unlike Troposphere, the Sceptre package creates a CLI tool available for your usage. You can verify the installation by running this command:

```
$ sceptre --version
Sceptre, version 2.1.3
```

That validates both that the sceptre command is available on your PATH and that it is an up-to-date version of Sceptre (e.g., 2.x).

Project Setup and Hooks Demonstration

With all of the dependencies installed, let's set up our first project with Sceptre, as seen in Listing 5-12.

Listing 5-12. Sceptre Project Setup

```
$ mkdir infrabook && cd infrabook
$ sceptre new project infrabook
Please enter a project_code [infrabook]:
Please enter a region []: us-east-1
```

---

[15]https://sceptre.cloudreach.com/2.1.5/docs/hooks.html#
[16]https://sceptre.cloudreach.com/latest/docs/resolvers.
  html#stack-output

```
$ tree
.
└── infrabook
    ├── config
    │   └── config.yaml
    └── templates

3 directories, 1 file

$ mkdir infrabook/config/prod
$ touch infrabook/config/prod/{app,config}.yaml
$ touch infrabook/templates/app.yaml
$ tree
.
└── infrabook
    ├── config
    │   ├── config.yaml
    │   └── prod
    │       ├── app.yaml
    │       └── config.yaml
    └── templates
        └── app.yaml

4 directories, 4 files
```

Since we used the CLI tool to create the project, the infrabook/config/config.yaml will already be populated as in Listing 5-13.

Listing 5-13. infrabook/config/config.yaml

```
project_code: infrabook
region: us-east-1
```

And infrabook/config/prod/app.yaml:

Listing 5-14. infrabook/config/prod/app.yaml

```
template_path: app.yaml
parameters:
  KeyName: infrabook
  OperatingSystem: AmazonLinux2
  InstanceType: m4.large
  PublicLocation: 0.0.0.0/0
hooks:
  after_create:
  - !cmd "ssh -i ~/.ssh/infrabook.pem ec2-user@$(aws cloud
  formation describe-stacks --stack-name infrabook-prod-app
  --query \"Stacks[0].Outputs[3].OutputValue\" --output text)"
  before_delete:
    - !cmd "echo About to be deleted!"
```

There's no need to show *infrabook/templates/app.yaml* here; it is the exact same file as is found in Listing 3-1. Let's now examine Listing 5-14. The **after_create** hook should ssh directly to the created instance once the deployment is complete. Before we try it out, it's probably worth pointing out that the hook as written will only work with a Linux-based operating system. It's also worth pointing out that the SSH key "infrabook.pem" is specific to my AWS account, housed on my local machine, and is located within my .ssh directory. Let's try it out! in Listing 5-15!

Listing 5-15. Sceptre Create

```
$ cd infrabook
$ sceptre create -y prod/app.yaml
[2019-07-30 23:32:48] - prod/app - Creating Stack
```

```
[2019-07-30 23:32:49] - prod/app infrabook-prod-app
AWS::CloudFormation::Stack CREATE_IN_PROGRESS User Initiated
[2019-07-30 23:32:53] - prod/app InstanceSg
AWS::EC2::SecurityGroup CREATE_IN_PROGRESS
[2019-07-30 23:32:57] - prod/app InstanceSg
AWS::EC2::SecurityGroup CREATE_IN_PROGRESS Resource creation
Initiated
[2019-07-30 23:32:57] - prod/app InstanceSg
AWS::EC2::SecurityGroup CREATE_COMPLETE
[2019-07-30 23:33:01] - prod/app EC2Instance AWS::EC2::Instance
CREATE_IN_PROGRESS
[2019-07-30 23:33:01] - prod/app EC2Instance AWS::EC2::Instance
CREATE_IN_PROGRESS Resource creation Initiated
[2019-07-30 23:33:35] - prod/app EC2Instance AWS::EC2::Instance
CREATE_COMPLETE
[2019-07-30 23:33:39] - prod/app infrabook-prod-app
AWS::CloudFormation::Stack CREATE_COMPLETE
The authenticity of host 'ec2-18-208-193-147.compute-1.
amazonaws.com (18.208.193.147)' can't be established.
ECDSA key fingerprint is SHA256:mwuNUZ3JubywuanJPU39v0y1U5UWnVV
ec3fD7sdT8lA.
Are you sure you want to continue connecting (yes/no)? yes
Warning: Permanently added 'ec2-18-208-193-147.compute-1.
amazonaws.com,18.208.193.147' (ECDSA) to the list of known hosts.
```

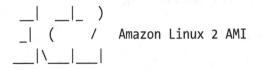

```
      __|  __|_  )
      _|  (     /   Amazon Linux 2 AMI
     ___|\___|___|
```

```
https://aws.amazon.com/amazon-linux-2/
7 package(s) needed for security, out of 16 available
Run "sudo yum update" to apply all updates.
[ec2-user@ip-172-31-23-162 ~]$
```

No doubt this is a useful trick if you're building some sort of automated configuration management solution to configure the instance, such as Ansible or Chef. Other obvious top-of-mind applications would be zipping up Lambda function code locally and uploading it to an S3 bucket in a before_create hook where the CloudFormation deployment aims to create the Lambda function using code stored in an S3 prefix. Doubtless there are a myriad of other applications as well – updating Jira tickets before a deployment, executing a workflow in ServiceNow, posting notifications in Slack, and so on. Before wrapping up in conclusion, we'll tear down our stack – which will also give us a chance to see our **before_delete** hook (from Listing 5-14) in action.

Listing 5-16. Sceptre Delete

```
$ cd infrabook
$ sceptre delete -y prod/app.yaml
The following stacks, in the following order, will be deleted:
prod/app
```

About to be deleted!
```
[2019-07-31 00:14:41] - prod/app - Deleting stack
[2019-07-31 00:14:42] - prod/app infrabook-prod-app
AWS::CloudFormation::Stack DELETE_IN_PROGRESS User Initiated
[2019-07-31 00:14:46] - prod/app EC2Instance AWS::EC2::Instance
DELETE_IN_PROGRESS
[2019-07-31 00:15:16] - prod/app EC2Instance AWS::EC2::Instance
DELETE_COMPLETE
[2019-07-31 00:15:16] - prod/app InstanceSg
AWS::EC2::SecurityGroup DELETE_IN_PROGRESS
[2019-07-31 00:15:20] - prod/app - delete complete
```

As you'll notice in the output in Listing 5-16, the bolded portion of the output corresponds to the desired output in the **before_delete** hook from Listing 5-14. As you can see from this example and the **after_create** example that we looked at previously, the hooks feature adds a layer of integration directly to your orchestrator as opposed to lots of cobbled-together scripts.

Conclusion

In this chapter, we took a closer look at a Python-based DSL in Troposphere, allowing us access to a full programming language with object orientation and inheritance. These features allow us to model our deployments in new and novel ways relative to what we are able to achieve by simply creating YAML-based templates – even when using some of the more complex native features of CloudFormation such as nested stacks. In this age of DevOps, tools like this provide a powerful bridge between development and operations teams, potentially enabling collaboration in ways not possible when using disparate toolchains.

Finally, we took a look at an orchestration tool, examining Sceptre. Sceptre provides a compelling feature set aimed at managing multiaccount, multi-deployment setups. It also provides a powerful, customizable set of hooks for integrating with existing automation tooling at multiple points in deployment lifecycle. Through an in-depth consideration of a single scenario, we demonstrated how to integrate hooks with existing AWS management tools and discussed the possibilities of how we could integrate deployments with other industry-standard tooling.

The use cases demonstrated here, though abbreviated, demonstrate the potential that both these classes of tools can have for you and your team if you are using or considering CloudFormation to manage your deployments. Though these examples certainly demonstrate the power and potential that these tools have to enable more efficient adoption of cloud services, in truth, we have just scratched the surface here. Your skill, imagination are your only constraints with these tools in your toolbelt.

CHAPTER 6

The AWS CDK and Pulumi

The AWS CDK[1] and Pulumi[2] each represent "next-generation" orchestration tools that work by building an abstraction over an existing orchestrator that allows the use of a full programming language. In the case of the CDK, the CloudFormation service provides the underlying functionality that the CDK uses to create and manage infrastructure. Similarly, Pulumi leverages Terraform's providers[3] to provide this sort of functionality. Right away, we see a difference in the extensibility of each tool, as the overall reach of the tool's functionality is constrained by its underlying orchestration technology: the CDK is limited to CloudFormation, while Pulumi has the ability to be supported by whatever Terraform providers are bridged[4] to Pulumi's specifications.

Looking at these tools together side-by-side in a single chapter may seem counterintuitive, but these tools are so similar in intent and implementation that looking at them together makes a great

---

[1]https://docs.aws.amazon.com/cdk/latest/guide/home.html
[2]www.pulumi.com/
[3]www.pulumi.com/docs/reference/vs/terraform/#using-terraform-providers
[4]https://github.com/pulumi/pulumi-terraform#how-it-works

© Bradley Campbell 2020
B. Campbell, *The Definitive Guide to AWS Infrastructure Automation*,
https://doi.org/10.1007/978-1-4842-5398-4_6

deal of sense. Each of them purposes to create an abstraction over an underlying orchestration engine with a general-purpose programming language, bringing the power of that language to that particular tool. In the case of the CDK, the underlying tool is CloudFormation; and with Pulumi, Terraform. While each tool supports multiple languages, we will stick with Python-based examples in this chapter in an effort to make an overall comparison more useful by not adding unneeded differences to the mix.

In this chapter, we will implement an EC2 instance and accompanying security group – similar to the infrastructure footprint that we've used in previous chapters. More specifically, we will take a look at

- *AWS CDK*

  - *Why CDK?* What advantages and benefits does the CDK offer us over CloudFormation?

  - *Getting Started*. How to get started with CDK – installation, and so on.

  - *EC2 Instance Build*. While the next chapter is wholly devoted to building an enterprise-ready VPC with multiple tools for comparison, we will build a simple deployment here just to get a feel for the CDK.

- *Pulumi*

  - *Why Pulumi?* What does Pulumi have to offer relative to Terraform?

  - *Getting Started*. Steps necessary to get Pulumi installed locally.

  - *EC2 Instance Build*. As with the CDK, we will build a simple EC2 instance with accompanying security group to get a feel for a project's flow with Pulumi.

Lastly, and perhaps most importantly, each of the examples in this chapter has the dependency that you have a VPC with subnets having the "Tier:Public" tag key/value combo. In the case of the CDK, the *Name* of the VPC is *prod*; in the case of Pulumi, the *Name* of the VPC is *dev*. In frequently building and tearing down VPCs for the purpose of writing these chapters, I used Terraform to manage the resources. The VPC itself is self-contained in a module, available in GitHub.[5]

AWS CDK

Why CDK?

Aligning to the benefits of the use of a tool like Troposphere, the CDK gives you the benefits of a real-world programming language – not a static markup language with logical enhancements. Table 6-1 takes a look at the CDK relative to simply using CloudFormation with respect to certain features; for good measure, I have also considered Troposphere in the comparison.

---

[5]https://github.com/geekmuse/terraform-module-aws-3tier-vpc/

Table 6-1. *CloudFormation/Troposphere/CDK Comparison Chart*

Tool →	CloudFormation	Troposphere	CDK
Feature ↓			
Supports a single programming language	No	Yes (Python)	Yes (multiple)
Supports multiple programming languages	No	No	Yes (Python, Node.js, Typescript, C#)
Reusable components	Yes, with nested stacks[6]	Yes, by building a class	Yes, by using a construct[7]
Supports looping mechanisms	No (no looping semantics)	Yes (supported by Python)	Yes (supported in all supported languages)
Pre-built Components by AWS	Certain cases (e.g., AWS pre-built templates)	No	Yes, many AWS-provided constructs exist[8]

(*continued*)

---

[6]This is not a "lightweight" implementation, however. Each nested stack is represented by a resource in the parent stack.

[7]https://docs.aws.amazon.com/cdk/latest/guide/constructs.html

[8]https://docs.aws.amazon.com/cdk/api/latest/docs/aws-construct-library.html

Table 6-1. (*continued*)

Tool →	CloudFormation	Troposphere	CDK
Requires separate pre-deployment orchestration	Yes, if using S3 (large templates) or nested stacks	Requires running Python commands locally to generate templates - Yes, if using S3 (large templates) or nested stacks	Self-contained CLI command does this for you
Deployment mechanism	AWS CLI, or upload to S3 and use console	AWS CLI, or upload generated template(s) to S3 and use console	Self-contained CLI commands
Provides pre-deployment changeset/diff	Possible using drift detection, but not provided "out-of-the-box"	Possible using drift detection, but not provided "out-of-the-box"	Yes
AWS Support[9]	Yes	Not directly (e.g., for Python code), but would be supported at the template/ deployment level	Not directly (e.g., for Python/JS code), but would be supported at the template/ deployment level

---

[9]Support levels will depend on support tier.

Table 6-1 tells a compelling story. To be clear, if you are heavily invested in the use of CloudFormation (or Troposphere) already with pre-built templates and well-oiled deployment mechanisms, I am not suggesting that you start from square one here. However, if you are in a position where you are choosing tools and approaches and considering what is right for your organization, I believe taking the information in Table 6-1 under advisement as you make that decision could be largely beneficial. Unless you prefer the simplicity of YAML, I can find few reasons to argue against giving the CDK a try.

Getting Started with the CDK

Getting started with the CDK is straightforward, assuming a working Node.js[10] and npm[11] are installed. While installs vary between OSes and individual machines, I was able to get a working setup on an Ubuntu 18.10 and 19.04 machine with the commands in Listing 6-1.

Listing 6-1. CDK Install on Ubuntu

```
$ sudo apt install nodejs
$ sudo apt install npm
$ sudo apt install python3
$ sudo apt install python3-pip
$ echo "alias python=\"python3\"" >> ~/.bashrc
$ echo "alias pip=\"pip3\"" >> ~/.bashrc
$ source ~/.bashrc
$ sudo npm install -g aws-cdk
$ sudo pip install --user aws-cdk.core
$ sudo apt-get install python3-venv
```

---

[10]https://nodejs.org/en/download/
[11]www.npmjs.com/get-npm

On my personal Mac, I use nvm[12] and pyenv[13] (along with pyenv-virtualenv[14]) to manage multiple versions of Node.js and Python (both of which are installed and managed themselves from Homebrew[15]), so in my case (using my localized versions of Node and Python, which are currently at v11.9.0 and 3.6.7, respectively), this is reduced to what we see in Listing 6-2.

Listing 6-2. CDK Install on MacOS with pyenv and nvm

```
$ npm install -g aws-cdk
$ pip install aws-cdk.core
```

Regardless of your OS and environmental setup, at the end of all this, you should be able to run the *cdk --version* command and get meaningful output, as in Listing 6-3. Your version may (and likely will) be different, but the point here is that some version is returned by the command (and not an error saying something like "cdk is not found in your PATH," or "cdk: command not found," and so on).

Listing 6-3. cdk --version

```
$ cdk --version
1.3.0 (build bba9914)
```

Once you have the CDK installed, bootstrapping, deploying, and managing deployments are all taken care of via the cdk command now available on your local machine.

---

[12]https://github.com/nvm-sh/nvm
[13]https://github.com/pyenv/pyenv
[14]https://github.com/pyenv/pyenv-virtualenv
[15]https://brew.sh/

Reprise – EC2 Instance with the CDK

Listing 6-4 shows how to set up a new project. The commands from this point assume you were able to successfully complete the setup in the previous section.

Listing 6-4. Getting Started with the CDK

```
$ mkdir cdk-app
$ cd cdk-app
$ cdk init app --language=python
Applying project template app for python
Executing Creating virtualenv...
```

\# Welcome to your CDK Python project!

This is a blank project for Python development with CDK.

The `cdk.json` file tells the CDK Toolkit how to execute your app.

This project is set up like a standard Python project. The initialization process also creates a virtualenv within this project, stored under the .env directory. To create the virtualenv, it assumes that there is a `python3`(or `python` for Windows) executable in your path with access to the `venv` package. If for any reason the automatic creation of the virtualenv fails, you can create the virtualenv manually.

To manually create a virtualenv on MacOS and Linux, use the following step:

```
```

```
$ python3 -m venv .env
```

```
```

After the init process completes and the virtualenv is created,
you can use the following
step to activate your virtualenv:

```
$ source .env/bin/activate
```

If you are on the Windows platform, you would activate the
virtualenv like this:

```
% .env\Scripts\activate.bat
```

Once the virtualenv is activated, you can install the required
dependencies:

```
$ pip install -r requirements.txt
```

At this point, you can now synthesize the CloudFormation
template for this code:

```
$ cdk synth
```

To add additional dependencies, for example, other CDK
libraries, just add them to your `setup.py` file and rerun the
`pip install -r requirements.txt`
command:

```
# Useful commands
 * `cdk ls`            list all stacks in the app
 * `cdk synth`         emits the synthesized CloudFormation
                       template
 * `cdk deploy`        deploy this stack to your default AWS
                       account/region
 * `cdk diff`          compare deployed stack with current state
 * `cdk docs`          open CDK documentation
```

Enjoy!

Once this setup is complete, the cdk-app directory will have contents similar to Listing 6-5.

Listing 6-5. cdk-app Directory Contents

```
$ tree
.
├── README.md
├── app.py
├── cdk.json
├── cdk_app
│   ├── __init__.py
│   └── cdk_app_stack.py
├── requirements.txt
└── setup.py

1 directory, 7 files
```

Following the instructions from the output in Listing 6-4 on my Mac, Listing 6-7 shows how to get everything set up. But first in Listing 6-6, we need to add a few necessary dependencies to our setup.py file, at approximately line 22. *Also, in many of the listings that follow, if the file is not a net-new file, changes made to that file will be bolded.*

Listing 6-6. setup.py

. . .

```
    install_requires=[
        "aws-cdk.core",
        "aws-cdk.ec2",
        "boto3",
    ],
```

. . .

As our application is largely dependent upon EC2 service features, we are adding that library to our setup.py file so we are able to use the library from our application. Now, let's activate the virtual environment and install our dependencies.

Listing 6-7. Virtual Environment and Dependencies

```
$ source .env/bin/activate
(.env) $ pip install -r requirements.txt
```

Python's pip utility will then output quite a bit of info to the console as the dependencies are installed. Once those dependencies are installed, we're ready to start developing. Feel free to explore the files as they currently exist, as the next few listings will demonstrate altered files to build a stack similar to the one we built in Listing 3-1. Next, let's have a look at the cdk.json file in Listing 6-8.

Listing 6-8. cdk.json

```
{
    "app": "python3 app.py",
      "context": {
        "Vpc": {
            "dev": null,
            "qa": null,
```

```
            "stg": null,
            "prod": "prod"
        },
        "ConnectPortByOs": {
            "Windows2016Base": 3389,
            "AmazonLinux2": 22
        },
        "AmiByOs": {
            "us-east-1": {
                "Windows2016Base": "ami-06bee8e1000e44ca4",
                "AmazonLinux2": "ami-0c6b1d09930fac512"
            },
            "us-west-2": {
                "Windows2016Base": "ami-07f35a597a32e470d",
                "AmazonLinux2": "ami-0cb72367e98845d43"
            }
        },
        "AllowedValues": {
            "DeployEnv": ["dev", "qa", "stg", "prod"],
            "InstanceType": ["t2.nano", "t2.micro", "t2.small",
            "t2.medium", "m4.large", "m4.xlarge"],
            "OperatingSystem": ["AmazonLinux2", "Windows2016Base"]
        },
        "Defaults": {
            "DeployEnv": "dev",
            "InstanceType": "t2.nano",
            "OperatingSystem": "AmazonLinux2",
            "KeyName": "",
            "PublicCidr": "0.0.0.0/0"
        }
    }
}
```

Looking back at Listing 3-1, this file will feel strikingly familiar. Essentially, the values of mappings and parameters have been incorporated here, allowing us to use these values within the CDK's runtime context mechanism.[16] Next, let's have a look at *cdk_app/cdk_app_ stack.py*.

Listing 6-9. cdk_app/cdk_app_stack.py

```python
import random
from aws_cdk import (
    aws_ec2 as ec2,
    core
)
import boto3

class CdkAppStack(core.Stack):
    def __init__(self, scope: core.Construct, id: str,
    **kwargs) -> None:
        super().__init__(scope, id, **kwargs)

        ec2b = boto3.client('ec2', region_name=kwargs['env']
        ['region'])
        vpc = ec2.Vpc.from_lookup(self, f'{id}-vpc',
        vpc_name=kwargs['env']['vpc'])
        subnets = []
        subnets_response = ec2b.describe_subnets(
            Filters=[
                {
                    'Name': 'tag:Tier',
                    'Values': ['public']
                },
```

---

[16]https://docs.aws.amazon.com/cdk/latest/guide/context.html

```
        {
            'Name': 'vpc-id',
            'Values': [vpc.vpc_id]
        }
    ]
)
for s in subnets_response['Subnets']:
    subnets.append(s['SubnetId'])

self.subnet_id = subnets[random.randint(0,
len(subnets)-1)]

sg = ec2.SecurityGroup(self, f'{id}-sg', vpc=vpc)
sg.add_ingress_rule(
    ec2.Peer.ipv4(kwargs['env']['cidr']),
    ec2.Port.tcp(kwargs['env']['port'])
)

inst = ec2.CfnInstance(self, f'{id}-inst',
    image_id=kwargs['env']['ami'],
    instance_type=kwargs['env']['inst_type'],
    security_group_ids=[sg.security_group_id],
    subnet_id=self.subnet_id
)
```

Here in Listing 6-9, we model our deployment using what the
CDK terms a Construct,[17] that is, a reusable module that encapsulates
infrastructure. Much like Terraform's data providers, the vpc = ec2.Vpc.
from_lookup line allows us to look up an existing infrastructure element –
something we're unable to do in any capacity (except perhaps with some
cleverly designed custom resources) with a native CloudFormation-based

---

[17]https://docs.aws.amazon.com/cdk/latest/guide/constructs.html

solution; here, however, we have first-class functionality to achieve this integration. Moving on from there, we create our security group resource, add the appropriate inbound rule to it, and then create our EC2 instance. Throughout this code, you will see that we are getting inputs from kwargs['env'], which are passed from the instantiation of a member of the CdkAppStack class, which we'll look at next.

This code incorporates the boto3 library to grab subnet IDs based on parameters, a feature which doesn't seem to be available for subnets (though, as we just discussed, this does work for finding the VPC itself). I don't particularly like the idea of having to include boto3, as I feel like from_lookup-esque functions should exist at a bare minimum for networking elements. But, until those features are implemented, I would suspect a CDK implementation – regardless of the language used – will probably incorporate that language's AWS SDK to interoperate cleanly within the context of existing resources. One additional assumption embedded in my example code is that a Tier tag exists on all subnets and that publicly routable subnets have the value public for this tag. Obviously, if you have a different tagging strategy you employ on your resources, the example can easily be modified to suit.

Listing 6-10. app.py

```
#!/usr/bin/env python3

import os
from aws_cdk import core
from cdk_app.cdk_app_stack import CdkAppStack
from cdk_app.helpers import Inputs

app = core.App()
i = Inputs()
```

```python
account = os.environ['CDK_DEFAULT_ACCOUNT']
region = os.environ['CDK_DEFAULT_REGION']
deploy_env = i.get(app, 'DeployEnv')
vpc = i.get(app, 'Vpc')[deploy_env]
cidr = i.get(app, 'PublicCidr')
os = i.get(app, 'OperatingSystem')
port = i.get(app, 'ConnectPortByOs')[os]
ami = i.get(app, 'AmiByOs')
inst_type = i.get(app, 'InstanceType')

CdkAppStack(app, "cdk-app",
        env={
            'account': account,
            'region': region,
            'deploy_env': deploy_env,
            'vpc': vpc,
            'cidr': cidr,
            'port': port,
            'os': os,
            'ami': ami[region][os],
            'inst_type': inst_type
        }
    )

app.synth()
```

Let's move on to Listing 6-10. In the imports, I'm importing a custom class to make grabbing inputs from context.json and falling back to defaults easier – we'll come to this file later. The next lines grab those inputs. Within the CdkAppStack instantiation, we now have the env block, which passes values down as seen in Listing 6-5. While not part of the CDK, the Inputs helper class makes grabbing context-based inputs a bit easier.

Listing 6-11. cdk_app/helpers.py

```python
class Inputs:

    def __init__(self):
        pass

    def _get_ck(self):
        return self.scope.node.try_get_context(self.key)

    def _param_get_default(self):
        if self.key in self.scope.node.try_get_context
        ('Defaults'):
            return self.scope.node.try_get_context('Defaults')
            [self.key]
        else:
            return self._get_ck()

    def _param_validate(self):
        if self.key in self.scope.node.try_get_context
        ('AllowedValues'):
            if self._get_ck() in self.scope.node.try_get_
            context('AllowedValues')[self.key]:
                return True
            else:
                return False
        else:
            return True

    def get(self, scope, key):
        self.scope = scope
        self.key = key
        return self._get_ck() if (self._get_ck() and self._
        param_validate()) else self._param_get_default()
```

Listing 6-11 is an implementation of a custom helper class. The class is mostly a wrapper around the try_get_context method provided by the CDK for grabbing context values, along with a fallback to a default value if one exists, and a validation of the provided value if a validation list is provided in the AllowedValues section of cdk.json. Now that we have our code all set up, let's first generate (or "synthesize," in CDK parlance) a CloudFormation template and then deploy our stack. Both of these commands will be run using the cdk command-line tool; before running these commands, it's worth pointing out that the synth command isn't necessary. The deploy command will create the resources in the target account without a synthesized template, but we run the synthesis in Listing 6-12 just to examine the outputted template.

Listing 6-12. cdk synth and Output

```
$ export CDK_DEFAULT_REGION=us-east-1
$ export CDK_DEFAULT_ACCOUNT=<your-aws-profile>
$ export AWS_PROFILE=<your-aws-profile>
$ export AWS_DEFAULT_REGION=us-east-1
$ cdk -c OperatingSystem=Windows2016Base -c DeployEnv=prod synth
Resources:
  cdkappsg4AAF3CFA:
    Type: AWS::EC2::SecurityGroup
    Properties:
      GroupDescription: cdk-app/cdk-app-sg
      SecurityGroupEgress:
        - CidrIp: 0.0.0.0/0
          Description: Allow all outbound traffic by default
          IpProtocol: "-1"
      SecurityGroupIngress:
        - CidrIp: 0.0.0.0/0
          Description: from 0.0.0.0/0:3389
```

```
            FromPort: 3389
            IpProtocol: tcp
            ToPort: 3389
        VpcId: vpc-XXXXXXXXXXXXXXXXX
      Metadata:
        aws:cdk:path: cdk-app/cdk-app-sg/Resource
  cdkappinst:
    Type: AWS::EC2::Instance
    Properties:
      ImageId: ami-06bee8e1000e44ca4
      InstanceType: t2.nano
      SecurityGroupIds:
        - Fn::GetAtt:
            - cdkappsg4AAF3CFA
            - GroupId
      SubnetId: subnet-XXXXXXXXXXXXXXXXX
    Metadata:
      aws:cdk:path: cdk-app/cdk-app-inst
  CDKMetadata:
    Type: AWS::CDK::Metadata
    Properties:
      Modules: aws-cdk=1.3.0,@aws-cdk/aws-cloudwatch=1.3.0,@
      aws-cdk/aws-ec2=1.3.0,@aws-cdk/aws-iam=1.3.0,@aws-cdk/
      aws-ssm=1.3.0,@aws-cdk/core=1.3.0,@aws-cdk/cx-api=1.3.0,@
      aws-cdk/region-info=1.3.0,jsii-runtime=Python/3.6.7
```

Less the Parameters and Mappings from Listing 3-1, you can see that this template is quite similar to Listing 3-1. Resources and resource associations are similarly constructed. Listing 6-13 shows how things look in the console when we deploy our stack.

Listing 6-13. cdk deploy Output

```
$ cdk -c OperatingSystem=Windows2016Base -c DeployEnv=prod deploy
This deployment will make potentially sensitive changes
according to your current security approval level
(--require-approval broadening).
Please confirm you intend to make the following modifications:

Security Group Changes
```

	Group	Dir	Protocol	Peer
+	${cdk-app-sg.GroupId}	In	TCP 3389	Everyone (IPv4)
+	${cdk-app-sg.GroupId}	Out	Everything	Everyone (IPv4)

```
(NOTE: There may be security-related changes not in this list.
See http://bit.ly/cdk-2EhF7Np)

Do you wish to deploy these changes (y/n)? y
cdk-app: deploying...
cdk-app: creating CloudFormation changeset...
 0/4 | 7:43:35 PM | CREATE_IN_PROGRESS    |
AWS::EC2::SecurityGroup | cdk-app-sg (cdkappsg4AAF3CFA)
 0/4 | 7:43:35 PM | CREATE_IN_PROGRESS    |
AWS::CDK::Metadata      | CDKMetadata
 0/4 | 7:43:38 PM | CREATE_IN_PROGRESS    |
AWS::CDK::Metadata        | CDKMetadata Resource creation Initiated
 1/4 | 7:43:38 PM | CREATE_COMPLETE       |
AWS::CDK::Metadata        | CDKMetadata
 1/4 | 7:43:40 PM | CREATE_IN_PROGRESS    |
AWS::EC2::SecurityGroup | cdk-app-sg (cdkappsg4AAF3CFA)
                          Resource creation Initiated
```

```
2/4 | 7:43:42 PM | CREATE_COMPLETE       |
AWS::EC2::SecurityGroup | cdk-app-sg (cdkappsg4AAF3CFA)
2/4 | 7:43:44 PM | CREATE_IN_PROGRESS    |
AWS::EC2::Instance      | cdk-app-inst (cdkappinst)
2/4 | 7:43:45 PM | CREATE_IN_PROGRESS    |
AWS::EC2::Instance        | cdk-app-inst (cdkappinst) Resource
                            creation Initiated
3/4 | 7:44:18 PM | CREATE_COMPLETE       |
AWS::EC2::Instance        | cdk-app-inst (cdkappinst)
4/4 | 7:44:19 PM | CREATE_COMPLETE       |
AWS::CloudFormation::Stack | cdk-app

 ✓  cdk-app

Stack ARN:
arn:aws:cloudformation:us-east-1:XXXXXXXXXXXX:stack/cdk-app/
24cd1170-be24-11e9-8e24-1202dd259b0c
```

One of the things I really like about how the CDK does things is that, as you'll notice in the preceding example, it notifies you of any security-sensitive changes you might be making. Additionally, you'll notice that it's actually creating a changeset and executing the changeset in order to update the stack. Though we'll not talk extensively about it here, the CDK's diff command provides very comprehensive output about the operations that will be carried out when performing an update on an existing stack from an updated codebase. In short, if CloudFormation is your tool of choice and you're not already using (or are heavily dependent upon) an orchestrator like Sceptre or an outside DSL tool like Troposphere, the CDK really deserves your attention. In my years of working in this space, I don't think I've seen rapid adoption of a tool like I've seen with the CDK since its

GA release, save for Terraform. I really do think the CDK has a lot to offer both ops and developers from many perspectives – namely, unified tooling that covers the day-to-day needs of both groups effectively. I am eager to see how AWS will mature the tool in the coming days, as even in its initial release it's an incredibly powerful tool that effectively leverages and builds upon the maturity of CloudFormation itself.

Pulumi

Why Pulumi?

Where the CDK attempts to overcome the shortcomings of CloudFormation, Pulumi aims to do the same for Terraform. Long have stood the complaints that YAML (CloudFormation) and HCL (Terraform) – each respective DSL language – lack the power and expressiveness needed to succinctly model complex infrastructure deployments. Each aims to solve that problem by wrapping a powerful orchestration runtime with a full-fledged programming language. Pulumi currently supports JavaScript, TypeScript, Go, and Python;[18] we'll have a look here at a Python-based example in an effort to create like-for-like comparisons.

First, however, let's look at a comparison between Pulumi and Terraform. Table 6-2 contains the comparison.

---

[18]www.pulumi.com/docs/reference/languages/

Table 6-2. *Pulumi/Terraform Comparison Chart*

Tool → Feature ↓	Terraform	Pulumi
Supports a single programming language	No	Yes (Python)
Supports multiple programming languages	No	Yes (JavaScript, TypeScript, Go, Python)
Supports looping mechanisms	Yes (count/for loops)	Yes
Reusable components	Yes, with modules	Yes, by building a Component[19]
Pre-built Components by AWS	Yes (Terraform registry[20])	No
Requires separate pre-deployment orchestration	Yes, if using remote state and state locking	No
Deployment mechanism	Built-in CLI commands	Built-in CLI commands
Provides pre-deployment changeset/diff	Yes	Yes
Has UI	Yes (Web/Terraform cloud)	Yes (Web)

---

[19]www.pulumi.com/docs/intro/concepts/programming-model/
 #components

[20]https://registry.terraform.io/browse/modules?provider=aws&verified=true

With the recent release of Terraform cloud,[21] users now have access to a web-based user interface – a feature whose absence has been long lamented by users of open source Terraform. Pulumi also provides a similar interface. Feature differences mostly lie in how you write the code that interacts with the underlying runtime.

Getting Started with Pulumi

Have a look at Pulumi's documentation regarding installation.[22] Installation is quite simple, especially relative to the installation of the CDK. For Linux users, the command in Listing 6-14 will get you going; MacOS users will only need Homebrew installed along with the command found in Listing 6-15.

Listing 6-14. Pulumi Install – Linux

```
$ curl -fsSL https://get.pulumi.com | sh
```

Listing 6-15. Pulumi Install – MacOS

```
$ brew install pulumi
```
Once you have Pulumi installed according to your specific operating system, the *pulumi* command should be available on your *PATH*.

First Pulumi Project – EC2 Instance

Let's begin our first Pulumi project in Listing 6-16.

---

[21]www.terraform.io/docs/cloud/index.html#about-terraform-cloud-and-terraform-enterprise

[22]www.pulumi.com/docs/reference/install/

Listing 6-16. Pulumi Project Setup

```
$ export AWS_PROFILE=<your-aws-profile>
$ mkdir pulumi
$ cd pulumi
$ pulumi new
Manage your Pulumi stacks by logging in.
Run `pulumi login --help` for alternative login options.
Enter your access token from https://app.pulumi.com/account/
tokens
    or hit <ENTER> to log in using your browser          :
We've launched your web browser to complete the login process.

Waiting for login to complete...
Please choose a template: aws-python            A minimal
                                                AWS Python
                                                Pulumi
                                                program
This command will walk you through creating a new Pulumi project.

Enter a value or leave blank to accept the (default), and press
<ENTER>.
Press ^C at any time to quit.

project name: (pulumi)
project description: (A minimal AWS Python Pulumi program)
Created project 'pulumi'

stack name: (dev)
Created stack 'dev'

aws:region: The AWS region to deploy into: (us-east-1)
Saved config
```

Your new project is ready to go! +⁺

To perform an initial deployment, run the following commands:

1. virtualenv -p python3 venv
2. source venv/bin/activate
3. pip3 install -r requirements.txt

Then, run 'pulumi up'

This will create several files in the directory and bootstrap your project. With the pulumi new command, you will be prompted to login to your Pulumi.com account (and to create an account first if you don't already have one created). Once that has been resolved, the process will continue as shown in the output in Listing 6-16. As you run the three commands indicated in the output numbered 1, 2, and 3, you'll have set up the necessary Python environment to run Pulumi. Once you've done that, you'll have a directory structure that looks like Listing 6-17.

Listing 6-17. Pulumi Directory Structure

```
$ tree -L 1
.
├── Pulumi.dev.yaml
├── Pulumi.yaml
├── __main__.py
├── requirements.txt
└── venv

1 directory, 4 files
```

The venv directory contains thousands of files, so I've omitted its contents here with -L 1 flag. The file containing our deployment is __main__.py. After bootstrapping, it will only contain a reference for an S3 bucket, as shown in Listing 6-18.

Listing 6-18. __main__.py

```
$ cat __main__.py
import pulumi
from pulumi_aws import s3

# Create an AWS resource (S3 Bucket)
bucket = s3.Bucket('my-bucket')

# Export the name of the bucket
pulumi.export('bucket_name', bucket.id)
```

Using Pulumi's *config set* command, let's build up a config.

Listing 6-19. CLI Commands to Build Config

```
$ pulumi config set AmiByOs.us-east-1.AmazonLinux2
ami-0c6b1d09930fac512
$ pulumi config set AmiByOs.us-east-1.Windows2016Base
ami-06bee8e1000e44ca4
$ pulumi config set AmiByOs.us-west-2.AmazonLinux2
ami-0cb72367e98845d43
$ pulumi config set AmiByOs.us-west-2.Windows2016Base
ami-07f35a597a32e470d
$ pulumi config set ConnectPortByOs.AmazonLinux2 22
$ pulumi config set ConnectPortByOs.Windows2016Base 3389
$ pulumi config set Os AmazonLinux2
$ pulumi config set InstanceType t2.nano
$ pulumi config set Az us-east-1c
```

Once these commands have been run, the dev config file (*Pulumi.dev. yaml*) should look like Listing 6-20.

Listing 6-20. Pulumi.dev.yaml

```
config:
  aws:region: us-east-1
  pulumi:AmiByOs.us-east-1.AmazonLinux2: ami-0c6b1d09930fac512
  pulumi:AmiByOs.us-east-1.Windows2016Base: ami-06bee8e1000
  e44ca4
  pulumi:AmiByOs.us-west-2.AmazonLinux2: ami-0cb72367e98845d43
  pulumi:AmiByOs.us-west-2.Windows2016Base: ami-07f35a597a
  32e470d
  pulumi:ConnectPortByOs.AmazonLinux2: "22"
  pulumi:ConnectPortByOs.Windows2016Base: "3389"
  pulumi:InstanceType: t2.nano
  pulumi:Os: AmazonLinux2
  pulumi:Az: us-east-1c
```

While the form is a bit different, this certainly looks like config files we've built for CloudFormation, Terraform, and the CDK. Pulumi doesn't support arbitrarily nested config files, so we play by its rules but still build in some notion of depth using a period to partition our data (as the colon is reserved by Pulumi). Cutting straight to the chase, let's have a look at the code that defines our stack in Listing 6-21.

Listing 6-21. __main__.py

```
import random
import pulumi
import pulumi_aws as aws
import boto3

## Get config and set some globals
conf = pulumi.Config()
_APP = 'pulumi'
_REGION = boto3.session.Session().region_name
```

```
_OS = conf.require('Os')
_AMI = conf.require(f'AmiByOs.{_REGION}.{_OS}')
_PORT = conf.require_int(f'ConnectPortByOs.{_OS}')
_INST_TYPE = conf.require('InstanceType')
_AZ = conf.require('Az')
_STACK = pulumi.get_stack()

## Instatiate boto client and gather context
ec2 = boto3.client('ec2', region_name=_REGION)
vpc = ec2.describe_vpcs(
        Filters=[
        {
            'Name': 'tag:Name',
            'Values': [_STACK]
        }]
    )['Vpcs'][0]['VpcId']

subnets_response = ec2.describe_subnets(
        Filters=[
            {
                'Name': 'tag:Tier',
                'Values': ['public']
            },
            {
                'Name': 'vpc-id',
                'Values': [vpc]
            }
        ]
    )
```

```
subnets = {}
for s in subnets_response['Subnets']:
    subnets[s['AvailabilityZone']] = s['SubnetId']

## Create security group resource
sg = aws.ec2.SecurityGroup(
        resource_name=f'{_APP}-sg',
        name=f'{_APP}-sg',
        vpc_id=vpc,
        ingress=[
            {
                'protocol': 'tcp',
                'from_port': _PORT,
                'to_port': _PORT,
                'cidr_blocks': ['0.0.0.0/0']
            }
        ],
        egress=[
            {
                'protocol': -1,
                'from_port': 0,
                'to_port': 0,
                'cidr_blocks': ['0.0.0.0/0']
            }
        ]
    )

## Create EC2 instance resource
inst = aws.ec2.Instance(
        resource_name=f'{_APP}-inst',
        associate_public_ip_address=True,
        subnet_id=subnets[_AZ],
        vpc_security_group_ids=[sg.id],
```

```
        ami=_AMI,
        instance_type=_INST_TYPE
   )

## Export values of interest
pulumi.export('public_ip', inst.public_ip)
pulumi.export('public_dns', inst.public_dns)
```

While the comments in the code serve to fairly well describe what each section of the code is doing, we'll walk through it quickly. Starting with the conf = ... line, we are grabbing configuration values from Pulumi (from the *Pulumi.dev.yaml* file), ending with the _STACK line. These values will be used throughout the rest of the Pulumi script. The next commented block uses a boto3 client to lookup a VPC ID and accompanying subnet IDs (based on the VPC ID and a tagging strategy); this block ends with us creating an object to create a map of availability zone (AZ) to subnet ID. The next block, starting with the sg = ... line, actually provisions our resources using Pulumi client libraries. First, we create a security group, followed by an EC2 instance; the instance uses the security group. Based on parameters passed in via our config, we determine the appropriate AMI and port to open up in the security group. Lastly, we create two outputs using the *pulumi.export* method. As we now have our code in place, let's provision the stack (Listing 6-22).

Listing 6-22. Provisioning a Stack with Pulumi

```
$ export AWS_PROFILE=<your-aws-profile>
$ pulumi up
Previewing update (dev):

     Type                        Name          Plan
 +   pulumi:pulumi:Stack         pulumi-dev    create
 +   ├─ aws:ec2:SecurityGroup    pulumi-sg     create
 +   └─ aws:ec2:Instance         pulumi-inst   create
```

267

```
Resources:
    + 3 to create

Do you want to perform this update? yes
Updating (dev):

    Type                          Name            Status
 +  pulumi:pulumi:Stack           pulumi-dev      created
 +   ├─ aws:ec2:SecurityGroup     pulumi-sg       created
 +   └─ aws:ec2:Instance          pulumi-inst     created

Outputs:
    public_dns: "ec2-35-153-213-177.compute-1.amazonaws.com"
    public_ip : "35.153.213.177"

Resources:
    + 3 created

Duration: 35s


Permalink: https://app.pulumi.com/XXXXXXXXX/pulumi/dev/
updates/4
```

The CLI command prompts you as to whether you want to provision
the stack or not; in Listing 6-22, we choose "yes," and Pulumi deploys our
resources and dutifully emits the outputs we have defined in our code.
One thing I find very interesting about Pulumi is its integration with its
SaaS tooling. Visiting the permalink provided in the output, we find a
lot of interesting additional metadata about the deployment. Figure 6-1
demonstrates what we see upon visiting the link provided.

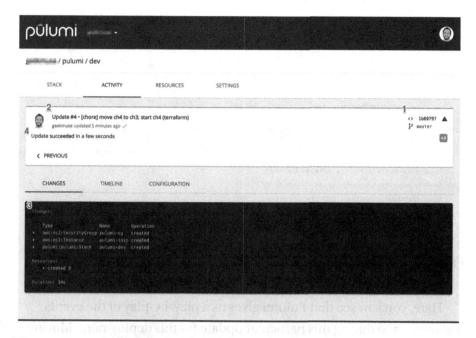

Figure 6-1. *Update Permalink*

The UI provides with a great deal of useful info. Moving through the numbered elements in the screenshot, we get the following:

1. The git SHA of the latest commit and the current branch of the repository that our Pulumi code is in when it is deployed via the CLI (if it is indeed in a git repository)

2. The git commit message of the latest commit of the repository that our code is in when deployed

3. A changeset of the deployment itself, including resources added, destroyed, or modified/updated

4. An approximate timestamp as to when the update occurred, as well as an indication of the user ID that initiated the update

In Figure 6-2, we see the contents of the *Timeline* sub-tab on the same page.

Figure 6-2. *Timeline Sub-tab*

Here, you can see that Pulumi gives us a play-by-play of the events that happened during this particular update for this deployment. Moving back up to the top of the page, the *Stack* tab gives us the info we'd see in the *Configuration* sub-tab, so we'll skip the sub-tab and have a look at the *Stack* tab in Figure 6-3.

/ pulumi / dev

| STACK | ACTIVITY | RESOURCES | SETTINGS |

Update #4 • [chore] move ch4 to ch3; start ch4 (terraform)
geekmuse updated 19 minutes ago ✓
Update succeeded in a few seconds

<> 1b69797   DETAILS
master

Outputs

Name ↑	Value
public_dns	ec2-35-153-213-177.compute-1.amazonaws.com
public_ip	35.153.213.177

Configuration

Name	Value
aws:region	us-east-1
pulumi:AmiByOs.us-east-1.AmazonLinux2	ami-0c6b1d89930fac512
pulumi:AmiByOs.us-east-1.Windows2016Base	ami-06bee8e1800e44ca4
pulumi:AmiByOs.us-west-2.AmazonLinux2	ami-0cb72367e98845d43
pulumi:AmiByOs.us-west-2.Windows2016Base	ami-07f35a597a32e470d
pulumi:Az	us-east-1c
pulumi:ConnectPortByOs.AmazonLinux2	22
pulumi:ConnectPortByOs.Windows2016Base	3389

Figure 6-3. *Stack Tab*

This isn't the content of the entire page, but it demonstrates the concept of what the page shows. It captures any outputs you define by an export, as well as showing you the latest configuration of your stack. Lastly, let's have a look at the *Resources* tab in Figure 6-4.

/ pulumi / dev

| STACK | ACTIVITY | RESOURCES | SETTINGS |

Resources

All resources ▾   🔍 Search for resources

Type	Name ↑	Status
pulumi:providers:aws	default_0_18_27	
aws:ec2:Instance	pulumi-inst	aws ☑
aws:ec2:SecurityGroup	pulumi-sg	aws ☑

Figure 6-4. *Resources Tab*

As you might expect, this tab lists all resources currently provisioned under this stack. If you notice at the far right of each resource's row, you'll notice an icon denoting a hyperlink. Clicking these links take you directly to the resource in the AWS console – obviously, you will need to be logged into the AWS console with the correct account for these links to function properly, but I really like that Pulumi gives you a quick jumping-off point to the AWS console straight from an administrative console in the provisioning tool.

Conclusion

As with any other tool we've given more than a cursory glance at in this book, these two tools could *easily* be the subject of their own volumes. Both of these tools are next-generation provisioning tools that, while possessing completely different lineages, share a lot in their approach toward their goal of overcoming perceived deficiencies in their forebears. Each provides an interface to several higher-level programming languages by creating an abstraction over tried-and-true infrastructure provisioning tooling. If you are already working with CloudFormation or Terraform, have a look at the CDK or Pulumi and determine if these features may make things easier for you working between developers and SREs/ops engineers.

While we looked at both of these tools in the context of their Python-based library offerings, it has been my experience that the TypeScript implementations are a bit more complete as of the time of this writing. While I imagine this is likely to change as more users adopt these tools and call for features (and that, if we follow from more overarching industry trends, these users will be using Python), it is worth having a look at the differences between offerings of TypeScript and your language of choice as you take up one of these tools.

CHAPTER 7

Let's Build a VPC

As the tools in this book (and many others) have arrived on the scene over the last few years, most have – in a very similar vein, that of the programming language counterparts – shown up with the de facto "Hello World"[1] example in tow. Often, these examples are so reductionistic as to hardly be useful, for example, creating an S3 bucket. In this chapter, we'll be creating a core component of networking infrastructure: a fully working three-tier[2] VPC, complete with public, private, and data subnets, gateways, routing tables, and the routes needed to ensure that traffic from each tier is appropriately routed. Our example will also enable flow logs[3] for the VPC, including needed IAM[4] constructs to grant trust to the CloudWatch Logs[5] service on behalf of the VPC service to allow the logs to be written appropriately.

As an added bonus, all of our builds will allow us to slightly alter the architecture as it is actually built out to differentiate the notion of a "high-availability" (and conversely non-high-availability) setup: this distinction

---

[1]https://en.wikipedia.org/wiki/%22Hello,_World!%22_program

[2]https://en.wikipedia.org/wiki/Multitier_architecture#Three-tier_architecture

[3]https://docs.aws.amazon.com/vpc/latest/userguide/flow-logs.html

[4]https://aws.amazon.com/iam

[5]https://docs.aws.amazon.com/AmazonCloudWatch/latest/logs/WhatIsCloudWatchLogs.html

© Bradley Campbell 2020
B. Campbell, *The Definitive Guide to AWS Infrastructure Automation*,
https://doi.org/10.1007/978-1-4842-5398-4_7

lies in how NAT gateways,[6] route tables,[7] and routes are provisioned. In the high-availability scenario, every availability zone gets its own NAT gateway and private route table; routes are added to this AZ-specific route table for the respective app and data subnet in that availability zone. This design provides a fault-tolerant design at the network level such that the loss of a single availability zone doesn't prevent the overall architecture from being able to function in the event of a loss of a single availability zone. Couple this with multi-AZ load balancers front multi-AZ autoscaling groups with resilient multi-AZ data-tier services like RDS or Aurora, and you have a very robust design for applications, even in the worst circumstances.

While a high-availability design is obviously beneficial in a production scenario where the loss of service could have a highly detrimental effect on your company both in direct (e.g. revenue from online sales) and indirect (e.g. reputation) ways, this design does carry additional costs that may not be desirable for every VPC you create. For example, in a development or QA VPC, the cost of additional NAT gateways and VPN hardware to achieve a completely fault-tolerant design may not be justifiable. In these cases, a single NAT gateway with a route table design that routes all private outbound traffic, regardless of AZ, through the single NAT gateway may be desired. As such, our design accounts for this, too. Non-high-availability designs can be delivered simply by setting the high-availability flag to false when building these VPCs. Though the particular syntax (i.e., variable name/value) will look different between each implementation, the delivery of these outcomes is the same. In this chapter, we'll have a look at how to deliver a VPC that meets these design criteria across several tools that we've already discussed, including

- *CloudFormation.* We will also use Sceptre in addition
  to our CloudFormation templates to handle parameter
  input storage and orchestration.

---

[6]https://docs.aws.amazon.com/vpc/latest/userguide/vpc-nat-gateway.html
[7]https://docs.aws.amazon.com/vpc/latest/userguide/VPC_Route_Tables.html

- *Terraform.* We will create a module to encapsulate our VPC and invoke that module to create the necessary resources.

- *AWS CDK.* We will model our VPC using a single CDK stack.

- *Pulumi.* We will create our VPC within a single project and use stacks to separate configurations.

In previous chapters regarding each of these tools, we discussed at length how to use them to set up new projects and how to use their native CLI interfaces to orchestrate provisioning of defined configurations in target environments. While we will deal with these concepts tangentially throughout the course of this chapter, these concepts are not the purpose of this chapter. Before we dive in though, let's have a look at the design of the VPC we will be creating.

Architecture

The two designs that follow show a high-level overview of the architecture to be created using the four selected tools.

High-Availability Design

The high-level overview shows subnets, route tables, routes, and gateways. There are additional elements, for instance, elastic IPs,[8] that aren't shown in the diagram. Additionally, the IAM elements and CloudWatch logs group that interface with VPC Flowlogs aren't shown here, but are common to both solutions.

---

[8]https://docs.aws.amazon.com/AWSEC2/latest/UserGuide/elastic-ip-addresses-eip.html

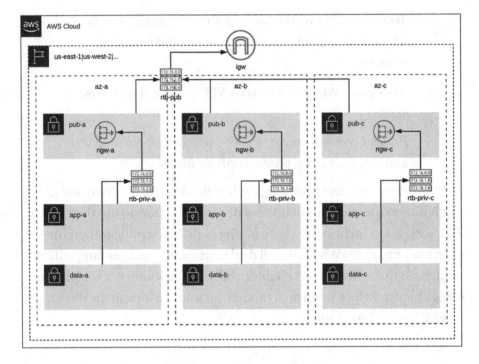

Figure 7-1. *High-Availability VPC Design*

Non-High-Availability Design

The intent with these diagrams is to display the key differences that exist between the two architectures, given that we will actually provide the capability to deliver either architecture from the same codebase.

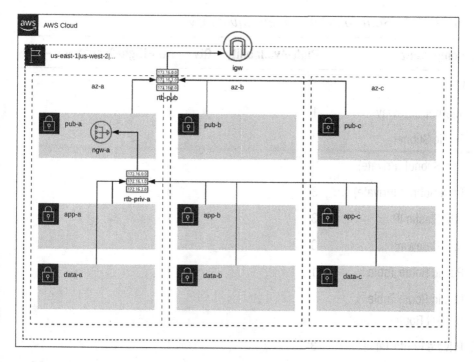

Figure 7-2. *Non-High-Availability VPC Design*

Table 7-1 provides a comprehensive inventory of all of the components that are built in each scenario.

Table 7-1. *Solution Component Inventory*

Component	High-Availability – Qty	Non-High-Availability – Qty
VPC	1	1
Internet Gateway	1	1
Public Subnet	3	3
App Subnet (Private)	3	3
Data Subnet (Private)	3	3
VPC Elastic IP	3	1
NAT Gateway	3	1
Public Route Table	1	1
Public Route Table Default Route	1	1
Private Route Table	3	1
Private Route Table Default Route	3	1
Subnet to Public Route Table Association	3	3
Subnet to Private Route Table Association	2 subnets x 3 route tables	6 subnets x 1 route table
CloudWatch Logs Group (FlowLogs)	1	1
IAM Role (Allow VPC to write FlowLogs to CloudWatch)	1	1
VPC FlowLogs Definition	1	1

Now that we have a clear idea of what these solutions will ultimately produce in terms of outputs, let's look at each respective implementation.

Solutions

CloudFormation

As mentioned in the chapter introduction, I am using sceptre in conjunction with vanilla CloudFormation templates to deliver this solution. The directory structure of this solution is as seen in Listing 7-1.

Listing 7-1. Tree Output – CloudFormation Solution Directory

```
$ tree
.
└── vpc
    ├── config
    │   ├── config.yaml
    │   ├── dev
    │   │   ├── config.yaml
    │   │   └── vpc.yaml
    │   └── prod
    │       ├── config.yaml
    │       └── vpc.yaml
    └── templates
        └── vpc.yaml

5 directories, 6 files
```

Let's move through the contents of these files, starting in the vpc/ config directory.

Listing 7-2. vpc/config/config.yaml

```
project_code: vpc
region: us-east-1
```

Listing 7-2 simply contains the Sceptre project descriptor and the target region (these values are gathered from the wizard interface of the CLI tool when creating the project with the sceptre project new command). Listings 7-6 and 7-7 contain parameters for dev and prod environments, respectively. It's also worth pointing out at this juncture that the *vpc/config/{dev,prod}/config.yaml* files are boilerplate created by Sceptre and will contain no values in this particular solution.

Listing 7-3. vpc/config/dev/vpc.yaml

```
template_path: vpc.yaml
parameters:
  AwsDns: 'true'
  BaseCidr: 10.0.0.0/16
  HighAvailability: 'false'
  Environment: dev
hooks:
  after_create:
    - !cmd "echo Vpc has been created."
  before_delete:
    - !cmd "echo Vpc will be deleted."
stack_tags:
  Environment: dev
  Provisioner: sceptre:/vpc/templates/vpc.yaml
```

Listing 7-4. vpc/config/prod/vpc.yaml

```
template_path: vpc.yaml
parameters:
  AwsDns: 'true'
  BaseCidr: 10.1.0.0/16
  HighAvailability: 'true'
  Environment: prod
hooks:
  after_create:
    - !cmd "echo Vpc has been created."
  before_delete:
    - !cmd "echo Vpc will be deleted."
stack_tags:
  Environment: prod
  Provisioner: sceptre:/vpc/templates/vpc.yaml
```

Let's now look at Listings 7-3 and 7-4. For the most part, there is nothing in these files that will look so foreign – we discussed how Sceptre passes parameters to the actual stacks and the functionality of hooks. The only differences here will be the stack_tags section,[9] which merely sets tags on the stack itself (resources that use resource tags inherit these tags from CloudFormation by default[10]). With our parameter files out of the way, the last thing to look at here is the template that defines the stack itself, which we have in Listing 7-5.

---

[9]https://sceptre.cloudreach.com/latest/docs/stack_config.html#stack_tags

[10]https://docs.aws.amazon.com/AWSCloudFormation/latest/UserGuide/aws-properties-resource-tags.html

Listing 7-5. vpc/templates/vpc.yaml

```
AWSTemplateFormatVersion: '2010-09-09'
Description: |
  Creates a three-tier VPC with high-availability toggle.

Parameters:
  AwsDns:
    Description: Use AWS DNS
    Type: String
    AllowedValues:
      - 'true'
      - 'false'
    Default: 'true'

  BaseCidr:
    Description: Base CIDR of the VPC
    Type: String
    Default: '10.0.0.0/16'
    ConstraintDescription: must be a string.

  HighAvailability:
    Description: Build with high-availability features (e.g.
    per-AZ NAT GW)
    Type: String
    AllowedValues:
      - 'true'
      - 'false'
    Default: 'false'

  Environment:
    Description: Environment identifier
    Type: String
```

```yaml
      AllowedValues:
        - dev
        - qa
        - stg
        - prod
      Default: dev

Conditions:
  AwsDns: !Equals [ !Ref AwsDns, 'true' ]
  HighAvailability: !Equals [ !Ref HighAvailability, 'true' ]

Resources:
  Vpc:
    Type: AWS::EC2::VPC
    Properties:
      CidrBlock: !Ref BaseCidr
      EnableDnsSupport: !If [ AwsDns, 'true', 'false' ]
      EnableDnsHostnames: !If [ AwsDns, 'true', 'false' ]
      InstanceTenancy: default
      Tags:
        - Key: Name
          Value: !Ref Environment

  FlowLogLogGroup:
    Type: AWS::Logs::LogGroup
    Properties:
      LogGroupName: !Sub "/flowlogs/${Environment}"
      RetentionInDays: 30

  FlowLogRole:
    Type: AWS::IAM::Role
    Properties:
      AssumeRolePolicyDocument:
```

```
        Version: '2012-10-17'
        Statement:
        - Effect: Allow
          Principal:
            Service: 'vpc-flow-logs.amazonaws.com'
          Action: 'sts:AssumeRole'
      Policies:
      - PolicyName: !Sub "flowlogs-policy-${Environment}"
        PolicyDocument:
          Version: '2012-10-17'
          Statement:
          - Effect: Allow
            Action:
            - 'logs:CreateLogStream'
            - 'logs:PutLogEvents'
            - 'logs:DescribeLogGroups'
            - 'logs:DescribeLogStreams'
            Resource: !GetAtt 'FlowLogLogGroup.Arn'
  FlowLog:
    Type: AWS::EC2::FlowLog
    Properties:
      DeliverLogsPermissionArn: !GetAtt FlowLogRole.Arn
      LogDestinationType: cloud-watch-logs
      LogGroupName: !Sub "/flowlogs/${Environment}"
      ResourceId: !Ref Vpc
      ResourceType: VPC
      TrafficType: ALL

  SubnetPub1:
    Type: AWS::EC2::Subnet
    Properties:
      VpcId: !Ref Vpc
```

```
CidrBlock:
  Fn::Select:
  - 0
  - !Cidr [ !Ref BaseCidr, 16, 12 ]
AvailabilityZone:
  Fn::Select:
  - 0
  - Fn::GetAZs: !Ref "AWS::Region"
MapPublicIpOnLaunch: true
Tags:
  - Key: Tier
    Value: public
  - Key: Name
    Value: !Join
    - '_'
    - - !Ref Environment
      - pub
      - Fn::Select:
        - 2
        - Fn::Split:
          - '_'
          - Fn::Select:
            - 0
            - Fn::GetAZs: !Ref "AWS::Region"
SubnetPub2:
  Type: AWS::EC2::Subnet
  Properties:
    VpcId: !Ref Vpc
    CidrBlock:
      Fn::Select:
```

```
      - 1
      - !Cidr [ !Ref BaseCidr, 16, 12 ]
    AvailabilityZone:
      Fn::Select:
      - 1
      - Fn::GetAZs: !Ref "AWS::Region"
    MapPublicIpOnLaunch: true
    Tags:
      - Key: Tier
        Value: public
      - Key: Name
        Value: !Join
          - '-'
          - - !Ref Environment
            - pub
            - Fn::Select:
              - 2
              - Fn::Split:
                - '-'
                - Fn::Select:
                  - 1
                  - Fn::GetAZs: !Ref "AWS::Region"

  SubnetPub3:
    Type: AWS::EC2::Subnet
    Properties:
      VpcId: !Ref Vpc
      CidrBlock:
        Fn::Select:
        - 2
        - !Cidr [ !Ref BaseCidr, 16, 12 ]
```

```
    AvailabilityZone:
      Fn::Select:
      - 2
      - Fn::GetAZs: !Ref "AWS::Region"
    MapPublicIpOnLaunch: true
    Tags:
      - Key: Tier
        Value: public
      - Key: Name
        Value: !Join
        - '_'
        - - !Ref Environment
          - pub
          - Fn::Select:
            - 2
            - Fn::Split:
              - '_'
              - Fn::Select:
                - 2
                - Fn::GetAZs: !Ref "AWS::Region"
SubnetApp1:
  Type: AWS::EC2::Subnet
  Properties:
    VpcId: !Ref Vpc
    CidrBlock:
      Fn::Select:
      - 4
      - !Cidr [ !Ref BaseCidr, 16, 12 ]
    AvailabilityZone:
      Fn::Select:
      - 0
      - Fn::GetAZs: !Ref "AWS::Region"
```

```
        MapPublicIpOnLaunch: false
        Tags:
          - Key: Tier
            Value: app
          - Key: Name
            Value: !Join
            - '-'
            - - !Ref Environment
              - app
              - Fn::Select:
                - 2
                - Fn::Split:
                  - '-'
                  - Fn::Select:
                    - 0
                    - Fn::GetAZs: !Ref "AWS::Region"
  SubnetApp2:
    Type: AWS::EC2::Subnet
    Properties:
      VpcId: !Ref Vpc
      CidrBlock:
        Fn::Select:
        - 5
        - !Cidr [ !Ref BaseCidr, 16, 12 ]
      AvailabilityZone:
        Fn::Select:
        - 1
        - Fn::GetAZs: !Ref "AWS::Region"
      MapPublicIpOnLaunch: false
      Tags:
        - Key: Tier
          Value: app
```

```
        - Key: Name
          Value: !Join
          - '-'
          - - !Ref Environment
            - app
            - Fn::Select:
              - 2
              - Fn::Split:
                - '-'
                - Fn::Select:
                  - 1
                  - Fn::GetAZs: !Ref "AWS::Region"
SubnetApp3:
  Type: AWS::EC2::Subnet
  Properties:
    VpcId: !Ref Vpc
    CidrBlock:
      Fn::Select:
      - 6
      - !Cidr [ !Ref BaseCidr, 16, 12 ]
    AvailabilityZone:
      Fn::Select:
      - 2
      - Fn::GetAZs: !Ref "AWS::Region"
    MapPublicIpOnLaunch: false
    Tags:
      - Key: Tier
        Value: app
      - Key: Name
        Value: !Join
        - '-'
```

```
          - - !Ref Environment
            - app
            - Fn::Select:
              - 2
              - Fn::Split:
                - '-'
                - Fn::Select:
                  - 2
                  - Fn::GetAZs: !Ref "AWS::Region"

SubnetData1:
  Type: AWS::EC2::Subnet
  Properties:
    VpcId: !Ref Vpc
    CidrBlock:
      Fn::Select:
      - 7
      - !Cidr [ !Ref BaseCidr, 16, 12 ]
    AvailabilityZone:
      Fn::Select:
      - 0
      - Fn::GetAZs: !Ref "AWS::Region"
    MapPublicIpOnLaunch: false
    Tags:
      - Key: Tier
        Value: data
      - Key: Name
        Value: !Join
        - '-'
        - - !Ref Environment
          - data
          - Fn::Select:
```

```
          - 2
          - Fn::Split:
            - '-'
            - Fn::Select:
              - 0
              - Fn::GetAZs: !Ref "AWS::Region"
SubnetData2:
  Type: AWS::EC2::Subnet
  Properties:
    VpcId: !Ref Vpc
    CidrBlock:
      Fn::Select:
      - 8
      - !Cidr [ !Ref BaseCidr, 16, 12 ]
    AvailabilityZone:
      Fn::Select:
      - 1
      - Fn::GetAZs: !Ref "AWS::Region"
    MapPublicIpOnLaunch: false
    Tags:
      - Key: Tier
        Value: data
      - Key: Name
        Value: !Join
        - '-'
        - - !Ref Environment
          - data
          - Fn::Select:
            - 2
            - Fn::Split:
              - '-'
```

```yaml
            - Fn::Select:
              - 1
              - Fn::GetAZs: !Ref "AWS::Region"
SubnetData3:
  Type: AWS::EC2::Subnet
  Properties:
    VpcId: !Ref Vpc
    CidrBlock:
      Fn::Select:
      - 9
      - !Cidr [ !Ref BaseCidr, 16, 12 ]
    AvailabilityZone:
      Fn::Select:
      - 2
      - Fn::GetAZs: !Ref "AWS::Region"
    MapPublicIpOnLaunch: false
    Tags:
      - Key: Tier
        Value: data
      - Key: Name
        Value: !Join
        - '-'
        - - !Ref Environment
          - data
          - Fn::Select:
            - 2
            - Fn::Split:
              - '-'
              - Fn::Select:
                - 2
                - Fn::GetAZs: !Ref "AWS::Region"
```

```
VpcIgw:
  Type: AWS::EC2::InternetGateway
  Properties:
    Tags:
    - Key: Name
      Value: !Ref Environment

VpcIgwAttach:
  Type: AWS::EC2::VPCGatewayAttachment
  Properties:
    InternetGatewayId: !Ref VpcIgw
    VpcId: !Ref Vpc

RteTblPub:
  Type: AWS::EC2::RouteTable
  Properties:
    VpcId: !Ref Vpc
    Tags:
      - Key: Name
        Value: !Sub "${Environment}-pub"

RtePubDefault:
  Type: AWS::EC2::Route
  Properties:
    DestinationCidrBlock: 0.0.0.0/0
    GatewayId: !Ref VpcIgw
    RouteTableId: !Ref RteTblPub

RteTblPubAssocSubnet1:
  Type: AWS::EC2::SubnetRouteTableAssociation
  Properties:
    RouteTableId: !Ref RteTblPub
    SubnetId: !Ref SubnetPub1
```

```
RteTblPubAssocSubnet2:
  Type: AWS::EC2::SubnetRouteTableAssociation
  Properties:
    RouteTableId: !Ref RteTblPub
    SubnetId: !Ref SubnetPub2

RteTblPubAssocSubnet3:
  Type: AWS::EC2::SubnetRouteTableAssociation
  Properties:
    RouteTableId: !Ref RteTblPub
    SubnetId: !Ref SubnetPub3

RteTblPriv1:
  Type: AWS::EC2::RouteTable
  Properties:
    VpcId: !Ref Vpc
    Tags:
      - Key: Name
        Value: !Sub "${Environment}-priv1"

Eip1:
  Type: AWS::EC2::EIP
  Properties:
    Domain: vpc

NatGw1:
  DependsOn: Eip1
  Type: AWS::EC2::NatGateway
  Properties:
    AllocationId: !GetAtt [ Eip1, AllocationId ]
    SubnetId: !Ref SubnetPub1
    Tags:
    - Key: Name
      Value: !Sub "${Environment}-ngw1"
```

```yaml
RtePriv1Default:
  Type: AWS::EC2::Route
  Properties:
    DestinationCidrBlock: 0.0.0.0/0
    NatGatewayId: !Ref NatGw1
    RouteTableId: !Ref RteTblPriv1

RteTblPrivAssocSnApp1:
  Type: AWS::EC2::SubnetRouteTableAssociation
  Properties:
    RouteTableId: !Ref RteTblPriv1
    SubnetId: !Ref SubnetApp1

RteTblPrivAssocSnData1:
  Type: AWS::EC2::SubnetRouteTableAssociation
  Properties:
    RouteTableId: !Ref RteTblPriv1
    SubnetId: !Ref SubnetData1

# If HighAvailability, create per-AZ
#   NAT GWs, private route tables, and route associations
#   for remaining AZs
RteTblPriv2:
  Condition: HighAvailability
  Type: AWS::EC2::RouteTable
  Properties:
    VpcId: !Ref Vpc
    Tags:
      - Key: Name
        Value: !Sub "${Environment}-priv2"
```

```
Eip2:
  Condition: HighAvailability
  Type: AWS::EC2::EIP
  Properties:
    Domain: vpc

NatGw2:
  Condition: HighAvailability
  DependsOn: Eip2
  Type: AWS::EC2::NatGateway
  Properties:
    AllocationId: !GetAtt [ Eip2, AllocationId ]
    SubnetId: !Ref SubnetPub2
    Tags:
    - Key: Name
      Value: !Sub "${Environment}-ngw2"

RtePriv2Default:
  Condition: HighAvailability
  Type: AWS::EC2::Route
  Properties:
    DestinationCidrBlock: 0.0.0.0/0
    NatGatewayId: !Ref NatGw2
    RouteTableId: !Ref RteTblPriv2

RteTblPrivAssocSnApp2:
  Type: AWS::EC2::SubnetRouteTableAssociation
  Properties:
    RouteTableId: !If [ HighAvailability, !Ref RteTblPriv2,
    !Ref RteTblPriv1 ]
    SubnetId: !Ref SubnetApp2
```

```
RteTblPrivAssocSnData2:
  Type: AWS::EC2::SubnetRouteTableAssociation
  Properties:
    RouteTableId: !If [ HighAvailability, !Ref RteTblPriv2,
    !Ref RteTblPriv1 ]
    SubnetId: !Ref SubnetData2

RteTblPriv3:
  Condition: HighAvailability
  Type: AWS::EC2::RouteTable
  Properties:
    VpcId: !Ref Vpc
    Tags:
      - Key: Name
        Value: !Sub "${Environment}-priv3"

Eip3:
  Condition: HighAvailability
  Type: AWS::EC2::EIP
  Properties:
    Domain: vpc

NatGw3:
  Condition: HighAvailability
  DependsOn: Eip3
  Type: AWS::EC2::NatGateway
  Properties:
    AllocationId: !GetAtt [ Eip3, AllocationId ]
    SubnetId: !Ref SubnetPub3
    Tags:
    - Key: Name
      Value: !Sub "${Environment}-ngw3"
```

```
RtePriv3Default:
  Condition: HighAvailability
  Type: AWS::EC2::Route
  Properties:
    DestinationCidrBlock: 0.0.0.0/0
    NatGatewayId: !Ref NatGw3
    RouteTableId: !Ref RteTblPriv3

RteTblPrivAssocSnApp3:
  Type: AWS::EC2::SubnetRouteTableAssociation
  Properties:
    RouteTableId: !If [ HighAvailability, !Ref RteTblPriv3,
    !Ref RteTblPriv1 ]
    SubnetId: !Ref SubnetApp3

RteTblPrivAssocSnData3:
  Type: AWS::EC2::SubnetRouteTableAssociation
  Properties:
    RouteTableId: !If [ HighAvailability, !Ref RteTblPriv3,
    !Ref RteTblPriv1 ]
    SubnetId: !Ref SubnetData3
```

As you can see, this template is quite lengthy (489 lines of code); as we work through subsequent examples written for other tools, you will see that we are able to accomplish the same solution as that created here, however with significantly less code. One of the most significant reasons for the LOC count in this chapter is that there are no looping constructs in vanilla CloudFormation templates (we can use a DSL like Troposphere where we can use loops, but even Troposphere must output per-resource statements for every resource described in a loop). For instance, you will see that each and every subnet must be described, each and every subnet must have its own route described in a routing table. These constraints lead to very easily intuited resource sets and relationships but create a "large template" situation that we have encountered here.

Terraform

From our foray into Terraform in Chapter 5, we already know that we aren't constrained to describing all our resources in a single template file. We'll be taking full advantage of that fact as we code our VPC implementation to logically divide resources into aptly named files to make things easier to understand. As we look at our code, let's first look at the overall directory structure of this project (Listing 7-6).

Listing 7-6. Terraform Project Directory

```
$ tree -I '*tfstate*' --dirsfirst
.
├── modules
│   └── vpc
│       ├── flowlog.tf
│       ├── gw.tf
│       ├── outputs.tf
│       ├── rtb-assoc.tf
│       ├── rtb.tf
│       ├── rte.tf
│       ├── sn.tf
│       ├── vars.tf
│       └── vpc.tf
├── main.tf
├── outputs.tf
├── provider.tf
└── vars.tf

2 directories, 13 files
```

Let's have a look at the *modules/vpc* files first, as they describe our VPC. I'll be looking at them in the order of control flow, looking first at inputs, looking next at resources in dependency order, and looking lastly at outputs. From there, we'll move up a directory, looking at how we create our providers, stage variables, and call an instance of the vpc module to actually provision resources. The first file we look at is the module's variables declarations in Listing 7-7, which also includes its data providers.

Listing 7-7. modules/vpc/vars.tf

```
data "aws_region" "current" {}

data "aws_availability_zones" "available" {
  state = "available"
}

locals {
  max_azs = 3
  num_azs = length(data.aws_availability_zones.available.names)
  azs     = data.aws_availability_zones.available.names
}

variable "base_cidr" {
  type    = string
  default = "10.0.0.0/16"
}

variable "aws_dns" {
  type = bool
}

variable "vpc_name" {
  type = string
}

variable "environment" {
  type = string
}
```

```
variable "high_availability" {
  type = bool
}
```

A further discussion of the nuance between locals and vars follows Listing 7-10. Since we talk about this at length there in light of the usage of locals within other parts of the codebase, there's not much else to say about the vars file. Listing 7-8 is short, sweet, and to the point: here, we create the base VPC which is a container for subsequent resources such as subnets and gateways.

Listing 7-8. modules/vpc/vpc.tf

```
resource "aws_vpc" "vpc" {
  cidr_block            = var.base_cidr
  instance_tenancy      = "default"
  enable_dns_support    = var.aws_dns
  enable_dns_hostnames  = var.aws_dns

  tags = {
    Name        = var.vpc_name
    Environment = var.environment
  }
}
```

Listing 7-9 contains the Internet gateway attached to the VPC, the Elastic IPs needed for the NAT gateways, and also provisions the NAT gateways. The number of Elastic IPs and NAT gateways provisioned is dependent on whether or not we're building the high-availability version of the solution.

Listing 7-9. modules/vpc/gw.tf

```
resource "aws_internet_gateway" "igw" {
  vpc_id = aws_vpc.vpc.id

  tags = {
    Name        = "${var.vpc_name}-igw"
    Environment = "${var.environment}"
  }
}

resource "aws_eip" "ngw_eip" {
  count       = var.high_availability ? (local.num_azs > local.
  max_azs ? local.max_azs : local.num_azs) : 1
  vpc         = true
  depends_on = ["aws_internet_gateway.igw"]

  tags = {
    Name        = "${var.vpc_name}-eip${count.index}"
    Environment = "${var.environment}"
  }
}

resource "aws_nat_gateway" "ngw" {
  count         = var.high_availability ? (local.num_azs >
  local.max_azs ? local.max_azs : local.num_azs) : 1
  allocation_id = aws_eip.ngw_eip[count.index].id
  subnet_id     = aws_subnet.public[count.index].id
  tags = {
    Name        = "${var.vpc_name}-ngw${count.index}"
    Environment = "${var.environment}"
  }
  depends_on = ["aws_internet_gateway.igw"]
}
```

In Listing 7-10, we create subnets across each availability zone for each of the three tiers of the solution. The count metaparameter of Terraform makes quick work of creating multiple resources with only three resource stanzas.

Listing 7-10. modules/vpc/sn.tf

```
resource "aws_subnet" "public" {
  count                   = local.num_azs > local.max_azs ?
                            local.max_azs : local.num_azs
  vpc_id                  = aws_vpc.vpc.id
  cidr_block              = cidrsubnet(var.base_cidr, 4,
                            count.index)
  availability_zone       = local.azs[count.index]
  map_public_ip_on_launch = true

  tags = {
    Name = "${var.vpc_name}-pub-${substr(local.azs[count.
    index], -2, 2)}"
    Tier = "public"
  }
}

resource "aws_subnet" "app" {
  count                   = local.num_azs > local.max_azs ?
                            local.max_azs : local.num_azs
  vpc_id                  = aws_vpc.vpc.id
  cidr_block              = cidrsubnet(var.base_cidr, 4, local.
                            max_azs + count.index)
  availability_zone       = local.azs[count.index]
  map_public_ip_on_launch = false
```

```
  tags = {
    Name = "${var.vpc_name}-app-${substr(local.azs[count.
    index], -2, 2)}"
    Tier = "app"
  }
}
resource "aws_subnet" "data" {
  count                    = local.num_azs > local.max_azs ?
                             local.max_azs : local.num_azs
  vpc_id                   = aws_vpc.vpc.id
  cidr_block               = cidrsubnet(var.base_cidr, 4,
                             (local.max_azs * 2) + count.index)
  availability_zone        = local.azs[count.index]
  map_public_ip_on_launch  = false

  tags = {
    Name = "${var.vpc_name}-data-${substr(local.azs[count.
    index], -2, 2)}"
    Tier = "data"
  }
}
```

One thing worth pointing out here is the power of Terraform's **locals** variables. Recalling from Chapter 5, locals are variables that are scoped locally to a module; additionally (and this is whence much of their power is drawn) they are calculated after variables and data providers are evaluated; hence, we can use values from variables and data providers in locals. If nothing, I recommend aliasing data providers to locals simply to save yourself some keystrokes. As a simple example, the count parameter in each of our subnet resources earlier is set as

```
count = local.num_azs > local.max_azs ? local.max_azs : local.
num_azs
```

In plain language, this means "if we have more AZs in this region than our defined max, use the defined max, else use the number of AZs available in the given region." Without the aliasing of data provider values to locals that happens in vars.tf, this expression would look like this:

```
count = length(data.aws_availability_zones.available.names) >
local.max_azs ? local.max_azs : length(data.aws_availability_
zones.available.names)
```

As the first is much more legible and concise than the latter, I encourage you to look for opportunities to take advantage of locals when possible to make your code more legible and easier to understand.

Listings 7-11, 7-12, and 7-13, respectively, provision the route tables, routes, and route table associations necessary for traffic to be appropriately routed through the respective gateway for a given subnet.

Listing 7-11. modules/vpc/rtb.tf

```
resource "aws_route_table" "pub" {
  vpc_id = aws_vpc.vpc.id

  tags = {
    Name        = "${var.vpc_name}-pub"
    Environment = var.environment
  }
}

resource "aws_route_table" "priv" {
  count   = var.high_availability ? (local.num_azs >
  local.max_azs ? local.max_azs : local.num_azs) : 1
  vpc_id = aws_vpc.vpc.id
```

```
  tags = {
    Name          = "${var.vpc_name}-priv${count.index}"
    Environment = var.environment
  }
}
```

Listing 7-12. modules/vpc/rte.tf

```
resource "aws_route" "pub_default" {
  route_table_id        = aws_route_table.pub.id
  destination_cidr_block = "0.0.0.0/0"
  gateway_id            = aws_internet_gateway.igw.id
  depends_on            = ["aws_route_table.pub"]
}

resource "aws_route" "priv_default" {
  count = var.high_availability ? (local.num_azs > local.max_
  azs ? local.max_azs : local.num_azs) : 1

  route_table_id        = aws_route_table.priv[count.index].id
  destination_cidr_block = "0.0.0.0/0"
  nat_gateway_id        = aws_nat_gateway.ngw[count.index].id
  depends_on            = ["aws_route_table.priv"]
}
```

Listing 7-13. modules/vpc/rtb-assoc.tf

```
resource "aws_route_table_association" "pub" {
  count           = local.num_azs > local.max_azs ? local.max_
                    azs : local.num_azs
  subnet_id       = aws_subnet.public[count.index].id
  route_table_id = aws_route_table.pub.id
}
```

```
resource "aws_route_table_association" "app" {
  count            = local.num_azs > local.max_azs ? local.max_
                     azs : local.num_azs
  subnet_id        = aws_subnet.app[count.index].id
  route_table_id = aws_route_table.priv[var.high_availability ?
                     count.index : 0].id
}

resource "aws_route_table_association" "data" {
  count            = local.num_azs > local.max_azs ? local.max_
                     azs : local.num_azs
  subnet_id        = aws_subnet.data[count.index].id
  route_table_id = aws_route_table.priv[var.high_availability ?
                     count.index : 0].id
}
```

Given the benefits of enabling FlowLogs for any VPC, we should certainly build it into configuration here. To enable FlowLogs, however, requires some additional configuration, namely, setting up a CloudWatch logs group for the logs information to pushed to, and an IAM role to grant the FlowLogs service the necessary privileges to allow it to send that information to CloudWatch logs. All of this configuration is contained in the *modules/vpc/flowlog.tf* file, which we see in Listing 7-14.

Listing 7-14. modules/vpc/flowlog.tf

```
resource "aws_cloudwatch_log_group" "flowlog" {
  name               = "/flowlogs/${var.environment}"
  retention_in_days = 30

  tags = {
    Name        = var.vpc_name
    Environment = var.environment
  }
}
```

```
data "aws_iam_policy_document" "flowlog_assume_role" {
  statement {
    actions = ["sts:AssumeRole"]

    principals {
      type        = "Service"
      identifiers = ["vpc-flow-logs.amazonaws.com"]
    }
  }
}

resource "aws_iam_role" "flowlog" {
  name                = "floglow-${var.environment}"
  path                = "/"
  assume_role_policy = data.aws_iam_policy_document.flowlog_
  assume_role.json
}

resource "aws_iam_role_policy" "flowlog" {
  name = "floglow-${var.environment}"
  role = aws_iam_role.flowlog.id

  policy = <<EOF
{
  "Version": "2012-10-17",
  "Statement": [
    {
      "Action": [
        "logs:CreateLogStream",
        "logs:PutLogEvents",
        "logs:DescribeLogGroups",
        "logs:DescribeLogStreams"
      ],
```

```
      "Effect": "Allow",
      "Resource": "${aws_cloudwatch_log_group.flowlog.arn}"
    }
  ]
}
EOF
}

resource "aws_flow_log" "flowlog" {
  iam_role_arn    = aws_iam_role.flowlog.arn
  log_destination = aws_cloudwatch_log_group.flowlog.arn
  traffic_type    = "ALL"
  vpc_id          = aws_vpc.vpc.id
}
```

The final point of business in our module is ensuring we expose a useful set of outputs for our caller(s). Assuming you would want to add application configurations to this same codebase somewhere down the line, having a useful set of outputs makes this much simpler.

Listing 7-15. modules/vpc/outputs.tf

```
output "vpc_id" {
  value = aws_vpc.vpc.id
}

output "azs" {
  value = slice(local.azs, 0, local.num_azs > local.max_azs ?
  local.max_azs : local.num_azs)
}

output "public_subnet_ids" {
  value = aws_subnet.public.*.id
}
```

```
output "app_subnet_ids" {
  value = aws_subnet.app.*.id
}

output "data_subnet_ids" {
  value = aws_subnet.data.*.id
}

output "public_subnet_cidrs" {
  value = aws_subnet.public.*.cidr_block
}

output "app_subnet_cidrs" {
  value = aws_subnet.app.*.cidr_block
}

output "data_subnet_cidrs" {
  value = aws_subnet.data.*.cidr_block
}
```

Let's now turn our attention to the module's outputs, which are shown in Listing 7-15. While it's clear from the output names, we're exporting the IDs of our newly created VPC and subnets, the CIDR blocks of all created subnets, and the AZs selected as a function of our call to the Terraform availability_zones data provider and a calculation of the number of AZs we're actually deploying into.

Now that we have the module defined for our VPC, how would we actually use it to create one? Let's have a look at the setup. First up, we'll look at our provider configuration. It's worth pointing out that unless otherwise specified, modules inherit the default provider in the root project. In this case, this will be the provider defined in Listing 7-16.

Listing 7-16. provider.tf

```
terraform {
  required_version = "= 0.12.6"
```

```
}

provider "aws" {
  version = "= 2.24.0"
}
```

Here, we declare that we're using the AWS provider. The other thing that's happening here – even if I've not discussed it at length – is an instance of runtime version[11] and provider version[12] pinning. This is a safety mechanism you can build it into your deployments to ensure that older (or newer) versions of the runtime or provider don't attempt to interoperate with your code, which can have unintended consequences, especially in situations where multiple users may be interacting with your deployment (and hence its statefile). With our provider declared, it's a short path to creating a VPC. Listing 7-17 shows our *main.tf* file, which shows our invocation of the module for which we've just walked through the code.

Listing 7-17. main.tf

```
module "dev_vpc" {
  source = "./modules/vpc"

  base_cidr         = "10.0.0.0/16"
  aws_dns           = true
  vpc_name          = "dev"
  environment       = "dev"
  high_availability = false
}
```

---

[11]www.terraform.io/docs/configuration/terraform.
html#specifying-a-required-terraform-version
[12]www.terraform.io/docs/configuration/terraform.
html#specifying-required-provider-versions

The module invocation is quite basic, with the underlying module itself handling the actual orchestration of resources with the provider. All subnet CIDRs are calculated based on the base_cidr parameter passed to the module. The use of AWS-provided DNS mechanisms within our VPC is toggled by the aws_dns parameter. The vpc_name and environment parameters allow us to create implementation-specific names for our resources and set appropriate tags on all resources. Lastly, the high_availability parameter – as we discussed at the outset of the chapter – is a convenient toggle that is extremely powerful, dictating a great portion of the overall network's design and connectivity.

As we've demonstrated how to use CLI commands to deploy resources described in our configuration files previously in Chapter 4, we won't revisit that here. What we will have a look at as we bring this section to a close are the *outputs.tf file* in our project root and what a set of outputs from an actual deployment look like.

Listing 7-18. outputs.tf

```
output "vpc_id" {
  value = module.dev_vpc.vpc_id
}

output "azs" {
  value = module.dev_vpc.azs
}

output "public_subnet_ids" {
  value = module.dev_vpc.public_subnet_ids
}

output "app_subnet_ids" {
  value = module.dev_vpc.app_subnet_ids
}
```

```
output "data_subnet_ids" {
  value = module.dev_vpc.data_subnet_ids
}

output "public_subnet_cidrs" {
  value = module.dev_vpc.public_subnet_cidrs
}

output "app_subnet_cidrs" {
  value = module.dev_vpc.app_subnet_cidrs
}

output "data_subnet_cidrs" {
  value = module.dev_vpc.data_subnet_cidrs
}
```

Given the straightforward naming conventions used in Listing 7-18, it should be clear what each of these outputs represents. Essentially, we are bubbling up resources from our module to our project root such that a terraform output command would surface them for us. Were we to have multiple sets of resources defined in the root of our project (perhaps a few EC2 instances and a load balancer deployed in the VPC we just created), we could then add outputs in this top-level outputs file to surface those values as well. Just as an example of what you might see were you to use this module and inspect its outputs, the output in Listing 7-19 is a capture of values from my own use of this module in a demo account.

Listing 7-19. terraform output

```
$ terraform output
app_subnet_cidrs = [
  "10.0.48.0/20",
  "10.0.64.0/20",
  "10.0.80.0/20",
]
```

```
app_subnet_ids = [
  "subnet-0386901a01181b941",
  "subnet-0c14ea9373dbbe8b5",
  "subnet-033ce8cf77b877fc2",
]
azs = [
  "us-east-1a",
  "us-east-1b",
  "us-east-1c",
]
data_subnet_cidrs = [
  "10.0.96.0/20",
  "10.0.112.0/20",
  "10.0.128.0/20",
]
data_subnet_ids = [
  "subnet-0c624f74f96c4f401",
  "subnet-081f846983b788c70",
  "subnet-091b06358f93105fd",
]
public_subnet_cidrs = [
  "10.0.0.0/20",
  "10.0.16.0/20",
  "10.0.32.0/20",
]
public_subnet_ids = [
  "subnet-0bc85b95882c00227",
  "subnet-014b20269e362a6a4",
  "subnet-00fd598d2f5e83842",
]
vpc_id = vpc-0f3389ff21ed09cdc
```

These outputs are incredibly useful, particularly the subnet CIDRs, as they're based on calculations Terraform performs based on the cidrsubnet function. If you're building modules, always try to think about what values consumers of your module will need as they use your module. While I could've simply left it at outputting the subnet IDs, I'd then put additional work on consumers who would then need to use those IDs to use the AWS SDK (or AWS CLI) to look up attributes about the specific subnet, such as CIDR and availability zone. Also, don't forget the -json flag that Terraform provides to provide these outputs in a machine-usable/script-friendly format (the output of this command is quite verbose and doesn't add any further value to the discussion at hand, so I won't be showing a demonstration of that output here – feel free to refer back to Chapter 4 for an example).

Wrapping up this section, it's quite obvious that there are substantial differences between a Terraform- and CloudFormation-based implementation to build a complex set of resources such as this. Terraform's count metaparameter essentially gives a pseudolooping construct that allows us to save a **lot** of boilerplate code. Listings 7-20 and 7-21 show the LOC counts for the CloudFormation and Terraform solutions, respectively.

Listing 7-20. Cloc Output – CloudFormation Solution

```
--------------------------------------------------------------------
Language              files        blank    comment        code
--------------------------------------------------------------------
YAML                      4           44          3         519
--------------------------------------------------------------------
SUM:                      4           44          3         519
--------------------------------------------------------------------
```

Listing 7-21. Cloc Output – Terraform Solution

Language	files	blank	comment	code
HCL	12	47	0	248
SUM:	12	47	0	248

No complex analysis is needed to demonstrate that Terraform solution delivers the same result in under half the code. Had I opted to use a nested stack approach for the CloudFormation-based solution instead of a single-template approach, this would have introduced additional code for the root stack. Additionally, it is my personal opinion that being able to split resources up according to purpose undeniably makes maintenance a less arduous task. With Terraform, this is essentially a "for-free" feature, whereas to do so in CloudFormation would mean creating several stacks by virtue of nested stacks or with Sceptre.

AWS CDK

One of the central themes of the CDK being its out-of-the-box constructs, which are "opinionated, well-architected, and handwritten by AWS"[13] implementations, our CDK-based VPC implementation relies heavily on the AWS-provided VPC construct.[14] Let's start out by looking at our local directory structure, shown in Listing 7-22.

---

[13]https://aws.amazon.com/blogs/aws/boost-your-infrastructure-with-cdk/
[14]https://docs.aws.amazon.com/cdk/api/latest/docs/@aws-cdk_aws-ec2. Vpc.html

Listing 7-22. Directory Listing

```
$ exa -T -I 'vpc_cdk.egg-info' --group-directories-first
.
├── vpc_cdk
│   ├── __init__.py
│   ├── helpers.py
│   └── vpc_cdk_stack.py
├── app.py
├── cdk.json
├── README.md
├── requirements.txt
└── setup.py
```

Let's have a look at the files that differ from the solution we looked at in the previous chapter. As the *vpc_cdk/__init__.py* is empty and we've already seen the *vpc_cdk/helpers.py* file, we'll start with the *vpc_cdk/vpc_cdk_stack.py* file (Listing 7-23), moving from there up into the root directory.

Listing 7-23. vpc_cdk/vpc_cdk_stack.py

```python
from aws_cdk import (
    core,
    aws_ec2 as ec2,
    aws_iam as iam,
    aws_logs as logs
)
import boto3
import sys

class VpcCdkStack(core.Stack):
```

```python
    def __init__(self, scope: core.Construct, id: str,
**kwargs) -> None:
        super().__init__(scope, id, **kwargs)
        self.max_azs = 3

        vpc = ec2.Vpc(self,
            f"{id}-{kwargs['env']['deploy_env']}-vpc",
            cidr=kwargs['env']['cidr'],
            default_instance_tenancy=ec2.DefaultInstanceTenancy.
            DEFAULT,
            enable_dns_hostnames=kwargs['env']['aws_dns'],
            enable_dns_support=kwargs['env']['aws_dns'],
            max_azs=self.max_azs,
            nat_gateways=self.max_azs if kwargs['env']['ha']
            else 1,
            subnet_configuration=[
                ec2.SubnetConfiguration(
                    name='public',
                    subnet_type=ec2.SubnetType.PUBLIC,
                    cidr_mask=20
                ),
                ec2.SubnetConfiguration(
                    name='app',
                    subnet_type=ec2.SubnetType.PRIVATE,
                    cidr_mask=20
                ),
                ec2.SubnetConfiguration(
                    name='data',
                    subnet_type=ec2.SubnetType.PRIVATE,
                    cidr_mask=20
                )
            ]
        )
```

```
flowlog_log_group = logs.LogGroup(self,
    f"{id}-{kwargs['env']['deploy_env']}-flowlog-log-
    group",
    log_group_name=f"/flowlogs/{kwargs['env']['deploy_
    env']}",
    retention=logs.RetentionDays.ONE_MONTH
)

iam_policy = iam.PolicyDocument(
    assign_sids=True,
    statements=[
        iam.PolicyStatement(
            actions=[
                "logs:CreateLogStream",
                "logs:PutLogEvents",
                "logs:DescribeLogGroups",
                "logs:DescribeLogStreams"
            ],
            effect=iam.Effect.ALLOW,
            resources=[
                flowlog_log_group.log_group_arn
            ]
        )
    ]
)
iam_role = iam.Role(self,
    f"{id}-{kwargs['env']['deploy_env']}-flowlog-role",
    assumed_by=iam.ServicePrincipal('vpc-flow-logs.
    amazonaws.com'),
    inline_policies={
```

```
                    f"{id}-{kwargs['env']['deploy_env']}-flowlogs":
                    iam_policy
            }
        )

    flowlog = ec2.CfnFlowLog(self,
        f"{id}-{kwargs['env']['deploy_env']}-flowlog",
        deliver_logs_permission_arn=iam_role.role_arn,
        log_destination_type='cloud-watch-logs',
        log_group_name=f"/flowlogs/{kwargs['env']
        ['deploy_env']}",
        traffic_type='ALL',
        resource_type='VPC',
        resource_id=vpc.vpc_id
    )
```

An instance of the VpcCdkStack class delivers a complete solution
vis-à-vis the CloudFormation and Terraform solutions we've already
looked at in this chapter. As hinted at by the AWS documentation,
built-in constructs are opinionated implementations of a core piece of
architecture. The ec2.Vpc construct delivers not just an empty VPC shell
but a full, working VPC, including subnets, gateways, routing tables, and
routes. Though not immediately apparent, what you will notice as you
provision this stack is that a great deal of flexibility in the way we name
resources is taken away from us as a result of delegating the buildout of
all resources to the CDK. While there is less control over naming and
tagging, the CDK does expose a useful set of tags; for instance, in lieu of
the Tier tag we had been using for our subnets, the CDK exposes an aws-
cdk:subnet-name tag, as shown in Figure 7-3.

Name	Subnet ID	State	VPC	IPv4 CIDR	Availabl
vpc-cdk/vpc-cdk-qa-vpc/appSubnet1	subnet-03c8d2026b713d5f2	available	vpc-007da6e17460c4019 | vpc-cdk/vpc-cdk-...	10.1.48.0/20	4091
vpc-cdk/vpc-cdk-qa-vpc/appSubnet2	subnet-0354330d6d785d228	available	vpc-007da6e17460c4019 | vpc-cdk/vpc-cdk-...	10.1.64.0/20	4091
vpc-cdk/vpc-cdk-qa-vpc/appSubnet3	subnet-080650e5b7f8534cb	available	vpc-007da6e17460c4019 | vpc-cdk/vpc-cdk-...	10.1.80.0/20	4091
vpc-cdk/vpc-cdk-qa-vpc/dataSubnet1	subnet-057546a56610eafad	available	vpc-007da6e17460c4019 | vpc-cdk/vpc-cdk-...	10.1.96.0/20	4091
vpc-cdk/vpc-cdk-qa-vpc/dataSubnet2	subnet-04e8deedab0bb90ef	available	vpc-007da6e17460c4019 | vpc-cdk/vpc-cdk-...	10.1.112.0/20	4091
vpc-cdk/vpc-cdk-qa-vpc/dataSubnet3	subnet-0cea3d4b0da02ceb4	available	vpc-007da6e17460c4019 | vpc-cdk/vpc-cdk-...	10.1.128.0/20	4091
vpc-cdk/vpc-cdk-qa-vpc/publicSubnet1	subnet-033523325da1ee868	available	vpc-007da6e17460c4019 | vpc-cdk/vpc-cdk-...	10.1.0.0/20	4090
vpc-cdk/vpc-cdk-qa-vpc/publicSubnet2	subnet-0529b192f7713cc0c	available	vpc-007da6e17460c4019 | vpc-cdk/vpc-cdk-...	10.1.16.0/20	4090
vpc-cdk/vpc-cdk-qa-vpc/publicSubnet3	subnet-09ad863658acc9c53	available	vpc-007da6e17460c4019 | vpc-cdk/vpc-cdk-...	10.1.32.0/20	4090

Subnet: subnet-0529b192f7713cc0c

| Description | Flow Logs | Route Table | Network ACL | **Tags** | Sharing |

Add/Edit Tags

Key	Value	
Name	vpc-cdk/vpc-cdk-qa-vpc/publicSubnet2	Hide Column
aws-cdk:subnet-name	public ←	Show Column
aws-cdk:subnet-type	Public	Show Column
aws:cloudformation:logical-id	vpccdkqavpcpublicSubnet2Subnet554113D1	Show Column
aws:cloudformation:stack-id	arn:aws:cloudformation:us-east-1:...stack/vpc-cdk/8cc2e780-cb4b-11e9-a2ec-129cd46a326a	Show Column
aws:cloudformation:stack-name	vpc-cdk	Show Column

Figure 7-3. *VPC Subnets Console*

Moving up into the parent directory, the *app.py* file (Listing 7-24) contains an instantiation of the class, which actually builds the resources when a `cdk deploy` command is issued.

Listing 7-24. app.py

```
#!/usr/bin/env python3

import os, sys
from aws_cdk import core
from vpc_cdk.vpc_cdk_stack import VpcCdkStack
from vpc_cdk.helpers import Inputs

app = core.App()
i = Inputs()

account = os.environ['CDK_DEFAULT_ACCOUNT']
region = os.environ['CDK_DEFAULT_REGION']
deploy_env = i.get_ck(app, 'DeployEnv')
```

```
base_cidr = i.get_ck(app, 'BaseCidr')[region][deploy_env]
aws_dns = i.get_ck(app, 'AwsDns')
high_availability = i.get_ck(app, 'HighAvailability')[deploy_env]

VpcCdkStack(app, "vpc-cdk",
    env={
        'cidr': base_cidr,
        'account': account,
        'region': region,
        'deploy_env': deploy_env,
        'aws_dns': aws_dns,
        'ha': high_availability,
    }
)

app.synth()
```

Of course, as we learned in the previous chapter, we can use context via the *cdk.json* file and directly on the CLI via the -c flag. Our cdk.json file (Listing 7-25) is the source of static context, while we rely on flags for dynamic context.

Listing 7-25. cdk.json

```
{
    "app": "python3 app.py",
    "context": {
        "BaseCidr": {
            "us-east-1": {
                "dev": "10.0.0.0/16",
                "qa": "10.1.0.0/16",
                "stg": "10.2.0.0/16",
                "prod": "10.3.0.0/16"
            },
```

```
    "us-west-2": {
        "dev": "10.10.0.0/16",
        "qa": "10.11.0.0/16",
        "stg": "10.12.0.0/16",
        "prod": "10.13.0.0/16"
    }
},
"AwsDns": true,
"HighAvailability": {
    "dev": false,
    "qa": false,
    "stg": true,
    "prod": true
}
}
}
```

With this setup, the only runtime context that needs to be passed in is a DeployEnv variable (which would be one of dev, qa, stg, or prod). This runtime value maps to selection of the VPC base CIDR and whether or not to build a high-availability solution. The only other change needed is to modify the install_requires section of *setup.py*, as shown in Listing 7-26.

Listing 7-26. Section of setup.py

```
install_requires=[
    "aws-cdk.core",
    "aws-cdk.aws_ec2",
    "aws-cdk.aws_iam",
    "aws-cdk.aws_logs",
    "boto3"
],
```

Once this file is updated, a `pip install -r requirements.txt` will add all of the required dependencies to the project. As the actual lifecycle of a stack through CLI commands was covered in the previous chapter, we won't revisit them here.

As we draw the CDK section to a close, let's compare the solution to the two previous solutions in terms of potential overall effort required to implement (though perhaps not the best measure, we'll be using lines of code as a proxy measure). With CloudFormation and Terraform weighing in at 519 and 248 lines, respectively, the CDK comes in much lighter, as we see in Listing 7-27.

Listing 7-27. CDK cloc Output

```
-------------------------------------------------------------------
Language                   files       blank      comment      code
-------------------------------------------------------------------
Python                         3          26            0       126
JSON                           1           0            0        26
-------------------------------------------------------------------
SUM:                           4          26            0       152
-------------------------------------------------------------------
```

Whereas Terraform was more than a 50% reduction relative to CloudFormation, the CDK represents approximately a 40% reduction relative to Terraform. Of course, in the case of the CDK, this measure is anecdotal, as there is a preexisting, AWS-built construct for a full VPC build. As that won't always be the case, it's best to avoid generalizations; however, in this case, it is a very powerful measure.

Pulumi

As we'll see, Pulumi code requires a bit more effort than the CDK, as it doesn't abstract away the complexity of the entire VPC. As a consequence, we are required to write code for each bit of the buildout, including subnets, routes, and route tables. As with our previous solutions, we'll first look at the directory structure of the finished solution (Listing 7-28) and then have a look at the relevant code.

Listing 7-28. Pulumi Solution Directory Structure

```
$ exa -T -I 'cdk.out|__pycache__|venv' --group-directories-
first
.
├── __main__.py
├── Pulumi.dev.yaml
├── Pulumi.yaml
└── requirements.txt
```

The Pulumi.yaml file is unchanged from its creation by the Pulumi CLI. We'll then have a look at the *requirements.txt, Pulumi.dev.yaml*, and *__main__.py* files. The *requirements.txt* file is showing in Listing 7-29.

Listing 7-29. requirements.txt

```
pulumi>=0.16.4
pulumi_aws>=0.16.2
boto3==1.9.213
```

In addition to the necessary Pulumi libraries, we'll be using the boto3 library (the Python AWS SDK) within our code to lookup aspects of the environment that aren't discoverable directly from Pulumi.

Knowing how Pulumi's config setup works from the previous chapter, the format of the config in Listing 7-30 shouldn't be too surprising – keep in mind as before that nested structures aren't supported directly in Pulumi's config files.

Listing 7-30. Pulumi.dev.yaml

```
config:
  aws:region: us-east-1
  vpc-pulumi:highAvailability: "false"
  vpc-pulumi:cidr.us-east-1: "10.100.0.0/16"
  vpc-pulumi:cidr.us-west-2: "10.101.0.0/16"
  vpc-pulumi:useAwsDns: "true"
  vpc-pulumi:maxAzs: 3
```

The configuration options are essentially the same as in previous solutions. Let's now look at the actual implementation of the solution.

Listing 7-31. __main__.py

```
from pulumi import (
    Config,
    Output,
    get_project,
    get_stack
)
from pulumi_aws import (
    ec2,
    cloudwatch as cw,
    iam
)
import boto3
import ipaddress

conf = Config()
ha = conf.require_bool('highAvailability')
_env = get_stack()
APP = f"{get_project()}-{_env}"
TIERS = ['public', 'app', 'data']
```

```python
region = boto3.session.Session().region_name
cidr = conf.require(f"cidr.{region}")
aws_dns = conf.require_bool('useAwsDns')
max_azs = conf.require_int('maxAzs')

client = boto3.client('ec2', region_name=region)

vpc = ec2.Vpc(
        resource_name=f'{APP}-vpc',
        cidr_block=cidr,
        enable_dns_hostnames=aws_dns,
        enable_dns_support=aws_dns,
        instance_tenancy='default',
        tags={
            'Name': APP,
            'Environment': _env
        }
    )

igw = ec2.InternetGateway(
        resource_name=f'{APP}-igw',
        vpc_id=vpc.id
    )

azs_response = client.describe_availability_zones(
        Filters=[
            {
                'Name': 'region-name',
                'Values': [region]
            },
            {
                'Name': 'state',
```

```
                'Values': ['available']
            }
        ]
    )

azs = [x['ZoneName'] for x in azs_response['AvailabilityZones']]
if len(azs) < max_azs:
    max_azs = len(azs)
subnet_cidrs = list(ipaddress.ip_network(cidr).subnets(new_
prefix=20))
subnets = {}
for i in TIERS:
    subnets[i] = {}
k = 0
for i in TIERS:
    for j in range(0, max_azs):
        subnets[i][j] = ec2.Subnet(
                resource_name=f"{APP}-{i}{j}",
                availability_zone=azs[j],
                cidr_block=str(subnet_cidrs[k]),
                map_public_ip_on_launch=True if i == 'public'
                else False,
                vpc_id=vpc.id,
                tags={
                    'Name': f"{i}{j}",
                    'Environment': _env,
                    'Tier': i
                }
            )

        k += 1
```

```
rtb_pub = ec2.RouteTable(
    f"{APP}-rtb-pub",
    vpc_id=vpc.id,
    tags={
        'Name': 'rtb-pub',
        'Environment': _env
    }
)

rte_pub = ec2.Route(
    f"{APP}-rte-pub",
    destination_cidr_block="0.0.0.0/0",
    gateway_id=igw.id,
    route_table_id=rtb_pub.id
)

for i in subnets["public"]:
    ec2.RouteTableAssociation(
        f"{APP}-rtb-assoc-pub{i}",
        route_table_id=rtb_pub.id,
        subnet_id=subnets["public"][i]
    )
rtb_privs = []
if not ha:
    eip = ec2.Eip(
        f"{APP}-eip0",
        vpc=True,
        tags={
            'Name': f"{APP}-eip0",
            'Environment': _env
        }
    )
```

```
ngw = ec2.NatGateway(
    f"{APP}-ngw0",
    allocation_id=eip.id,
    subnet_id=subnets["public"][0],
    tags={
        'Name': f"{APP}-ngw0",
        'Environment': _env
    }
)
rtb_priv = ec2.RouteTable(
    f"{APP}-rtb-priv0",
    vpc_id=vpc.id,
    tags={
        'Name': 'rtb-priv',
        'Environment': _env
    }
)
rtb_privs.append(rtb_priv)
rte_priv = ec2.Route(
    f"{APP}-rte-priv0",
    destination_cidr_block="0.0.0.0/0",
    nat_gateway_id=ngw.id,
    route_table_id=rtb_priv.id
)
for i in subnets["app"]:
    ec2.RouteTableAssociation(
        f"{APP}-rtb-assoc-app{i}",
        route_table_id=rtb_priv.id,
        subnet_id=subnets["app"][i]
    )
```

```
        for i in subnets["data"]:
            ec2.RouteTableAssociation(
                f"{APP}-rtb-assoc-data{i}",
                route_table_id=rtb_priv.id,
                subnet_id=subnets["data"][i]
            )
else:
    for i in range(0, max_azs):
        eip = ec2.Eip(
            f"{APP}-eip{i}",
            vpc=True,
            tags={
                'Name': f"{APP}-eip{i}",
                'Environment': _env
            }
        )
        ngw = ec2.NatGateway(
            f"{APP}-ngw{i}",
            allocation_id=eip.id,
            subnet_id=subnets["public"][i],
            tags={
                'Name': f"{APP}-ngw{i}",
                'Environment': _env
            }
        )
        rtb_priv = ec2.RouteTable(
            f"{APP}-rtb-priv{i}",
            vpc_id=vpc.id,
            tags={
```

```
                'Name': f'rtb-priv{i}',
                'Environment': _env
            }
        )
        rtb_privs.append(rtb_priv)
        ec2.Route(
            f"{APP}-rte-priv{i}",
            destination_cidr_block="0.0.0.0/0",
            nat_gateway_id=ngw.id,
            route_table_id=rtb_priv.id
        )
        ec2.RouteTableAssociation(
            f"{APP}-rtb-assoc-app{i}",
            route_table_id=rtb_priv.id,
            subnet_id=subnets["app"][i]
        )
        ec2.RouteTableAssociation(
            f"{APP}-rtb-assoc-data{i}",
            route_table_id=rtb_priv.id,
            subnet_id=subnets["data"][i]
        )
log_group = cw.LogGroup(
    f"{APP}-flowlog-lg",
    name=f"/{get_project()}/flowlogs/{_env}",
    retention_in_days=30,
    tags={
        'Name': f"{APP}-flowlog-lg",
        'Environment': _env
    }
)
```

```
cw_info = Output.all(log_group.arn)
policy_doc = cw_info.apply(
    lambda info: """{{
    "Version": "2012-10-17",
    "Statement": [
        {{
            "Action": [
                "logs:CreateLogStream",
                "logs:PutLogEvents",
                "logs:DescribeLogGroups",
                "logs:DescribeLogStreams"
            ],
            "Effect": "Allow",
            "Resource": "{0}"
        }}
    ]
}}
""".format(info[0]))

assume_role_policy_doc = """{
    "Version": "2012-10-17",
    "Statement": [
        {
            "Sid": "cwTrust",
            "Effect": "Allow",
            "Action": "sts:AssumeRole",
            "Principal": {
                "Service": "vpc-flow-logs.amazonaws.com"
            }
        }
    ]
}
"""
```

```
policy = iam.Policy(
    f"{APP}-flowlog-policy",
    name=f"{APP}-flowlog",
    path="/",
    policy=policy_doc
)

role = iam.Role(
    f"{APP}-flowlog-role",
    assume_role_policy=assume_role_policy_doc,
    name=f"{APP}-flowlog-role",
    path="/",
    tags={
        'Name': f"{APP}-flowlog-role",
        'Environment': _env
    }
)
attach_info = Output.all(role.name, policy.arn)
role_attach = attach_info.apply(
    lambda info: iam.RolePolicyAttachment(
        f"{APP}-flowlog-role-attach",
        policy_arn=info[1],
        role=info[0]
    )
)

flowlog_info = Output.all(role.arn, log_group.arn)
flowlog = flowlog_info.apply(
    lambda info: ec2.FlowLog(
        f"{APP}-flowlog",
        iam_role_arn=info[0],
        log_destination=info[1],
```

```
        traffic_type="ALL",
        vpc_id=vpc.id,
        tags={
            'Name': f"{APP}-flowlog",
            'Environment': _env
        }
    )
)
```

The code in Listing 7-31 is relatively straightforward for the Python programmer. The only thing particularly worth calling out is the necessity of using Pulumi's Outputs mechanism[15] to retrieve attributes outputted on resources as they're created. Essentially, these serve as signals to the underlying Terraform provider to help it understand the dependencies between resources. We discussed previously the necessity for the incorporation of boto in certain situations, this being one of them. Enumerating the availability zones in the region is only done through boto (as seen in the `client.describe_availability_zones()` block of code), as unfortunately access to a data provider-like interface doesn't currently exist in Pulumi (though I would suspect this is something the Pulumi team is working toward in a future release).

Relative to the other solutions in terms of effort, the line count for the Pulumi solution (Listing 7-32) is similar to the Terraform solution (Listing 7-21).

---

[15]www.pulumi.com/docs/intro/concepts/programming-model/#outputs

Listing 7-32. Pulumi cloc Output

```
------------------------------------------------------------------
Language                 files       blank     comment        code
------------------------------------------------------------------
Python                       1          20          28         233
YAML                         1           0           0           7
------------------------------------------------------------------
SUM:                         2          20          28         240
------------------------------------------------------------------
```

Conclusion

Having looked at the same target architecture built using each of these four solutions, it is evident that CloudFormation presents a higher burden of work on an implementer than our other solutions. Even with that fact in hand, the underlying tenet of AWS Support still holds true for the CloudFormation service – and so its use still bears consideration. Figure 7-4 contains a decision tree that captures the decision points you'll want to consider as you choose between these tools.

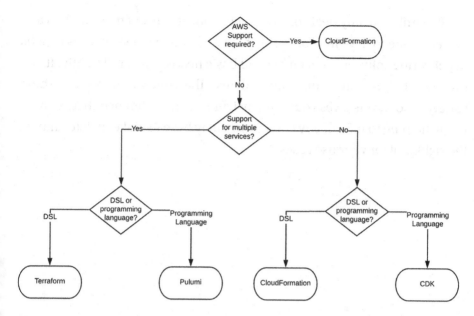

Figure 7-4. *Tool Decision Tree*

This matrix doesn't take into account the "burden of implementation" metric we discussed in terms of line counts to deliver each solution; as that metric certainly factors into the total cost of ownership (TCO) to deliver any project, it's worth considering as you make a decision. However, the TCO equation will vary from organization to organization, so it's worth using Figure 7-4 as a starting point for developing your own decision-making framework. Also, take into consideration the services you leverage in building out your services and your adoption curve: if you're an early adopter, Terraform may be a better choice for you. There are many aspects to be considered; as stated, make sure you capture the ones important to your organization in your decision-making process.

Regardless of any decision you might come to, any of these tools is a powerful one to have in your toolbelt. As we've shown here, each is capable of delivering solutions that go beyond basic needs, albeit differently. It is my hope that demonstrating how to deliver the same solution across these variety of solutions gives you some insight into the differences between them, helping to inform any choices you may have to make in determining the right tool for your use cases.

CHAPTER 8

Conclusion

As we started our journey, we lived a few days in the life of a budding cloud engineer who needed a solution to manage their cloud estate's resources in a robust, manageable way. In the hypothetical world in which no tooling exists to deal with the situation, our engineer resorted to creating and attempting to manage a bespoke set of tools to manage a situation of ever-increasing complexity. The stage set, we dove into the current landscape of infrastructure management tools, looking at the major players, the ecosystems that have emerged around them, and next-generation tools that build upon the success, power, and stability of these tools. If you've walked away from this book with anything, it's probably a sense of how vast this ecosystem and the choices you must make to figure out what tool (or tools) are best for you and the needs of your organization. So, instead of providing a recap of everything I've said already in this book, I'm going to leave you with two more thoughts.

Thought #1: Look Past Your Own Biases in Choosing a Tool

After a few years of using Terraform extensively in its nascent years, I had a strong bias toward the tool. In my estimation, it made me more efficient and allowed me to solve a wider array of problems than I found myself able to with CloudFormation. I soon found myself in the midst of a large

© Bradley Campbell 2020
B. Campbell, *The Definitive Guide to AWS Infrastructure Automation*,
https://doi.org/10.1007/978-1-4842-5398-4_8

migration project within a large organization where the team expressed an interest in using Terraform. While this particular organization wanted to use Terraform for their project, the overall history of projects delivered within the organization had been quite successful with CloudFormation. Due to the reasons behind this success (i.e., AWS support, shallower learning curve for adoption, institutional knowledge of and prior experience with CloudFormation), I was encouraged by a few others who had successfully delivered migration projects within the organization to use CloudFormation. I pressed forward with what I thought best, building out an extremely complex solution using Terraform (the app itself had quite complex requirements).

A few months after building out the solution, I was somewhat dismayed to learn that the team who eventually owned the solution had not really progressed in their understanding or usage of Terraform, putting them in a position to not truly own the solution – hence not truly making the project a success. At the end of the day, I could have delivered their application using any choice of tool. CloudFormation made the most sense for them in every practical dimension, but I used the team's desire to use Terraform feed my bias to use it for a project for which it was not ultimately the best fit in the human dimension.

Consider who will be using the solutions you build and who will be maintaining them. As much as it may seem a harmless decision made in a vacuum to choose one of these tools over another, there are real-world implications to your choices. DSLs present much simpler "interfaces" than programming language-based tools – however, if your team has extensive programming experience, then a tool like the CDK or Pulumi (or perhaps a DSL like Troposphere) may make a lot of sense and give the team a great amount of flexibility down the road. There is no "one-size-fits-all" solution here. While I have provided very generalized guidance in picking a tool in the previous chapter, there are a wide array of factors to consider. Ultimately though, your customer (and I use that word in a very wide sense: whether another member of your own team, a member of another internal team in your company, or perhaps a client in a consulting context) should be where you start from in your decision to solution a project. Consider their needs first and work backward from there – even if it doesn't align to your biases. In fact, you may even wind up getting to learn something new as you work your way through a new tool or framework to build that best solution.

Thought #2: Build a Learning Strategy

This book covers a lot of material across four separate tools, with peripheral coverage of a small subsection of tools which comprise ecosystems around these four tools. I dare say 1,000 pages would begin to do some justice to a systematic, in-depth treatment of these tools and their deepest capabilities. Even with those thousand pages, more would need to be added on almost a daily basis to keep pace with the rate of innovation going on in this space. Between the time I started the first chapter of this book and now, Terraform has hit a *major* milestone in its 0.12 release. The 0.12 release saw Terraform radically changing the way its parser works and, along with it, the way the HCL works; needs for workarounds in HCL that have been necessary for years have disappeared. As well, the promise of more changes and long-awaited features are still promised in 0.12 minor releases. In the same span of time, the CDK has gone from beta release to generally available and has gone through quite a few minor version releases. My compulsion to finish this book **before** re:Invent is underscored by the fact that I know there's a good chance that I would need another chapter or appendix just to talk about potential changes to CloudFormation or the CDK as a result of things announced at the conference. The point I am trying to make is this: I have tried in this book to provide a foundation for your understanding of this ecosystem, the tools as they exist now, and the problems they were intended to solve.

Every day, the problems change, and the tools and approaches we use them in conjunction with change as well. Staying relevant in this industry carries an implied subtext of being informed, and you can't do that without building a strategy to stay informed. Even if it's as simple as subscribing to a few blogs, figure out what works for you and build a habit of consistently staying in-the-know about what's going on in the industry. Assuming you identify with Thought #1 which preceded this section, having a wide variety of tools available to you to solve problems puts you in the best position to solve the most problems – keeping you relevant, valuable, and employable in an industry whose only constant is change. I have included in the Appendix a few of my favorite resources in this regard, and I hope they help you as you navigate the technology landscape.

And Finally

Your time is valuable. In a world that offers innumerable ways to spend your time, you've chosen to invest the time – your time – reading this book. For that, I am grateful. It is my sincere hope that you learned something that you didn't know when you started this book. As you continue to learn, grow, and mature in your career, consider the impact that sharing your knowledge will have on others.

There is a lot of headroom left for cloud computing in the industry, despite the foothold it already has. As you've worked through the use of these tools in this book, I do hope you've considered some of the realities I laid out in the beginning: that with a simple shell script or YAML file run through CloudFormation, you can provision an entire data center for your organization in a matter of minutes. With the knowledge of these tools, you'll be empowered to tap into that power.

Appendix

CloudFormation DSLs/Generators

Name of Tool	Language	URL
Cfn	Perl	https://metacpan.org/pod/Cfn
Paws::Cloudformation	Perl	https://metacpan.org/pod/Paws::CloudFormation
SparkleFormation	Ruby	www.sparkleformation.io/
GoFormation	Golang	https://github.com/awslabs/goformation
go-cloudformation	Golang	https://github.com/crewjam/go-cloudformation
Lono	Ruby	https://github.com/tongueroo/lono
cloudformation-template-generator	Scala	https://github.com/MonsantoCo/cloudformation-template-generator
cfndsl	Ruby	https://github.com/cfndsl/cfndsl
VaporShell	PowerShell	https://vaporshell.io/

(continued)

© Bradley Campbell 2020
B. Campbell, *The Definitive Guide to AWS Infrastructure Automation*,
https://doi.org/10.1007/978-1-4842-5398-4

Name of Tool	Language	URL
cloud-seeder	Haskell	http://hackage.haskell.org/package/cloud-seeder
cloudformation-builder	Java	https://github.com/scaleset/cloudformation-builder
Humidifier	C#	https://github.com/jakejscott/Humidifier
Humidifier	Ruby	https://github.com/kddeisz/humidifier
cloudformal	Scala	https://github.com/mshibuya/cloudformal
cloudform	TypeScript	https://github.com/bright/cloudform
cloud-formation-dsl	TypeScript	https://github.com/stephenh/cloud-formation-dsl
posh-awscfn	PowerShell	https://github.com/ezshield/posh-awscfn
coffin	CoffeeScript	http://chrisfjones.github.io/coffin/
cloudformation-ruby-dsl	Ruby	https://github.com/bazaarvoice/cloudformation-ruby-dsl
AWS CDK	Python, Java, C#/.NET, JavaScript, TypeScript	https://docs.aws.amazon.com/cdk/latest/guide/what-is.html

(*continued*)

Name of Tool	Language	URL
cfhighlander	Ruby	`https://github.com/theonestack/cfhighlander`
cfoo	YAML	`https://github.com/drrb/cfoo`
cfn-include	JSON, YAML	`www.npmjs.com/package/cfn-include`
kombusion	- YAML (templates) - Golang (custom plugins)	`https://github.com/KablamoOSS/kombustion`

CloudFormation Orchestrators

Name of Tool	URL
cumulus	`https://github.com/peterkh/cumulus`
stacker	`https://github.com/cloudtools/stacker`
stackformation	`https://github.com/AOEpeople/StackFormation`
stack_master	`https://github.com/envato/stack_master`
qaz	`https://github.com/daidokoro/qaz`
bora	`https://github.com/pkazmierczak/bora`

Learning Resources

Name	Type	URL
Jeff Barr's Blog	Blog	`https://aws.amazon.com/blogs/aws/author/jbarr/`
Last Week in AWS	Newsletter	`www.lastweekinaws.com/`
r/Devops (Reddit)	Web site	`www.reddit.com/r/devops/`
cloudskills.fm	Podcast	`https://cloudskills.fm/`
Real World DevOps	Podcast	`www.realworlddevops.com/`
AWS Podcast	Podcast	`https://aws.amazon.com/podcasts/aws-podcast/`
A Cloud Guru Blog	Blog	`https://read.acloud.guru/`

Index

Printed in the United States
By Bookmasters